My
Windows® 8.1
Computer *for* Seniors

Michael Miller

que®

800 East 96th Street,
Indianapolis, Indiana 46240 USA

My Windows® 8.1 Computer for Seniors

Copyright © 2014 by Pearson Education, Inc.

ISBN-13: 978-0-7897-5329-8
ISBN-10: 0-7897-5329-4

Library of Congress Control Number: 2013949971

Printed in the United States of America

Second Printing: June 2014

Trademarks

All terms mentioned in this book that are known to be trademarks or service marks have been appropriately capitalized. Que Publishing cannot attest to the accuracy of this information. Use of a term in this book should not be regarded as affecting the validity of any trademark or service mark.

Warning and Disclaimer

Every effort has been made to make this book as complete and as accurate as possible, but no warranty or fitness is implied. The information provided is on an "as is" basis. The author and the publisher shall have neither liability nor responsibility to any person or entity with respect to any loss or damages arising from the information contained in this book.

Special Sales

For information about buying this title in bulk quantities, or for special sales opportunities (which may include electronic versions; custom cover designs; and content particular to your business, training goals, marketing focus, or branding interests), please contact our corporate sales department at corpsales@pearsoned.com or (800) 382-3419.

For government sales inquiries, please contact governmentsales@pearsoned.com.

For questions about sales outside the U.S., please contact international@pearsoned.com.

Editor-in-Chief
Greg Wiegand

Executive Editor
Rick Kughen

Development Editor
Charlotte Kughen
The Wordsmithery LLC

Managing Editor
Kristy Hart

Project Editor
Lori Lyons

Copy Editor
Charlotte Kughen
The Wordsmithery LLC

Senior Indexer
Cheryl Lenser

Proofreader
Sarah Kearns

Technical Editor
Karen Weinstein

Publishing Coordinator
Kristin Watterson

Compositor
Bronkella Publishing

Cover Designer
Mark Shirar

Contents at a Glance

Table of Contents

14 Storing and Sharing Pictures with Loved Ones **283**

About the Author

Michael Miller is a prolific and popular author of non-fiction books, known for his ability to explain complex topics to everyday readers. He writes about a variety of topics, including technology, social networking, business, and music. Mr. Miller has written more than 150 books over the past two decades, as well as a variety of online and print articles. His best-selling books for Que include *My Facebook for Seniors, Facebook for Grown-Ups, Easy Facebook, Easy Computer Basics, Absolute Beginner's Guide to Computer Basics*, and *My Pinterest*. Collectively, his books have sold more than 1 million copies worldwide.

Find out more at the author's website: www.molehillgroup.com

Follow the author on Twitter: molehillgroup

Dedication

To my late grandfather, Albert Blickenstaff, who taught me everything I know about being a grandpa.

Acknowledgments

Thanks to all the folks at Que who helped turn this manuscript into a book, including Rick Kughen, Greg Wiegand, Charlotte Kughen, Lori Lyons, Todd Brakke, and technical editor Karen Weinstein.

We Want to Hear from You!

As the reader of this book, *you* are our most important critic and commentator. We value your opinion and want to know what we're doing right, what we could do better, what areas you'd like to see us publish in, and any other words of wisdom you're willing to pass our way.

We welcome your comments. You can email or write to let us know what you did or didn't like about this book—as well as what we can do to make our books better.

Please note that we cannot help you with technical problems related to the topic of this book.

When you write, please be sure to include this book's title and author as well as your name and email address. We will carefully review your comments and share them with the author and editors who worked on the book.

Email: feedback@quepublishing.com

Mail: Que Publishing
        ATTN: Reader Feedback
        800 East 96th Street
        Indianapolis, IN 46240 USA

Reader Services

Visit our website and register this book at quepublishing.com/register for convenient access to any updates, downloads, or errata that might be available for this book.

Keyboard

Mouse

In this prologue you learn how to operate Windows 8.1 with your mouse or keyboard, or with touch-screen gestures.

→ Using Windows with a Mouse or Touchpad
→ Using Windows with a Keyboard
→ Using Windows on a Touchscreen PC

Prologue: Basic Operations

Whether you're completely new to computers or just new to Windows 8 or 8.1, there are some basic operations you need to master. On any PC, you can operate Windows with your keyboard or mouse (or, on a notebook PC, your touchpad). On a touchscreen PC, you can also use touch gestures for many operations. Choose whichever approach is more comfortable and convenient for you.

Using Windows with a Mouse or Touchpad

To use Windows efficiently on a desktop or notebook PC, you need to master a few simple operations with your mouse or touchpad, such as pointing and clicking, dragging and dropping, and right-clicking.

Mouse and Touchpad Operations

Of the various mouse and touchpad operations, the most common is pointing and clicking—that is, you point at something with the onscreen cursor, and then click the appropriate mouse or touchpad button. Normal clicking uses the left button; however, some operations require that you click the right button instead.

(1) To single-click (select) an item, position the cursor over the onscreen item and click the left mouse or touchpad button.

(2) To double-click (select or open) an item, position the cursor over the onscreen item and click the left mouse or touchpad button twice in rapid succession.

(3) To right-click an item (to display a context-sensitive options menu), position the cursor over the onscreen item, and then click the *right* mouse button.

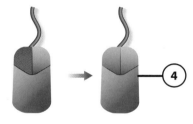

(4) To drag and drop an item from one location to another, position the cursor over the item, click and hold the left mouse button, drag the item to a new position, and then release the mouse button.

(5) To scroll through a window, click the up or down arrow on the window's scrollbar.

(6) To move to a specific place in a long window or document, click the scroll box (between the up and down arrows) and drag it to a new position.

Scroll Wheel

If your mouse has a scroll wheel, you can use it to scroll through a long document. Just roll the wheel back or forward to scroll down or up through a window. Likewise, some notebook touchpads let you drag your finger up or down to scroll through a window.

(7) To display the Start screen, mouse over the lower-left corner of the screen and click the Start button. (The Start button is always present on the Windows desktop, at the far left side of the taskbar.)

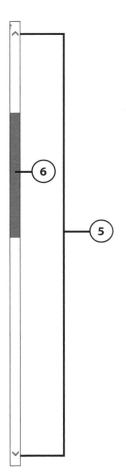

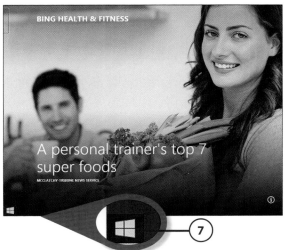

(8) To open the Charms bar, mouse over the lower-right or upper-right corner of the screen.

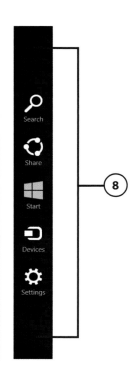

Mouse Over

Another common mouse operation is called the *mouse over*, or *hovering*, where you hold the cursor over an onscreen item without pressing either of the mouse buttons. For example, when you mouse over an icon or menu item, Windows displays a *ToolTip* that tells you a little about the selected item.

Using Windows with a Keyboard

You don't have to use your mouse or touchpad to perform many operations in Windows. Many users prefer to use their keyboards, as it enables them to keep their hands in one place when they're entering text and other information.

Keyboard Operations

Many Windows operations can also be achieved from your computer keyboard, without touching your mouse or touchpad. Several of these operations use special keys that are unique to Windows PC keyboards, such as the Windows and Application keys.

To scroll down any page or screen, press the PageDown key.

 To scroll up any page or screen, press the PageUp key.

 To launch a program or open a file, use the keyboard's arrow keys to move to the appropriate item and then press the Enter key.

 To display a context-sensitive pop-up menu (the equivalent of right-clicking an item), use the keyboard's arrow keys to move to that item and then press the Application key.

 To cancel or "back out" of the current operation, press the Esc key.

 To rename a file, use the keyboard's arrow keys to move to that file and then press the F2 key.

 To access an application's Help system, press the F1 key.

 To display the Start screen, press the Windows key.

 To open the Charms bar, press the Windows+C keys.

Using Windows on a Touchscreen PC

If you're using Windows 8 or 8.1 on a computer or tablet with a touchscreen display, you'll be using your fingers instead of a mouse to do what you need to do. To that end, it's important to learn some essential touchscreen operations.

It's Not All Good

Touchscreen PCs

The majority of PCs sold today do not have touchscreen displays, as this technology typically adds $100 or so to the computer's price. There's no point in touching or swiping a non-touchscreen display, as it won't do anything. Save your touch gestures for PCs with true touchscreen displays.

Touchscreen Operations

Windows 8 and 8.1 were designed with touchscreens in mind. Most operations can be performed without a mouse or keyboard, using simple touch gestures instead.

 To "click" or select an item on a touchscreen display, tap the item with the tip of your finger and release.

 To "right-click" an item on a touchscreen display (typically displays a context-sensitive options menu), press and hold the item with the tip of your finger.

 To scroll up or down a page, swipe the screen in the desired direction.

 To open the Charms bar, touch the right edge of the screen and swipe to the left.

To display the Start screen, open the Charms bar and then tap Start.

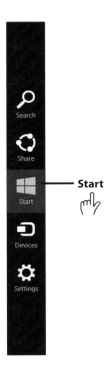

Start

Notebook PC

All-in-one desktop PC

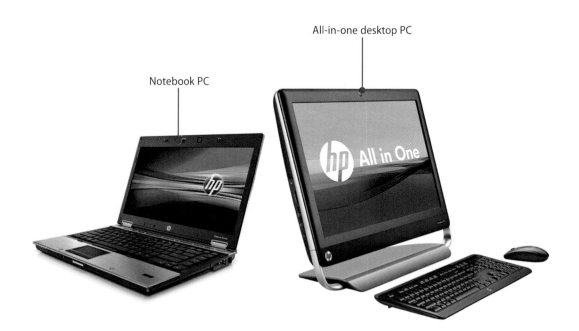

In this chapter you find out what components are in a typical computer system—what they are and how they work.

Understanding Computer Basics

How do computers work? What should you look for if you need a new PC? And how do you connect everything together?

These are common questions for seniors, and for anyone just getting started out with computers. Read on to learn more about the key components of a typical computer system—and how they all work together.

Examining Key Components

All computers do pretty much the same things, in pretty much the same ways. There are differences, however, in the capacities and capabilities of key components, which can affect how fast your computer operates. And when you're shopping for a new PC, you need to keep these options in mind.

Hard Disk Drive

All computers feature some form of long-term storage for your favorite documents, photos, music, and videos. This storage is typically in the form of an *internal hard disk drive*. This is a device that stores data magnetically, on multiple metallic platters—kind of like a high-tech electronic juke box.

Lettered Drives

All storage drives are assigned specific letters by Windows. On most systems, the main hard drive is called the c: drive. If you have a second hard drive, it will be the d: drive. Any external drives attached to your PC pick up the lettering from there.

Most computers today come with very large hard drives, capable of storing just about anything you can imagine. In terms of capacity, you can find hard drives with anywhere from 300 gigabytes (GB) to 2 terabytes (TB) of storage space. The more hard disk storage the better, especially if you have lots of digital photos or videos to store.

Kilobytes, Megabytes, Gigabytes, and Terabytes

The most basic unit of digital storage is called a *byte*; a byte typically equals one character of text. One thousand bytes equal one *kilobyte* (KB). One thousand kilobytes, or one million bytes, equal one *megabyte* (MB). One thousand megabytes, or one billion bytes, equal one *gigabyte* (GB). One thousand gigabytes, or one trillion bytes, equal one *terabyte* (TB).

Some notebook PCs offer solid state devices instead of hard disks for long-term storage. Unlike traditional hard disks, solid state storage devices have no moving parts; instead they store data electronically on silicon microchips. That makes solid state storage smaller, lighter, and faster than hard disk storage, but also more expensive. For that reason, PCs with solid state storage typically provide much less storage space than those with traditional hard drives. For most of us, traditional hard drives are the better choice.

Memory

Hard disks provide long-term storage for your data. Your computer also needs short-term storage to temporarily store documents as you're working on them or photos you're viewing.

This short-term storage is provided by your PC's *random access memory*, or RAM. Most PCs today offer anywhere from 2 to 8 megabytes (MB) of RAM. The more memory in your computer, the faster it operates.

Processor

The other major factor that affects the speed of your PC is its *central processing unit* (CPU) or *processor*. The more powerful your computer's CPU, measured in terms of megahertz (MHz), the faster your system runs.

Today's CPUs often contain more than one processing unit. A dual-core CPU contains the equivalent of two processors in one unit and should be roughly twice as fast as a comparable single-core CPU; a quad-core CPU should be four times as fast as a single-core CPU.

System Unit

On a typical desktop computer, the hard disk, memory, and CPU are contained within a separate system unit that also sports various connectors and ports for monitors and other devices. On an all-in-one desktop, the system unit is built into the monitor display. On a notebook PC, the hard disk and other components are all part of the notebook itself.

Display

All computers today come with liquid crystal display (LCD) screens. The screen can be in an external monitor (for desktop systems) or built into a notebook PC. Screens come in a variety of sizes, from 10" diagonal in small notebook PCs to 24" or more in larger desktop systems. Naturally, you should choose a screen size that's easy for you to read.

LCD monitor

Some LCD monitors offer touch-screen operation, which is useful with the Windows 8.1 operating system; Windows 8.1 was built with touch-screen operation in mind. With a touch-screen monitor, you can perform many operations with the swipe of a fingertip. Unfortunately, touch-screen displays cost more than traditional displays, so they're found primarily on higher-end units.

Keyboard

When it comes to typing letters and emails, as well as posting updates to Facebook, you need an alphanumeric keyboard. On a desktop PC, the keyboard is an external component (called a *peripheral*); the keyboard is built into all notebook PCs.

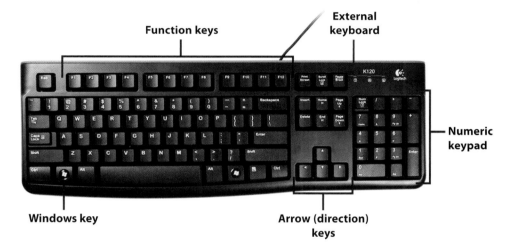

Computer keyboards include typical typewriter keys, as well as a set of so-called *function keys* (designated F1 through F12) aligned on the top row of the keyboard; these function keys provide one-touch access to many computer functions. For example, pressing the F1 key in many programs brings up the program's help system.

There are also several keys that aren't letters or numbers that perform general functions. For example, the Escape (Esc) key typically undoes the current action, the Backspace key deletes the previous character, and the Delete (Del) key deletes the current character. And, as you learn later in this book, there are also Windows and Menu keys that have specific functionality within the Windows operating system.

In addition, most external (and some notebook) keyboards have a separate numeric keypad, which makes it easier to enter numbers. There are also number keys beneath the function keys on all computer keyboards.

External Input on a Notebook PC

Even though notebook PCs come with built-in keyboards and touchpads, you can still connect external keyboards and mice if you like, via the PC's USB ports. (Read more about USB ports later in this chapter.) Some users prefer the feel of full-size keyboards and mice to the smaller versions included in their notebooks.

Pointing Device

You use a pointing device of some sort to move the cursor from place to place on the computer screen. On a desktop PC, the pointing device of choice is called a *mouse*; it's about the size of a bar of soap, and you make it work by rolling it across a hard surface, such as a desktop.

Left button ——   —— Scroll wheel
                                   —— Right button

External mouse

Most notebook PCs have a built-in pointing device called a *touchpad*. You move your fingers across the touchpad to move the cursor across the computer screen.

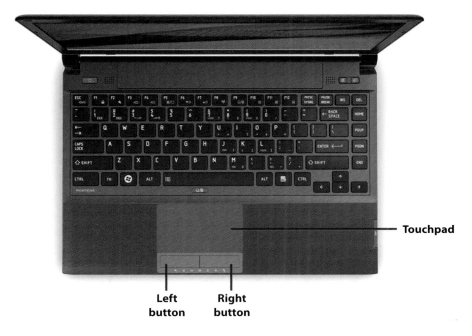

Touchpad

Left button   **Right button**

Both mice and touchpads have accompanying buttons that you click to perform various operations. Most devices include both left and right buttons; clicking the left button activates most common functions, whereas clicking the right button provides additional functionality in select situations.

Virtual Buttons

Some touchpads don't have discrete buttons. Instead, the lower part of the touchpad is designated as the button area; you tap on the lower-left quadrant to left-click, and tap on the lower-right quadrant to right-click.

Connectors

Every computer comes with a variety of connectors (called *ports*) to which you can connect external components (called *peripherals*), such as keyboards, printers, and the like. There are a number of different connectors available, and not all computers offer the same assortment.

On today's computers, the most common type of connector is called the *universal serial bus*, or *USB*. Most external devices connect to your computer via USB.

Desktop computers (and most notebooks) also have a connector for an external monitor. This can be a traditional video graphics array (VGA) connector, or a newer digital visual interface (DVI) connector. If DVI is available, you should use that.

HDMI

Some notebook computers come with an additional HDMI connector. This port transmits both video and audio, and is typically used to connect a computer to a living room TV. (HDMI is also used to connect DVD players, Blu-ray players, cable boxes, and other devices to television sets.)

Most computers today also have an Ethernet port to connect to wired home and office networks. Notebook computers also offer wireless network connectivity, via a technology called *Wi-Fi*. If your computer has Wi-Fi, you don't have to connect via Ethernet.

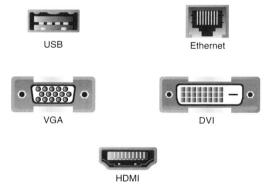

USB

Ethernet

VGA

DVI

HDMI

Exploring Different Types of PCs

If you're in the market for a new PC, there are two general types available—desktops and notebooks. All types of computers do pretty much the same thing, and they do it in similar ways; the differences between desktop and notebook computers are more about how they're configured than how they perform.

Desktop PCs

The first general type of PC is the desktop system. A desktop computer is designed to be used in one place; it's a stationary computer, not a portable one.

All desktop PCs have a separate keyboard and mouse, used for typing and navigating the screen. You also have a monitor, or computer screen, and a system unit that houses all the internal electronics for the entire system.

In a traditional desktop PC system, the monitor and system unit are two separate components; you can store the system unit under your desk or in some other out-of-the-way place. So-called all-in-one systems combine the monitor and system unit (as well as speakers) into one piece of equipment, which reduces the number of connections you have to make. Some all-in-ones offer touch-screen monitors.

Monitor

Desktop PC
system unit

Keyboard

Mouse

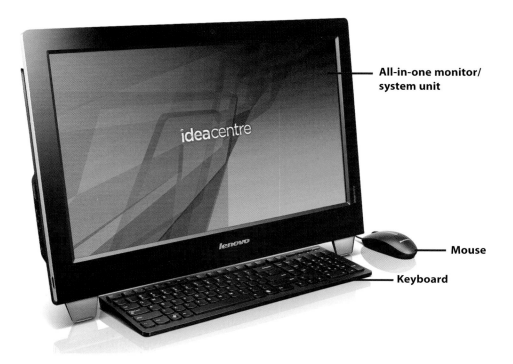

All-in-one monitor/
system unit

Mouse

Keyboard

For seniors, the major advantage of a desktop PC is the larger monitor screen, full-size keyboard, and separate mouse. It's easier to read many documents on a larger desktop monitor, and most full-size keyboards also offer numeric keypads, which are easier for entering numbers when you're doing online banking or budgeting. Many seniors also find the separate mouse easier to use than the small touchpad found on most notebook PCs.

Monitor Screens

Most desktop computer monitors have screens that measure 19" to 22" diagonal. Most notebook PC screens measure 12" to 16" diagonal—considerably smaller than their desktop counterparts.

On the downside, a desktop PC isn't portable; you have to leave it in one place in your home. In addition, a desktop system is more complicated to set up, with all its external components. And you'll likely pay a little more for a desktop system than you will for a similarly configured notebook PC.

Notebook PCs

A notebook PC, sometimes called a laptop computer, combines all the components of a desktop system into a single unit with built-in screen, keyboard, and touchpad. Notebook PCs are not only small and lightweight, but also portable because they're capable of operating from a built-in battery that can last anywhere from 2 to 4 hours on a charge. (Naturally, a notebook PC can also be plugged into a wall to use standard AC power.)

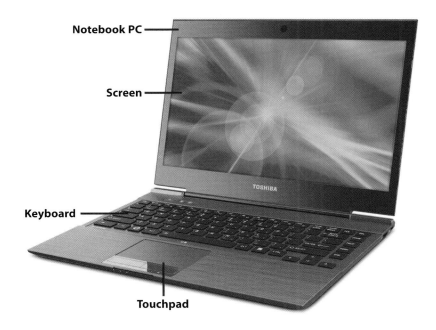

Most seniors today opt for notebook PCs, primarily because they're much easier to set up. In fact, there's little in the way of hardware to set up; just plug it in (or not, if you're using battery power), open the case, and it's ready to go. There are no cords or cables to connect.

In addition, you can take a notebook PC just about anywhere. You can move your notebook to your living room or bedroom as you desire, and even take it with you when you're traveling or use it in public places such as coffeehouses.

On the downside, the typical notebook PC has a smaller screen than a desktop system, which could be problematic if you experience deteriorating vision. In addition, the compact keyboard of a notebook model might be more difficult for you to type on. Most notebook PCs also use a small touchpad to navigate onscreen, as opposed to the larger mouse of a desktop system, which some seniors might find difficult to use.

DIFFERENT TYPES OF NOTEBOOKS

Most people opt for traditional notebooks, which typically have a 14" to 16" display and hard disk storage. Traditional notebooks run anywhere from $300 to $700, and are what you'll find the most of at most retail stores.

If you want a smaller and lighter notebook, consider an *ultrabook*. Ultrabooks typically have smaller screens, no CD/DVD drive, and use solid state storage instead of traditional hard drive storage. This results in longer battery life, but at an increased price—approaching $1,000 in many cases.

If you want a larger screen and don't plan on transporting your notebook much, if at all, consider a *desktop replacement* model. These notebooks have larger screens (17" or so), bigger hard drives, and more powerful processors. They also have very limited battery life and also cost more than traditional notebooks.

Finally, there is a new breed of device that combines the features of a notebook PC with those of a tablet, such as the iPad. These are called *hybrid PCs*, and typically have a touch-screen display and can be operated with or without a removable or disappearing keyboard. Hybrid PCs tend to cost more than traditional notebooks, however, which make them less popular than other models.

Which Type of PC Should You Buy?

Which type of PC you purchase depends on how and where you plan to use your new computer. Here are some recommendations:

- If you need a larger screen and like a full-sized keyboard and mouse, go with a desktop PC. Consider an all-in-one system for easier setup.

- If you don't want to bother connecting cables and external devices, go with a notebook PC.

- If you want to be able to use your computer in different rooms of your home, go with a notebook PC.

- If you want to be able to easily take your computer with you when you travel, go with a notebook PC.

Naturally, every person has his or her unique needs and preferences. Always try out a system in the store to see if the system is comfortable for you before making a purchase.

Setting Up Your New Computer System

After you purchase a new PC, you need to set up and connect all of the system's hardware. As you might suspect, this is easier to do with a notebook PC than it is with a desktop system.

Hardware and Software

All the physical parts of your computer—the screen, the system unit, the keyboard, and so forth—are referred to as *hardware*. The programs and apps and games you run on your computer are called *software*.

Set Up a Notebook PC

If you have a notebook PC, there isn't much you need to connect; everything's inside the case. Just connect your printer (and any other external peripherals), plug your notebook into a power outlet, and you're ready to go.

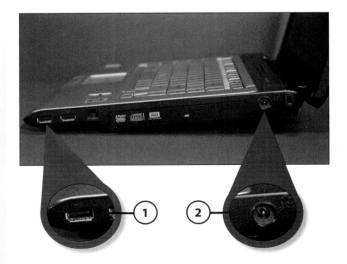

(1) Connect one end of your printer's USB cable to a USB port on your notebook; connect the other end of the cable to your printer.

(2) Connect one end of your computer's power cable to the power connector on the side or back of your notebook.

(**3**) Connect the other end of the computer's power cable to a power source and then connect your printer and other powered external peripherals to the same power source.

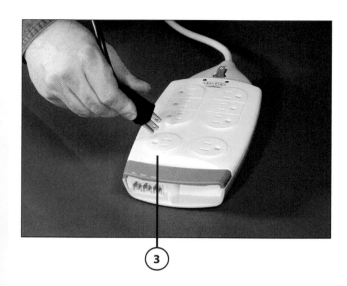

3

Use a Surge Suppressor

For extra protection, connect the power cable on your system unit to a surge suppressor rather than directly into an electrical outlet. This protects your PC from power-line surges that can damage its delicate internal parts.

Set Up a Traditional Desktop PC

If you have a traditional desktop computer system, you need to connect all the pieces and parts to your computer's system unit before powering it on. When all your peripherals are connected, you can connect your system unit to a power source.

(**1**) Connect the mouse cable to a USB port on the back of your system unit.

(**2**) Connect the keyboard cable to a USB port on the back of your system unit.

Mice and Keyboards

Most newer mice and keyboards connect via USB. Some older models, however, connect to dedicated mouse and keyboard ports on your system unit. You should use whatever connection is appropriate.

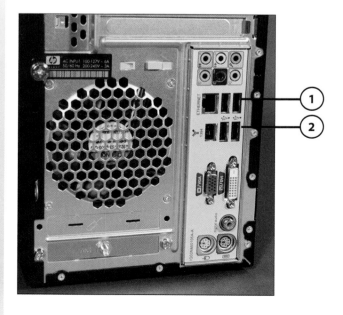

3 Connect the blue VGA monitor cable to the blue monitor port on the back of your system unit; make sure the other end is connected to your video monitor.

Digital Connections

Many newer computer monitors use a DVI connection instead of the older VGA-type connection. If you have a choice, a DVI connection delivers a crisper picture than the older VGA (analog) connection—although a DVI cable is a bit more expensive than a VGA cable.

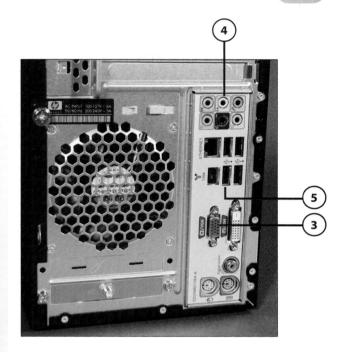

4 Connect the green phono cable from your main external speaker to the audio out or sound out connector on your system unit; connect the other end of the cable to the speaker.

5 Connect one end of your printer's USB cable to a USB port on the back of your system unit; connect the other end of the cable to your printer.

6 Connect one end of your computer's power cable to the power connector on the back of your system unit.

(7) Connect the other end of the power cable to a power source and then connect your printer and other powered external peripherals to the same power source.

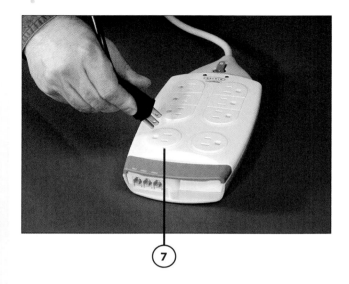

Set Up an All-in-One Desktop PC

In an all-in-one desktop PC, the speakers and system unit are built into the monitor, so there are fewer things to connect—just the mouse, keyboard, and any external peripherals, such as a printer. This makes for a much quicker and easier setup.

(1) Connect the mouse cable to a USB port on the monitor.

(2) Connect the keyboard cable to a USB port on the monitor.

(3) Connect one end of your printer's USB cable to a USB port on the monitor; connect the other end of the cable to your printer.

(4) Connect one end of your computer's power cable to the power connector on the monitor.

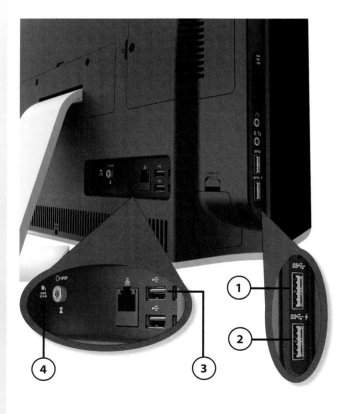

5 Connect the other end of the power cable to a power source and then connect your printer and other powered external peripherals to the same power source.

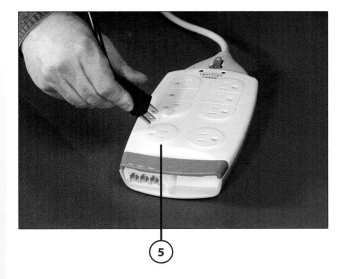

5

Start screen

Desktop tile

Apps button

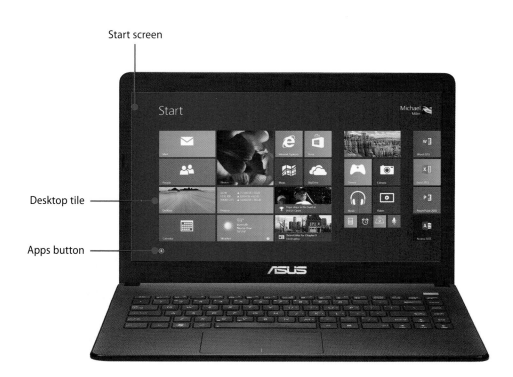

In this chapter you find out how to turn on and
start using a new Windows 8.1 computer.

→ Powering Up and Powering Down
→ Finding Your Way Around Windows

2

Using Windows 8.1—If You've Never Used a Computer Before

Many people our age have used computers before, and probably
have owned at least one PC over the years. But not everyone is an
experienced computer user, and if you've just purchased your first PC,
there's a lot to learn—especially when it comes to using the Windows
operating system.

This chapter, then, is for those of you just starting out with your first PC.
If you're a more experienced user, feel free to skip ahead to Chapter 3,
"Using Windows 8.1—If You've Used Windows Before"; otherwise, read on
to learn how to get started with your new computer and Windows 8.1.

Powering Up and Powering Down

If you've already read Chapter 1, "Understanding Computer Basics,"
you've learned how to connect all the components of your new
computer system. Now that you have everything connected, it's time to
turn everything on.

Booting Up

Technical types call the procedure of starting up a computer *booting* or *booting up* the system. Restarting a system (turning it off and then back on) is called *rebooting*.

Turn On and Configure Your New PC—for the First Time

The first time you power up your new PC, you're led through an initial setup and configuration process so that you can get Windows ready to use.

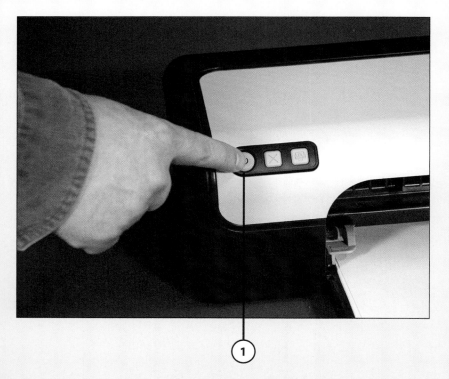

(1) Turn on your printer, monitor (for a traditional desktop PC), and other powered external peripherals.

Go in Order

Your computer is the *last* thing you turn on in your system, after all other connected devices. That's because when it powers on, it has to sense all the other components—which it can do only if the other components are plugged in and turned on.

(**2**) If you're using a notebook PC, open the notebook's case so that you can see the screen and access the keyboard.

(**3**) Press the power or "on" button on your computer. Windows starts up and begins displaying a series of Setup windows and screens.

④ In the first Setup window, Windows prompts you to select Language to Install, Time and Currency Format, and Keyboard or Input Method. Most users accept the settings as Windows offers them (the *default settings*), although you can change any setting as necessary. Click Next to proceed.

⑤ Select Install Now. Windows begins the installation process.

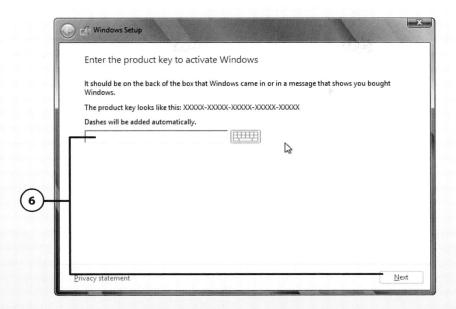

6 If you're prompted to enter a Product Key, do so now. (The Product Key is a combination of 25 letters and numbers, typically found on the back or bottom of your computer, or somewhere in the accompanying instructions or paperwork.) Just enter the numbers and letters; Windows adds the dashes automatically. Click Next. The License Terms window opens.

Product Key

The Windows product key is *not* case sensitive, which means it doesn't matter whether you enter lowercase or uppercase letters. Be careful not to confuse the number 0 with the uppercase O; the 0 (zero) should have a slash mark through it in the product key.

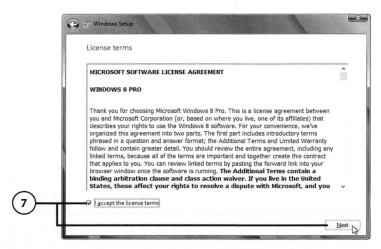

7 You can read the Windows license, if you like, but you must check I Accept the License Terms to continue using your new PC. Click Next to proceed, and Windows completes the Setup process; your computer may turn off and back on during this process.

8 When the Setup is complete, you see the Personalize screen. Click the color scheme you'd like to see on your new computer. Each scheme is a combination of foreground and background colors.

9 Enter a name for your computer into the PC Name box. The name should be descriptive but *not* include any spaces, such as *BobsLaptop*. You can include a hyphen (-), but no other special characters.

10 Click the Next button. The Settings screen displays.

Wireless Network

If there are wireless networks available, the installation process prompts you to select your network from the list; do so and then click Connect. If no network is available, select Connect to a Wireless Network Later. Learn more about connecting wirelessly in Chapter 8, "Browsing and Searching the Web."

(11) Click Use Express Settings to quickly complete the setup. (You can go back later and fine-tune individual Windows settings; there's no need to do so now.) You see the Sign In to Your PC screen.

(12) To get full use out of your new Windows 8.1 PC, you need to create a Microsoft Account. (It's free.) Start by clicking Sign Up for a New Email Address.

Create a New Microsoft Account

If you have a Microsoft Account (from Hotmail or another Microsoft site), enter your email address for that account into the Email Address box and then click Next.

(13) Enter your desired email address into the Email Address box.

(14) Enter your desired password into the New Password box, then re-enter it into the Reenter Password box.

(15) Enter your name into the First Name and Last Name boxes.

(16) Click the Country/Region list and select your country.

(17) Enter your ZIP Code into the ZIP Code box.

(18) Click Next.

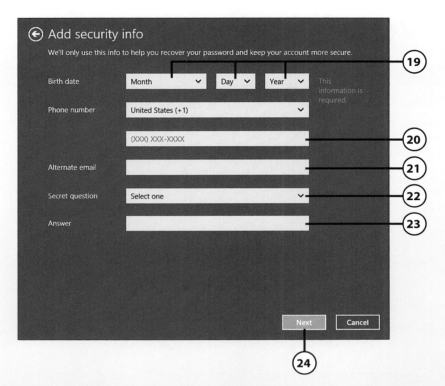

(19) Use the Birth Date controls to enter your month, day, and year of birth.

(20) Enter your phone number into the Phone Number box.

(21) If you have a second email address, enter it into the Alternate Email box. (If you don't have an alternate email address, you can skip this step.)

(22) Pull down the Secret Question list and select a question; you'll be asked this question if you ever have to reset your password.

(23) Enter the answer to your secret question into the Answer box.

(24) Click Next.

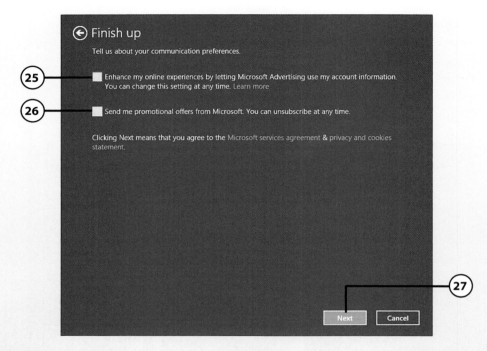

25 If you want Microsoft to use your personal information for advertising purposes (why would you?), check the first box.

26 If you want Microsoft to send you promotional offers via email, check the second box.

27 Click Next, and Windows completes the Setup process. When the process is complete, the Start screen displays.

WINDOWS ACCOUNTS

The first time you power up a new PC, you're asked to perform some basic setup operations, including activating and registering Windows and configuring your system for your personal use. Part of this process involves creating a *user account* for this computer.

You use your email address to create the new user account. If you don't have an existing email address (or don't want to use it, for some reason or another) Microsoft lets you create a new email account at the same time you're activating Windows.

Learn more about user accounts, passwords, and the like in Chapter 4, "Setting Up User Accounts."

Turn On Your System— Normally

Each subsequent time you turn on your computer, you go through pretty much the same routine—but without the initial configuration steps.

(**1**) Turn on your printer, monitor (for a traditional desktop PC), and other powered external peripherals.

(**2**) If you're using a notebook PC, open the notebook's case so that you can see the screen and access the keyboard.

(**3**) Press the power or "on" button on your computer. Windows launches automatically and displays the Lock screen.

Lock Screen Information
The Windows lock screen displays a photographic background with some useful information on top—including the date and time, power status, and Wi-Fi (connectivity) status.

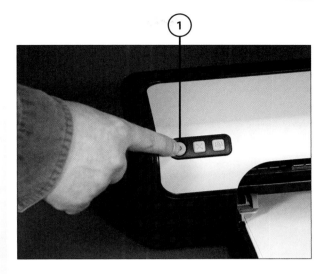

(4) Press any key or move your mouse to display the sign-in screen.

(5) Enter your password (if necessary).

(6) Press the Enter key on your keyboard or click the right arrow.

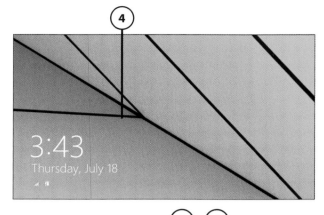

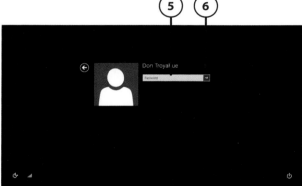

Turn Off Your Computer

How you turn off your PC depends on what type of computer you have. If you have a notebook or tablet model, you shut things down by pressing the unit's power (on/off) button. If you have a desktop PC, however, you want to shut down your system through Windows. (You can also use this process to shut down a notebook or tablet PC.)

New to Windows 8.1

In Windows 8, you had to open the Charms bar to shut down your PC. The ability to shut down from the Quick Access menu is new to Windows 8.1.

(1) Right-click the Start button at the lower-left corner of any screen to display the Quick Access menu.

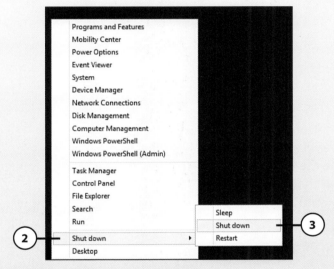

(2) Click Shut Down to display the submenu of options.

(3) Click Shut Down.

Sleep Mode

If you're using a notebook PC, Windows includes a special Sleep mode that keeps your computer running in a low-power state, ready to start up quickly when open the lid or turn it on again. You can enter Sleep mode from the Quick Access menu—or, with many units, by closing the lid of your notebook.

Finding Your Way Around Windows 8.1

When it comes to finding your way around Windows 8.1, you need to know three important elements—the Start screen, the Charms bar, and the Desktop.

Display the Start Screen

Everything in Windows 8 and 8.1 revolves around the Start screen. That's where you start out and where you launch new apps and software programs. You can display the Start screen using your mouse, keyboard, or touchscreen display.

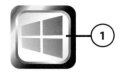

(1) From your keyboard, press the Windows key. *Or…*

(2) …with your mouse or touchpad, click the Start button at the lower-left corner of any screen. (If you don't see the Start button, mouse over the bottom-left corner to display it.)

(3) …on a touchscreen device, touch the right edge of the screen, swipe to the left to open the Charms bar, and then tap Start.

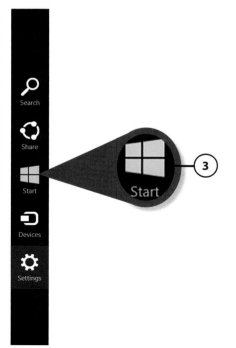

Use the Start Screen

The Start screen consists of a series of tiles. Each tile represents a particular app, program, document, or function. For example, the Weather tile represents Windows' Weather app; the tile displays basic weather information, and if you want to open the full Weather app, all you have to do is click or tap the tile.

Different Looks

Your Start screen probably looks a little different from the ones shown in this chapter—in particular, the tiles you see. That's because every person's system is different, depending on the particular programs and apps you have installed on your PC.

(1) To display the horizontal scrollbar, move your mouse.

(2) To scroll to the right, press the PageDown key on your keyboard, click and drag the on-screen scrollbar with your mouse, or (if you have a touchscreen PC) swipe with your finger.

(3) To scroll to the left, press the PageUp key on your keyboard, click and drag the onscreen scrollbar with your mouse, or (if you have a touchscreen PC) swipe with your finger.

(4) To launch an app, click a tile with your mouse, move to the tile and press Enter on your keyboard, or (if you have a touchscreen PC) tap the tile with your finger.

(5) To see all the apps displayed on your PC, click or tap the Apps button to display the Apps screen.

(6) To sign out of Windows or switch users, click or tap your name.

New to Windows 8.1

The Apps button (the down arrow) on the Start screen is new to Windows 8.1.

Display the Charms Bar

Windows 8.1 has more functions up its sleeve, although they're not obvious during normal use. These are a series of system functions, called *Charms*, which you access from a Charms bar that appears on the right side of the screen. You can display the Charms bar using your keyboard, mouse, or touchscreen.

(1) From your keyboard, press Windows+C (the Windows and C keys together). Or…

(2) With your mouse or touchpad, mouse over the upper-right or lower-right corner of the screen. Or…

(3) On a touchscreen device, touch the right edge of the screen and swipe your finger to the left.

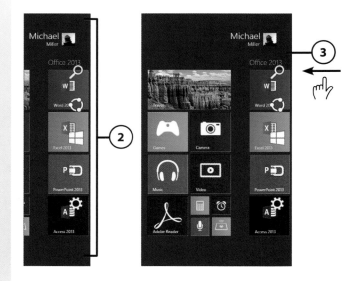

Use the Charms Bar

You use the Charms bar to access various Windows functions, as well as configure various Windows settings.

(**1**) Click or tap Search to search your computer for apps and documents.

(**2**) Click or tap Share to share the content of the current app with other apps or users (via email and other services).

(**3**) Click or tap Start to return to the Start screen.

(**4**) Click or tap Devices to print the current document or access other external devices.

(**5**) Click or tap Settings to access and configure various Windows or application settings.

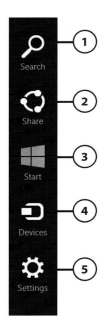

Notification Panel

Whenever the Charms Bar is displayed, Windows also displays a notification panel (at the bottom left of the screen) with the current date and time, Internet connection status, and power status. This panel pretty much duplicates the information shown on the Windows 8.1 Lock screen.

Display the Desktop

Windows 8.1 is fully compatible with most older software programs. These programs—not specifically designed for Windows 8 or 8.1—run in a special environment dubbed the Desktop. When you open an older program, it automatically launches from within the Desktop environment. You can also open the Desktop separately, by clicking or tapping the Desktop tile on the Start screen.

You can "pin" frequently used programs to the Taskbar that runs along the bottom of the Desktop; these pins appear on the left side of the Taskbar. The right side of the Taskbar displays icons for various system activities (such as date, time, wireless network signal strength, and remaining battery life) in what is called the *notification area*.

1. Click or tap the program's icon to open any program docked to the Taskbar.

2. Double-click or tap a shortcut icon to open any program shortcut on the Desktop itself. (Shortcut icons have a small upward-pointing arrow in the lower-left corner.)

3. To minimize all open programs and display the Desktop background, click the far-right corner of the Taskbar.

4. To return to the Start screen, click the Start button at the far-left side of the Taskbar.

Start screen

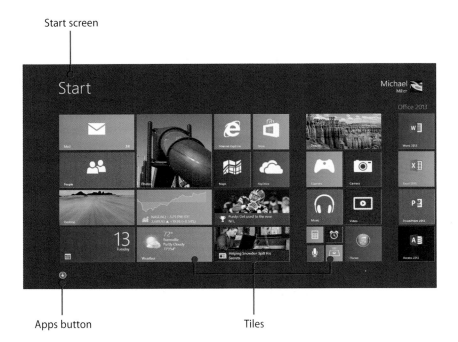

Apps button

Tiles

In this chapter you find out how to do your current tasks on a new Windows 8.1 computer.

→ What's New in Windows 8.1?
→ Logging in with the New Lock Screen
→ Launching Apps from the New Start Screen
→ Accessing the Desktop and Traditional Apps
→ Exploring Improved System Tools
→ Configuring Options from the Charms Bar
→ Relearning Essential Operations
→ Making Windows 8.1 More Like Windows 7

Using Windows 8.1—If You've Used Windows Before

If you've used a computer before, it's likely that you find Windows 8.1 a tad confusing. That's natural; the new Windows 8.1 interface (actually introduced in Windows 8) is unlike anything you've seen before.

You see, Windows 8.1 represents a new approach to computing. Starting with Windows 8, Microsoft's goal was to introduce a single operating system that provides a consistent experience across different types of devices—computers, tablets, and smartphones. To that end, Windows 8 and 8.1 adopt many features formerly found on tablets and smartphones, such as full-screen applications and touchscreen operation, and adapts them to the computer screen.

These changes make it somewhat challenging for you to use your new Windows 8.1 computer to do the same tasks you did with older (pre-Windows 8) versions of Windows. There's a lot that's different, which means you need to relearn how to use Windows—and rediscover where Microsoft put everything.

What's New in Windows 8.1?

Let's start by detailing exactly what's new and different about Windows 8.1. If you've been using Windows 7, Windows Vista, or Windows XP, there's a ton of changes to the Windows operating system. There's even a lot that's changed between Windows 8 and Windows 8.1.

Windows 8.1 Update

If you have a computer running Windows 8, you can (and should) update to Windows 8.1; the new features and fixes make Windows 8.1 a lot more usable than Windows 8 was. For more details about the free update, go to windows.microsoft.com.

Changes from Windows 7 to Windows 8

Windows 8 was a big shock to users of previous versions of Windows. Microsoft essentially changed how people use the operating system, designing an interface better suited to touchscreen devices, such as tablets, than to traditional desktop and notebook computers.

What were these changes? Here's a short list of what Microsoft did with Windows 8:

- Removed the Start button and Start menu from the traditional desktop
- Introduced a new Start screen to launch all applications—part of what Microsoft dubbed the "Modern" interface
- Introduced full-screen Modern apps
- Introduced a new Windows Store to purchase and download Modern apps
- Incorporated touchscreen operation for the Modern interface (actually, designed the Modern interface for touchscreen use)
- Removed the desktop's "Aero" interface in favor of a flatter, non-transparent look
- Removed all "gadgets" that could be used on the traditional desktop

- Introduced the concept of online user accounts, so you could log into Windows using your Microsoft account information

- Integrated the operating system with Microsoft's SkyDrive cloud storage service

- Included Internet Explorer 10, in both desktop and full-screen Modern versions

- Renamed Windows Explorer to File Explorer, and added a ribbon interface

- Completely overhauled the Task Manager tool to make it more functional

- Included the new Windows Defender antivirus/anti-spyware tool, free of charge

- Introduced options to both refresh and reset the operating system in case of severe system problems

That's a lot of changes, and they weren't all received warmly by experienced users. People were particularly annoyed by the removal of the Start button and Start menu, and of being forced to use the new Modern interface and Start screen—even if all they wanted to do was run traditional desktop apps. It was as if in embracing the burgeoning market for tablet computers, Microsoft was abandoning its existing user base and forcing hundreds of millions of existing users to learn a new way of doing things, for no good reason.

Changes from Windows 8 to Windows 8.1

Microsoft listened (a little) to the huge number of customer complaints and made some significant changes to Windows 8.1. These changes, which primarily affect the Modern interface, help users work more consistently in a single environment (either Modern or traditional desktop) without having to needlessly shift between the two.

So if you've been using Windows 8, here's what you'll find new and improved in Windows 8.1:

- Returned the Start button to the desktop—although there's still no Start menu; instead clicking the Start button displays the Modern Start screen

- Enabled users to "boot" directly to the desktop on startup, bypassing the Start screen
- Made the Start screen more customizable, including the introduction of two new tile sizes
- Enabled users to use the desktop background as the background for the Start screen
- Added photo slideshow capabilities to the lock screen
- Incorporated more system configuration options within the Modern interface (you don't have to open the desktop Control Panel to make most changes)
- Added Bing web search to the traditional Windows file/system search
- Integrated SkyDrive cloud storage more fully throughout the operating system
- Introduced additional "snap" options for displaying multiple Modern apps onscreen at the same time
- Revamped the Windows Store to make it easier to use
- Revamped the Xbox Music, Xbox Video, and Photos apps
- Added several new Modern apps, including Calculator, Alarm, Health & Fitness, and Food & Drink
- Included Internet Explorer 11, in both desktop and Modern versions—with major interface changes to the Modern version

Some of these changes are relatively minor, some more noticeable. All are designed to make Windows 8.1 more useable on either a touchscreen or traditional computing device. If you've been complaining about Windows 8, you'll find that the Windows 8.1 update addresses most of your issues.

Logging in with the New Lock Screen

Prior to Windows 8, you logged into Windows from a fairly innocuous log-in screen, using your own unique username and password. (Maybe; you could have opted to log in without a password.) This sort of user-specific log-in remains in Windows 8.1, but is now done from what is called the lock screen.

The Windows 8.1 lock screen resembles the lock screen you find on an iPhone or iPad. The lock screen itself consists of a background image and some key pieces of "live" information, such as current weather or how many unread email messages are waiting for you. You can configure the lock screen to display a slideshow of your digital photos, if you like. It's also where you log into your Windows user account with your own unique password.

How you configure your user account is something else that's different in Windows 8/8.1. Unlike previous versions of Windows, where each Windows user account was local (that is, specific to a given PC), Windows 8/8.1 encourages you to log into Windows using your web-based Microsoft Account. This option enables you to access information from other Microsoft sites (such as Outlook and Bing) on your new computer. It also lets you keep your configuration settings when you move to another Windows 8.1 computer; just log in with the same Microsoft Account and the new computer will look the same as your previous one.

Local Account

You can still opt to log into your Windows 8.1 computer the traditional way, using a local user account. Note that local accounts don't have the same functionality as accounts linked to your Microsoft Account online; in particular, you won't be able to share or tap into content stored online, such as your online contacts or personalized news and weather information.

Log into Windows

Logging into your Windows 8.1 PC is a fairly straightforward affair. Just select your user account and enter your password.

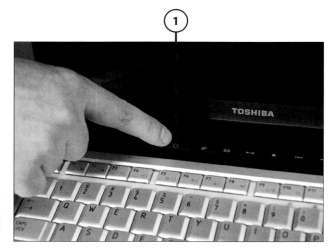

(1) Power on your computer.

(2) After a brief period, the Windows lock screen displays; press any key or tap anywhere on the screen to display your username.

(3) Enter your password.

(4) Press Enter or click/tap the right-arrow button to display the Windows Start screen.

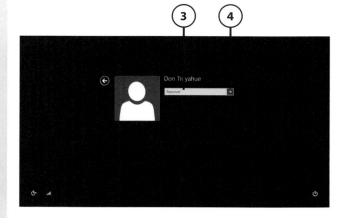

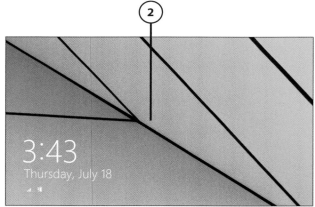

Launching Apps from the New Start Screen

After you log into your Windows 8.1 computer, by default you're greeted with the Start screen. If you've used an older version of Windows, you're probably used to seeing the Windows desktop (which still exists; more on that later), but instead you see a collection of large, colorful, sometimes animated tiles against a colored background. This is your new home base in Windows 8.1.

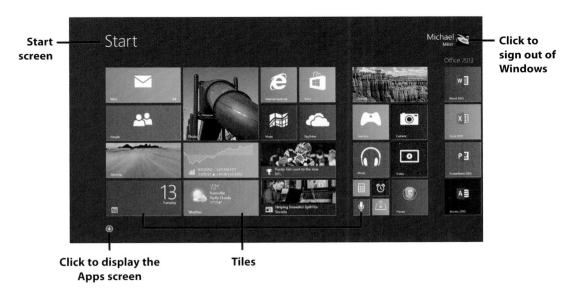

Start screen — **Start** — **Michael Miller** — **Click to sign out of Windows**

Click to display the Apps screen — **Tiles**

Bypass the Start Screen

Although the Start screen appears by default, Windows 8.1 lets you bypass the Start screen and go directly to the traditional desktop. You can also opt to display the Apps screen (which displays all the apps on your PC) instead of the Start screen. Both these options are discussed in Chapter 5, "Personalizing Windows."

The Start screen is where you find and launch your favorite programs, applications, and utilities. Instead of using a Start menu on the desktop, as was the case with all versions of Windows since Windows 95, you now find most of the same options and operations on the Start screen.

The main area of the Start screen consists of a series of tiles. Each tile represents a particular app, program, document, or function. At the top-right corner of the screen is your name and profile picture. Click or tap your name to sign out of Windows, lock the screen, or change your account picture.

Many users find the Start screen more functional than the old Start menu. Instead of displaying only the name of a program, the Start screen often displays "live" information from an application. For example, the tile for the Weather app displays the current temperature and weather conditions; the tile for the News app displays a scrolling display of current headlines. Some tiles even display current content—for example, the Photos tile displays a slideshow of your pictures, and the Desktop tile displays the desktop background. This lets you view some information without having to launch the actual applications.

Customizing Your Tiles

You can easily rearrange the tiles on the Start screen, as well as add new tiles and delete unused ones. Learn more in Chapter 5.

Display the Start Screen

Because there is no longer a Start menu in Windows 8/8.1, you have to return to the Start screen when you want to open a new application or document. There are several ways to do this, depending on how you like to use your computer.

(1) From your computer keyboard, press the Windows key. *Or…*

(2) …with your mouse, click the Start button in the lower-left corner of any screen. (You may need to mouse over the corner to make the Start button visible.) *Or…*

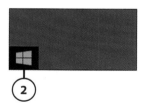

(3) …with your mouse, mouse over the lower-right or upper-left corner of the screen to display the Charms bar and then click Start. *Or…*

(4) …on a touchscreen device, touch the right edge of the screen and swipe left to display the Charms bar and then tap Start.

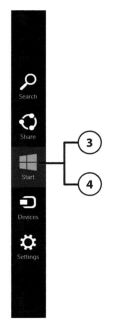

Scroll Through the Start Screen

There are probably more tiles on your Start screen than can be displayed on a single screen of your computer display. To view all your Start tiles, you need to scroll the screen left or right. There are several ways to do this.

(1) To scroll with your mouse, click and drag the horizontal scrollbar at the bottom of the screen, or click the right and left scroll arrows on either side of the scrollbar. If your mouse has a scroll wheel, you can use the scroll wheel to scroll right (down) or left (up) through the tiles. *Or…*

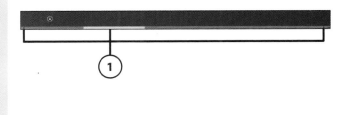

(2) …to scroll with your keyboard, one screen at a time, press the PageDown button (scrolls right) or the PageUp button (scrolls left). To scroll one tile at a time, press the left arrow or right arrow buttons. *Or…*

(3) ...to scroll with a touchscreen display, swipe the screen with your finger right to left to scroll right, or left to right to scroll left.

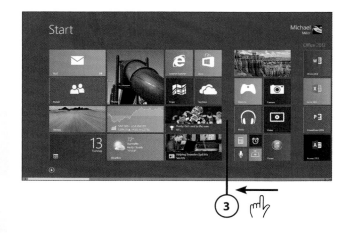

Open a Tile

Each tile on the Start screen represents a specific app or document. There are three ways to launch an app or open a document from these tiles.

(1) To open a tile with your mouse, click the tile, using the left mouse button. Or...

(2) ...to open a tile with your keyboard, use your keyboard's arrow keys to move to that tile, then press the Enter key. Or...

(3) ...to open a tile on a touchscreen display, tap the tile with your finger.

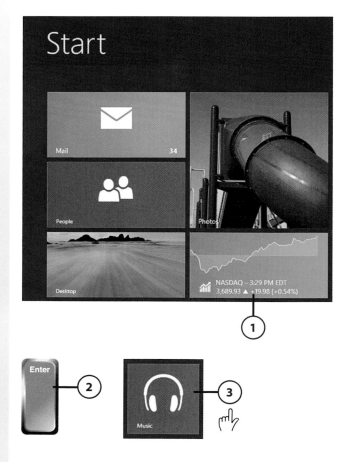

Find Additional Apps and Utilities

The Start screen is where you find most of your favorite apps and utilities. When you install a new app, however, it doesn't automatically appear on the Start screen; you have to manually add the app to the Start screen.

If you want to view *all* the apps and utilities installed on your PC, you use Windows 8.1's Apps screen, instead. You can easily access this screen from the Start screen.

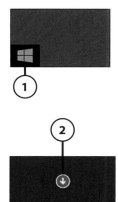

(**1**) Click the Start button or press the Windows key to open the Start screen.

(**2**) Click or tap the Apps (down arrow) button to display the All Apps screen.

(**3**) Click or tap an app's tile to open it.

Add to the Start Screen

To add an app to the Start screen, right-click the app on the Apps screen to display the Options bar along the bottom of the screen, and then click Pin to Start.

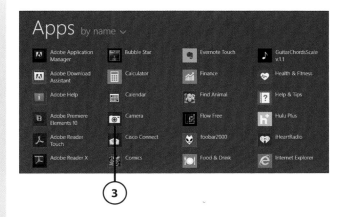

Apps by name ⌄

Adobe Application Manager	Bubble Star	Evernote Touch	GuitarChordsScale v.1.1
Adobe Download Assistant	Calculator	Finance	Health & Fitness
Adobe Help	Calendar	Find Animal	Help & Tips
Adobe Premiere Elements 10	Camera	Flow Free	Hulu Plus
Adobe Reader Touch	Cisco Connect	foobar2000	iHeartRadio
Adobe Reader X	Comics	Food & Drink	Internet Explorer

Accessing the Desktop and Traditional Apps

With Windows 8.1 you have to get used to using a mix of new Modern apps and traditional desktop apps. We've already talked about how to launch a Modern app from the Start screen. Traditional apps run on the Windows desktop, which in Windows 8.1 kind of functions as its own app in the operating system.

Open the Desktop

Windows 8.1 lets you run traditional software applications, such as Microsoft Office or Adobe Photoshop Elements, by retaining a version of the Windows desktop. This version of the traditional desktop is pretty much like the desktop you're used to from previous versions of Windows. In fact, if you have a lot of older programs that you like to use, it's likely that you'll spend most of your time in desktop mode.

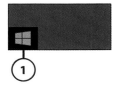

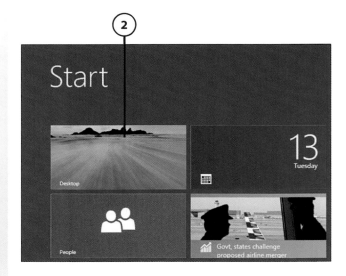

1. Click the Start button or press the Windows key to open the Start screen.

2. Click or tap the Desktop tile.

Open a Traditional Desktop App

The Windows 8.1 desktop looks and works much the same as the traditional desktop in Windows 7 or Windows Vista. That is, applications open in separate windows that can be resized and moved around the desktop. And you can still "pin" application shortcuts directly to the desktop or to the Taskbar that appears at the bottom of the desktop.

There are some changes to the desktop, however. First, you no longer have the see-through windows found in the Aero interface of Windows 7 and Windows Vista; all window frames are solid. More important, there is no longer a Start menu on the desktop that you use to open new programs and utilities. When you want to open a new application or utility, you have to return to the Start screen, which you do by clicking the Start button. You might find this more time-consuming than using the old Start menu, and I'd agree—but that's how Microsoft designed it.

1. Click the Start button or press the Windows key to open the Start screen.

2. Scroll to and then click or tap the tile for the application you want to open.

3. The desktop opens, with the selected application in its own window. You can now use the application as you would normally.

Exploring Improved System Tools

You might find Windows 8.1's new Modern interface takes some getting used to, but Microsoft made several other improvements in the operation system that are immediately useful. In particular, Microsoft has improved some of the most-used system utilities to make them more intuitive and easier to use.

For example, the new File Explorer, which replaces the old Windows Explorer, features an improved ribbon interface, like the one in recent versions of Microsoft Office. Instead of using pull-down menus to access obscure file management commands, the File Explorer ribbons put the most common operations front and center—and make them easier to do, too. Instead of pulling down the File menu to cut, copy, and paste files, just use the Move To and Copy To buttons on the File Manager's Home ribbon. It's a major improvement.

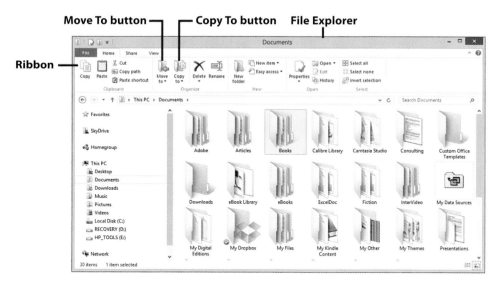

In addition, the Task Manager in Windows 8.1 is much easier to use and more informative than the one found in previous versions of Windows. You can use the new Task Manager to close frozen applications, view system performance, and even manage which programs automatically open when Windows starts up. (To open the Task Manager, right-click the lower-left corner on the Desktop and select Task Manager.)

Click to view system performance

Currently open apps and processes

Task Manager

Click to manage startup apps

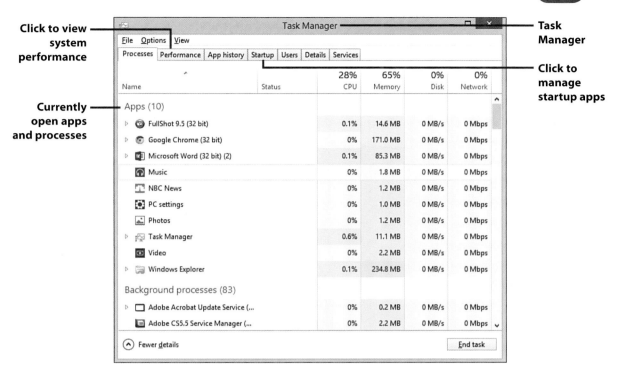

Finally, I've found that Windows 8.1 runs faster and more reliably than older versions of Windows—even on older PCs. So if you upgraded an old PC to Windows 8.1, it should seem zippier than it did before.

Configuring Options from the Charms Bar

In previous versions of Windows, you configured various system options from the Control Panel. Although the Control Panel still exists in Windows 8.1 (it's accessible from the Apps screen in the Windows System group), many common options are configurable from a new Charms bar.

The Charms bar slides in from the right side of the screen when you move your mouse to either the top-right or bottom-right corner of any screen. You can also open the Charms bar by pressing Windows+C.

Configure Windows 8.1 from the Charms Bar

The Charms bar is context-sensitive. That is, the detailed options available vary from program to program. When you open the Charms bar from the Start screen, you see Windows-specific options; when you open it from other applications, you see options specific to that program.

(1) Click or tap Search to search your computer for apps and documents.

(2) Click or tap Share to use email and other services to share the content of the current app.

(3) Click or tap Start to return to the Start screen from any other location.

(4) Click or tap Devices to print the current document or to configure any external devices connected to your computer.

(5) Click or tap Settings to access and configure various Windows and application settings and to shut down your computer.

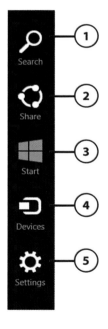

Relearning Essential Operations

As previously noted, Windows 8 and 8.1 were designed with tablets and smartphones in mind. What these devices have in common is a touchscreen display—that is, you operate your tablet or phone with your fingers, not with a keyboard or mouse.

Similarly, you can operate Windows 8.1 with touch gestures—if your PC has a touchscreen display, that is. In fact, many operations, such as displaying the Charms bar or viewing running apps, are much easier and more intuitive on a touchscreen display.

All of these features are nice if your new PC has a touchscreen display—which few existing computers do. If your PC doesn't have a touchscreen display, you have to learn the keyboard shortcuts or mouse movements necessary to replicate the touch gestures.

Touchscreens on New PCs

If you're in the market for a new PC, you'll find that many all-in-one and notebook models come with touchscreen displays. Expect to pay $100 or so more for a touchscreen model than a similar one without the touchscreen, however.

To ease your way into using Windows 8.1 on your new computer, the following table details how to perform some of the most useful operations—with a keyboard, mouse, or touchscreen display. (Note that not all operations can be performed in all three ways.)

Essential Windows 8.1 Operations

Operation	Keyboard	Mouse	Touchscreen
Close currently running app or window	Alt+Q	Drag the top of the app to the bottom of the screen; for Desktop apps, click the X button in top-right corner of window.	Touch the top edge of the screen and swipe down about halfway through the screen.
Display Apps screen	Ctrl+Tab (from the Start screen)	Click the Apps (down arrow button) on the Start screen	Tap the Apps (down arrow button) on the Start screen
Display Charms bar	Windows+C	Mouse over the upper- or lower-right corner of screen.	Touch the right edge of the screen and swipe to the left.
Display context-sensitive options menu	Application (menu) key	Right-click.	Press and hold the item with your finger.
Display Options bar	Windows+Z	Right-click anywhere on the screen.	Touch the top or bottom of the screen and swipe toward the middle.
Display two or more Modern apps side-by-side (snap the apps)	N/A	Mouse over the top-left corner of the screen and then move the cursor down to display thumbnails of all open apps; select the app to snap and drag its (large) thumbnail to either the left or right side of the screen and then release the mouse button.	Touch the left edge of the screen, drag your finger to the right, and then quickly drag it back to the left to display the switcher panel; press and drag the app you'd like to snap to the right and then drop it on either the left or right edge of the screen.
Lock computer	Win+L	From the Start screen, click *username*, Lock (where *username* is the username you use).	From the Start screen, tap *username*, Lock (where *username* is the username you use).
Move an item to a new location	N/A	Click and drag, then release.	Press and hold, drag to new location, and then release.
Open a program or document	Enter	Click (sometimes double-click).	Tap.
Open Windows Help	Windows+F1	From the Charms bar, click Settings, Help.	From the Charms bar, tap Settings, Help.

Operation	Keyboard	Mouse	Touchscreen
Return to Start screen	Windows key	Click the Start button.	Open the Charms bar and tap Start.
Scroll down	PageDown or down arrow	Click and drag the scrollbar or click the scroll arrows; use the mouse scroll wheel.	Swipe up.
Scroll left	PageUp or left arrow	Click and drag the scrollbar or click the scroll arrows; use the mouse scroll wheel.	Swipe right.
Scroll right	PageDown or right arrow	Click and drag the scrollbar or click the scroll arrows; use the mouse scroll wheel.	Swipe left.
Scroll up	PageUp or up arrow	Click and drag the scrollbar or click the scroll arrows; use the mouse scroll wheel.	Swipe down.
Search	Windows+Q or Windows+S	Display the Charms bar and click Search.	Display the Charms bar and tap Search.
Shut down Windows	Alt+F4	Right-click Start button then select Shut Down, Shut Down.	From the Charms bar, tap Settings, Power, Shut Down.
Switch to previous application	N/A	N/A	Touch the left edge of the screen and swipe rapidly to the right.
View or switch to other open apps	Alt+Tab	Mouse over the top-left corner of the screen and then move the cursor downward to display thumbnails of all open documents; click a thumbnail to switch to that item.	Touch the left edge of the screen, drag your finger to the right, and then quickly drag it back to the left; you can then tap any app thumbnail to switch to that app.
Zoom in to the Start screen	N/A	Click anywhere on the zoomed out screen; or press Ctrl key then use the mouse scroll wheel.	Use two fingers to touch two adjacent points on the screen and then move your fingers apart.
Zoom out of the Start screen	N/A	Click the – button in the lower-right corner of the Start screen; or press the Ctrl key and then use the mouse scroll wheel.	Use two fingers at two distant points on the screen and then pinch your fingers in toward each other.

Making Windows 8.1 More Like Windows 7

One of the big complaints about Windows 8 was how different it was from Windows 7. Microsoft listened and made some changes to Windows 8.1 that let you configure the new operating system to more closely work and look like the older one.

Boot to the Desktop

If you do most of your work with traditional desktop apps, there's no reason you need to land on the Start screen every time you turn on your PC. Fortunately, Windows 8.1 lets you bypass the Start screen and go directly to the desktop whenever you sign into Windows.

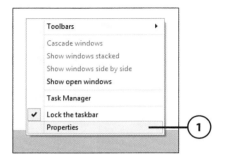

1. From the Windows desktop, right-click the taskbar and click Properties to display the Taskbar and Navigation Properties dialog box.

2. Click the Navigation tab.

3. Go to the Start Screen section and check Go to the Desktop Instead of Start When I Sign In.

4. Click the OK button.

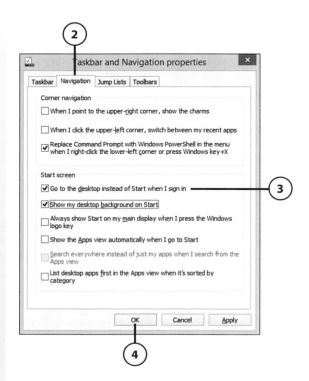

Display Your Desktop Background on the Start Screen

One of the things that users found jarring about Windows 8 was the transition from the desktop to the Start screen, which had totally different backgrounds. (The Windows 8 Start screen didn't display background images, only color and some simple graphics.) Windows 8.1 provides a more uniform look throughout by letting you display the same background image on the Start screen as you do on the desktop. This simple change makes the transition from desktop to Start screen feel much more natural.

1. From the Windows desktop, right-click the taskbar and click Properties to display the Taskbar and Navigation Properties dialog box.

2. Click the Navigation tab.

3. Go to the Start Screen section and check Show My Desktop Background on Start.

4. Click the OK button.

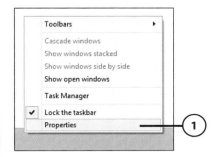

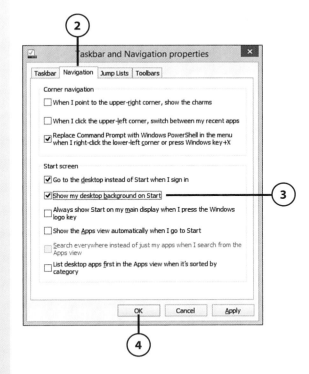

Disable Live Corners

Windows 8 introduced the notion of "live" corners that activate specific functions when you tap them or mouse over them. This is fine if you're using a touchscreen PC, but some people using a mouse on a traditional PC find that live corners actually get in the way of normal operations. To that end, Windows 8.1 lets you disable the upper-left and upper-right live corners, so you won't activate things by mistake.

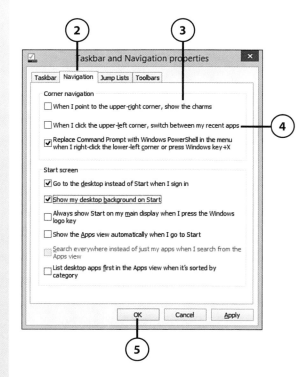

1. From the Windows desktop, right-click the taskbar and click Properties to display the Taskbar and Navigation Properties dialog box.

2. Click the Navigation tab.

3. Go to the Corner Navigation section and uncheck When I Point to the Upper-Right Corner, Show the Charms.

4. Uncheck When I Click the Upper-Left Corner, Switch Between My Recent Apps.

5. Click the OK button.

Show Desktop Apps First

Windows 8.1's Apps screen is the de facto replacement for the traditional Start menu, in that it displays every single app and utility installed on your system. You can sort the apps on this screen in a number of different ways—by name, date installed, most used, or category. If you primarily use traditional desktop apps, choose to sort apps on the Apps screen by category, and configure Windows to display desktop apps first.

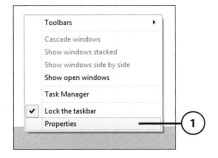

(1) From the Windows desktop, right-click the taskbar and click Properties to display the Taskbar and Navigation Properties dialog box.

(2) Click the Navigation tab.

(3) Go to the Start Screen section and check List Desktop Apps First in the Apps View When Its Sorted By Category.

(4) Click the OK button.

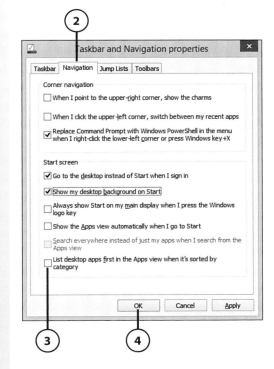

>>Go Further

GETTING THE START MENU BACK

If you've been using Windows for a while, it's hard to understand why Microsoft made so many changes in Windows 8 and 8.1—especially the change that removed the Start menu. These changes force us to relearn how to do many tasks we've been doing the same way for years, and most people—especially seniors—don't particularly like having to relearn this sort of stuff. I know I don't.

There are, however, some options for replacing the absent Start menu in Windows 8.1. These options don't come from Microsoft, but rather from third parties who have created add-on utilities that return the functionality of the old Start menu to the new Windows 8.1 desktop. Most of these utilities are free, and they're all relatively easy to download and install on your Windows 8.1 PC.

I recommend the following Start menu replacement programs:

- Classic Shell (www.classicshell.net)

- IOBit StartMenu8 (www.iobit.com/iobitstartmenu8.php)

- Pokki (www.pokki.com/windows-8-start-menu)

- Start8 (www.stardock.com/products/start8/)

With one of these Start menu replacements installed, you don't ever have to back out to the Start screen to launch new programs. Just log into Windows 8.1, open the desktop, and stay there—using the Start menu replacement just as you did the old Start menu before.

Click to select user

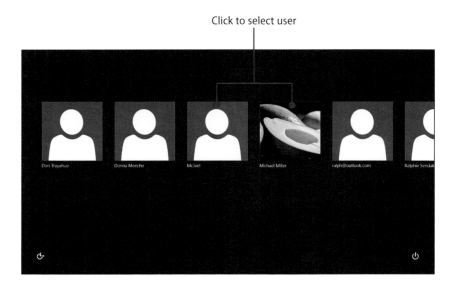

In this chapter you discover how to configure your computer for multiple users.

→ Understanding User Accounts
→ Setting Up a New Account on Your PC
→ Switching Users

Setting Up User Accounts

Chances are you're not the only person using your computer; it's likely that you'll be sharing your PC with your spouse and maybe even your grandkids. Fortunately, you can configure Windows so that different people using your computer sign on with their own custom settings—and access to their own personal files.

Understanding User Accounts

The best way for multiple people to use a single computer is to assign each person his or her own password-protected *user account*. For a given person to use the PC and access her own programs and files, she has to sign into the computer with her personal password. If a person doesn't have an account or the proper password, she can't use the computer.

Windows 8.1 lets you create two different types of user accounts— online and local. The default is the online account, which comes with some unique benefits.

Sign In Options

When you set up a new user account, you can choose from three different ways to sign into your PC. You can sign into your account with a traditional password, with a personal identification number (PIN), or with something new, called a picture password. Most of us will choose the traditional password option, as it's easiest to set up and less confusing to use.

Microsoft Accounts

An online account is linked to a new or existing Microsoft Account, and lets you synchronize your account settings between multiple computers. That is, you can sign into another Windows 8.1 computer with your Microsoft Account and see the same Start screen, apps, and favorites you have on your home computer.

In addition, when you use a Microsoft Account on your computer, Windows displays information from other Microsoft sites you use. For example, Windows displays the latest weather conditions in the Weather app, the latest news headlines in the News app, and the latest stock quotes in the Stock app—all based on settings you make when you configure your Microsoft Account. Local accounts cannot access this personalized data.

The good news is that you might already have a Microsoft Account. If you use Outlook.com or Hotmail for email, you have a Microsoft Account. If you use the online version of Microsoft Office, or Microsoft's SkyDrive online storage, you have a Microsoft Account. If you subscribe to the Xbox Live online gaming service (or, more likely, if your grandkids do), you have a Microsoft Account.

If you don't yet have a Microsoft Account, it's easy enough to create one while you're setting up a new user account on your PC. It's free, and doesn't take much time.

Local Accounts

The second type of account is a local account exclusive to your current computer. This is the only type of account you could create in older versions of Windows. In Windows 8.1, you can still use local accounts, even though online accounts are more versatile.

The chief advantage of a local account is privacy. With an online account, all your activities are linked to a central account, which Microsoft stores and manages. With a local account, your offline activities are not transmitted back to Microsoft.

Unfortunately, local accounts cannot provide personalized information for many Windows 8.1 apps. If you want to take full advantage of the News, Weather, Sports, and Stock apps, for example, you don't want to choose the local account option.

VALUE OF SEPARATE ACCOUNTS

When you get your PC set up just the way you like, you may be hesitant to let anybody else use it. This goes doubly so for your grandchildren; you love 'em, but don't want them to mess up your computer with their games and tweeting and whatnot.

This is where creating separate user accounts has value. Create a user account for each user of your PC—for you, your spouse, and each of your grandkids—and then make everybody sign in under their own personal accounts. Your grandkids can personalize their accounts however they want and there's nothing they can break, and nothing they can change. The next time you sign in, everything should look just the way you left it—no matter who used your computer in the meantime.

Setting Up a New Account on Your PC

You create one user account when you first launch Windows on your new PC. At any time you can create additional user accounts for other people using your computer.

Set Up a New User with a Microsoft Account

By default, Windows will use an existing Microsoft Account to create your new Windows user account. So if you have an Outlook.com, Hotmail, Windows Live Mail, Xbox Live, Windows Phone, or other Microsoft account, you can use that account to sign into Windows on your computer.

1. From the Start screen, press Windows+C to display the Charms Bar.

2. Click or tap Settings to display the Settings panel.

3. Click or tap Change PC Settings to display the PC Settings page.

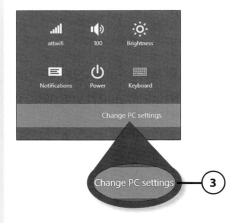

(4) Click or tap Accounts in the left column to display the Accounts page.

(5) Click or tap Other Accounts in the left column.

(6) Click or tap the Add a User button to display the How Will This User Sign In? page.

(7) Enter the person's email address into the Email Address box. If this person currently has a Microsoft Account, such as an Outlook.com or Xbox Live account, use that email address for that account.

(8) Click or tap the Next button.

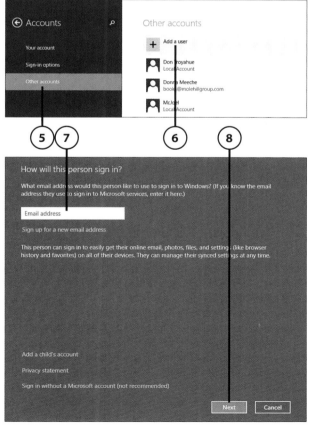

9 If the email address you entered is not for a Microsoft account, you'll be prompted to set up a Microsoft account. Enter the desired password into the New Password and Reenter Password boxes.

10 Enter the person's name into the First Name and Last Name boxes.

11 Enter the person's ZIP Code into the ZIP Code box.

12 Click the Next button.

13 When prompted to add security information, enter this person's birthdate, phone number, and alternate email address.

14 Choose a secret question and enter an answer for it.

15 Click the Next button.

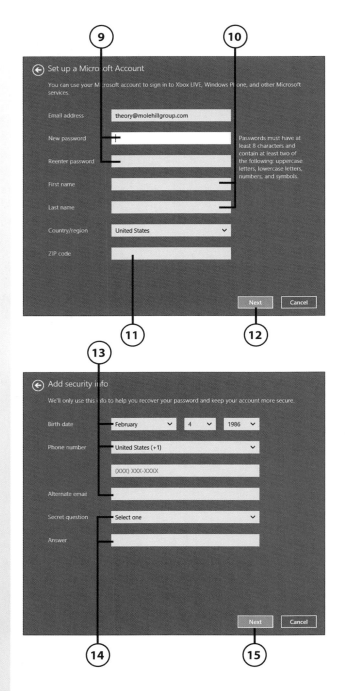

16 Choose whether you want to let Microsoft Advertising use your account information and whether you want to receive promotional offers from Microsoft. (You probably don't want to do either.)

17 Enter the indicated characters into the bottom box.

18 Click the Next button.

19 Click the Finish button.

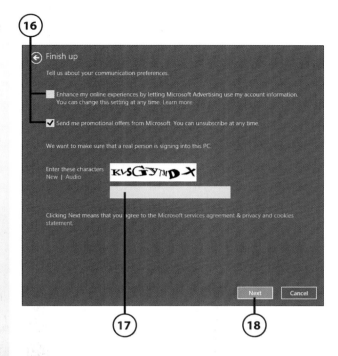

Set Up a New User with a Local Account

If a new user does not have an existing Microsoft Account of any kind and does not want one, or if the user only needs access to this particular PC, you can create a local account for this person.

(**1**) Follow the instructions in the previous section until you get through step 6.

(**2**) Go to the bottom of the screen and click or tap Sign In Without a Microsoft Account.

(**3**) Click or tap the Local Account button.

(**4**) Enter the desired username into the User Name box.

(**5**) Enter the desired password into the Password box and then type it into the Reenter Password box.

(**6**) Enter some sort of hint about the password into the Password Hint box.

(**7**) Click or tap the Next button.

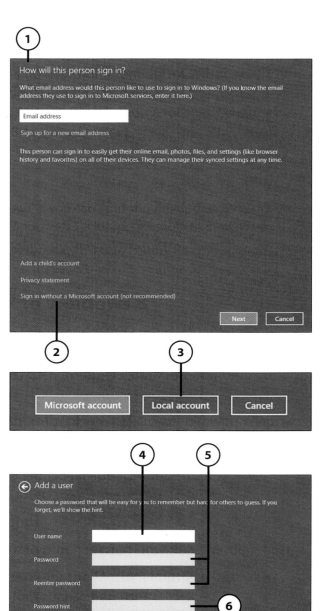

8 Click or tap the Finish button on the final screen.

CHILD ACCOUNTS

>>>Go Further

If you're setting up an account on your computer for one of your grandchildren, you might want to make that account a special *child account*. You see this option when you first click or tap Add a User; click Add a Child's Account from the options at the bottom of the How Will This Person Sign In? screen. (You also have the option of making a new account a child account when you reach the end of the normal account creation process.)

The big difference between a child account and a regular account is that Windows enables Family Safety Monitoring for the child account. With Family Safety Monitoring you can turn on web filtering (to block access to undesirable websites), limit when your grandkids can use the PC and what websites they can visit, set limits on games and Windows Store app purchases, and monitor your grandkids' PC activity.

You do all this from the Family Safety console, which you access from the User Accounts and Family Safety section of the Windows Control Panel. From there you can turn on and off Family Safety and activity reporting, as well as configure web filtering, time limits, Windows Store and game restrictions, and app restrictions for any account.

It's all about making Windows—and your Windows computer—safer for younger users. Your grandkids will be the better for it.

Switching Users

If other people are using your computer, they'll want to sign in with their own accounts. Fortunately, it's relatively easy to sign in and out of different accounts, and switch users.

Change Users

You can change users on your PC without restarting it.

(1) From the Start screen, click or tap your username and picture in the top-right corner.

(2) Click or tap the next user's name.

(3) When prompted, enter the new user's password.

(4) Press Enter or click or tap the next arrow.

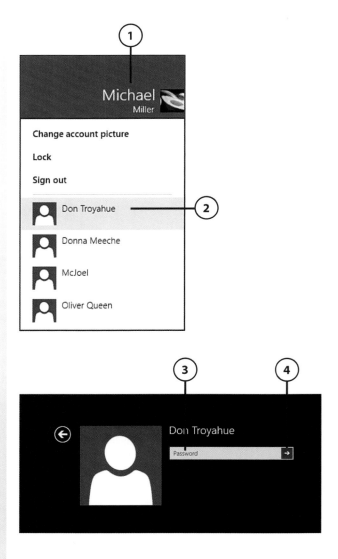

Sign Out of Windows

When you switch users, both accounts remain active; the original user account is just suspended in the background. You can also opt to log completely out of a given account and return to the Windows lock screen.

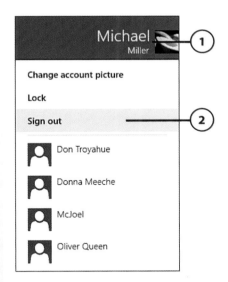

1. From the Start screen, click or tap your username and picture in the top-right corner.

2. Click or tap Sign Out.

Sign In with Multiple Users

If you have more than one user assigned to Windows, the sign-in process is slightly different when you start up your computer.

1. Power up your computer.

2. When the Windows lock screen appears, press any key on your keyboard or gently tap the screen (if you have a touch-screen display) to display the sign-in screen.

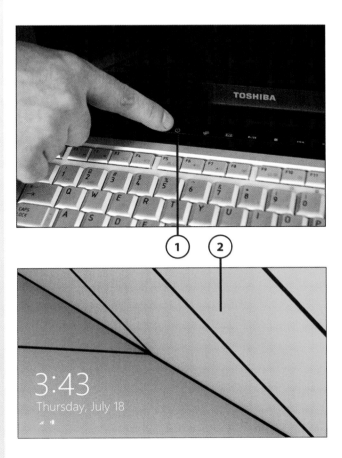

(**3**) If you see a single-person sign-in screen, click or tap the left arrow to display all the users on this PC.

(**4**) Click or tap your username to display your personal sign-in screen.

(**5**) Enter your password as normal.

(**6**) Press the Enter key or click/tap the right-arrow button to display your personal Start screen.

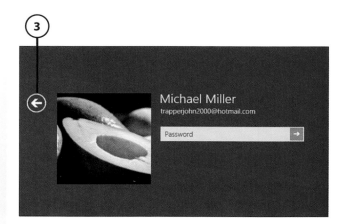

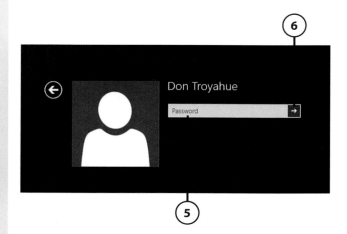

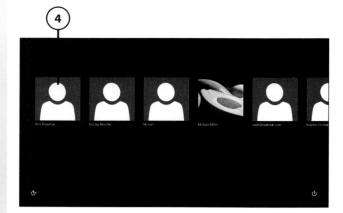

Selected lock
screen

Choose lock screen
background

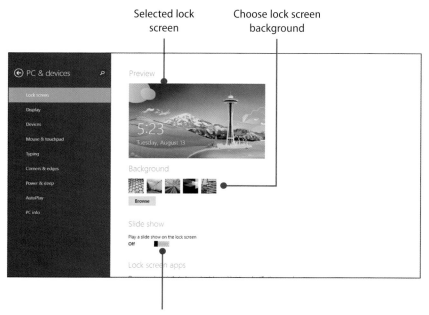

Display slide show on lock screen

In this chapter you find out how to customize the look and feel of Windows to your own personal satisfaction.

→ Personalizing the Start Screen
→ Personalizing the Lock Screen
→ Configuring Other Windows Settings

Personalizing Windows

Whether you're new to computers or have some experience under your belt, Windows 8.1 is a horse of a different color. Lots of different colors, actually, as you can see from the colorful tiles on the Start screen.

Fortunately, there are some simple things you can do to personalize Windows. You can rearrange the tiles on the Start screen, pick different background colors and images, and otherwise make Windows 8.1 your own.

Personalizing the Start Screen

Let's start with the Start screen, your own personal home base in Windows 8.1. As you know, the Start screen consists of a number of tiles that you use to open apps and files.

You don't have to settle for the default Start screen that Windows gives you, however. You can easily change the background color of the Start screen, choose to display your desktop background as the background for the Start screen, and determine which tiles are displayed—and how.

Change the Background Color and Pattern

When you first turned on and configured your new computer, you were asked to choose a color scheme for Windows. This color scheme is what you see when you display the Windows Start screen. But you're not locked into this initial choice; you can change the color scheme and background image for your Start screen (and various subsidiary screens) at any time and as often as you like.

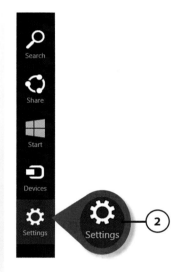

(1) From the Start screen, press Windows+C to display the Charms bar.

(2) Click or tap Settings to display the Settings panel.

(3) Click or tap Personalize to display the Personalize panel.

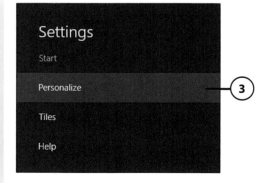

(**4**) Select a background color from the Background Color chooser.

(**5**) Select an accent color from the Accent Color chooser *or…*

(**6**) …select a background theme from the selection at the top of the bar. (This option preselects background and accent colors to match the selected pattern.)

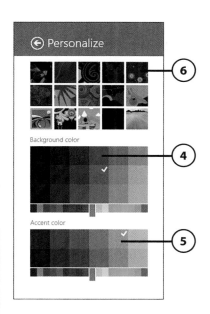

Immediate Changes

The changes you make are immediate and interactive. You don't have to "save" them; they're applied automatically.

Show Your Desktop Background on the Start Screen

In Windows 8.1, you can display the same background picture on the Start screen as you do on the Windows desktop. This makes the transition from the desktop environment to the Modern Start screen less visually jarring.

New to Windows 8.1

The ability to display a background picture on the Start screen is new to Windows 8.1.

(**1**) From the Start screen, click the Desktop tile to display the Windows desktop.

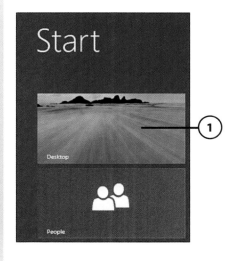

(2) Right-click an open area of the
taskbar and select Properties
to display the Taskbar and
Navigation Properties dialog
box.

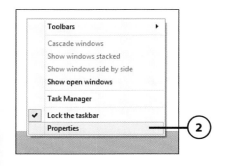

(3) Click the Navigation tab.

(4) Go to the Start Screen section
and check Show My Desktop
Background on Start.

(5) Click the OK button.

Change the Desktop Background

To change the background picture on
the desktop (and the Start screen, if
you have them linked), right-click the
desktop and select Personalize.

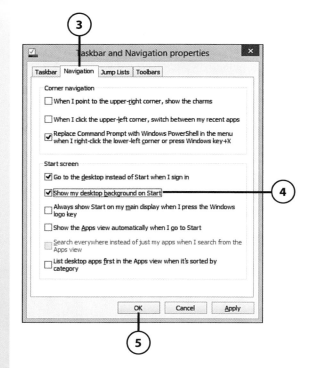

Make a Tile Larger or Smaller

The Start screen is composed of dozens of individual tiles, each representing an app, program, operation, or file. There are four sizes of tiles— small, medium, wide, and large.

New to Windows 8.1

The small and large tile sizes are new to Windows 8.1 Not all tiles are available in all sizes, however.

① Go to the Start screen and right-click the tile you want to change. This adds a check mark to the tile and displays the pop-up Options bar at the bottom of the screen.

② Click Resize.

③ Click the new size you want for this tile.

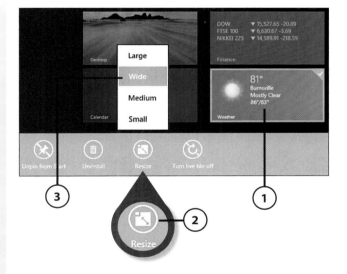

Rearrange Tiles

If you don't like where a given tile appears on the Start screen, you can rearrange the order of your tiles. It's a good idea to rearrange your tiles to put your most-used tiles first, or to group your tiles according to the way you use Windows day-to-day.

(1) With your mouse, click and drag a given tile to a new position. *Or…*

(2) …on a touchscreen display, use your finger to press and drag a given tile to a new position.

Move to Another Group

As discussed in the next section, you can organize tiles on the Start screen into groups. To move a tile to a different group, click and drag the tile from one group to another.

Organize Tiles into Groups

You can organize the tiles on the Start screen into multiple groups of like tiles. For example, you might want to group the tiles for all of the Office apps into a Microsoft Office group. You can create new tile groups at any time.

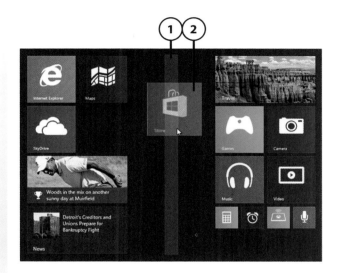

(1) Click and drag an existing tile to the right of its current group until you see a shaded vertical bar.

(2) Drop the tile onto that bar. This creates a new group with that tile as the first tile.

SHRINK THE START SCREEN TO REARRANGE GROUPS

You can shrink the Start screen in order to see more tiles and complete groups. Move your cursor to the bottom-right corner of the Start screen and click the Zoom (–) button. (Or, on a touchscreen device, pinch the screen to shrink it.)

With the Start screen shrunk, you can easily rearrange your tile groups by clicking and dragging a complete group from one position to another. Click an open area of the screen to return to the full-size view.

Name Groups of Tiles

You can give each tile group a name
so that you know what's where. For
example, you might want to organize
all your media-related (photos, music,
and video) tiles into one group and
call it Media.

(1) Right-click any empty area of
the Start screen to display the
options bar.

(2) Click Customize.

(3) Move the cursor to the text box
above the group of tiles, enter a
name for that group, and press
Enter.

Remove a Name

To remove the name from a tile group,
right-click the Start screen to display
the Options bar, click Customize,
mouse over the current name, and
then click the X next to the name.

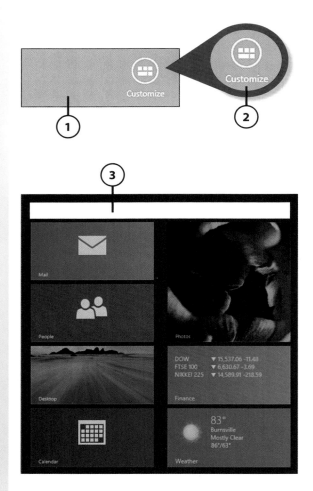

Right click on
    empty area
Name Groups
Spaces appear
Type names
To Remove
    cursor over
    name group groups
    X appears away
    click it.
Right click Stop Naming
                    group

Remove a Tile

You might find that there are one or more tiles on your Start screen that you never use. You can remove unused tiles to get them out of your way and make room for additional tiles.

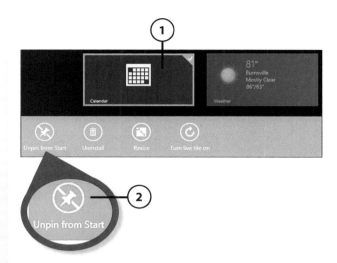

Tile Goes, App Stays

Removing a tile from the Start screen does not delete the corresponding app from your system. The tile for that app will still appear on the Apps screen.

(1) Right-click the tile you want to remove from the Start screen. A check mark appears in the corner of the tile and displays the pop-up Options bar at the bottom of the screen.

(2) Click Unpin from Start.

Add a New Tile

If you accidently remove a tile from the Start screen, or you want to add a tile for an app that isn't already there, you can do so.

(1) Click the Apps button at the bottom left of the Start screen to display the Apps screen.

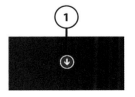

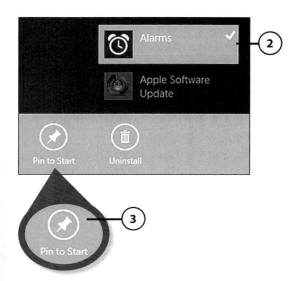

(**2**) Right-click the item you want to add; this displays the Options bar at the bottom of the screen.

(**3**) Click or tap Pin to Start.

New Tiles

Each new tile you add appears at the end of your existing tiles on the Start screen. You can move a new tile to a new position by clicking and dragging it with your mouse or finger.

Turn On or Off a Live Tile

Many tiles on the Start screen are "live," meaning that they display current information or a selected document for that app. For example, the Weather tile displays the current weather conditions; the Photos tile displays a slideshow of photographs stored on your computer.

As useful as that sounds, all the blinking and shifting of the live tiles can be distracting. If you don't like the constant action of a live tile, you can turn it off—that is, display a default tile icon instead.

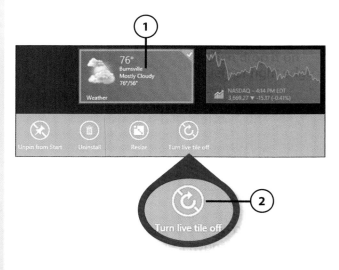

(**1**) Right-click the tile you want to change; this adds a check mark to the corner of the tile and displays the Options bar at the bottom of the screen.

(**2**) Click Turn Live Tile Off.

Turn On a Live Tile

To turn on a live tile, repeat these steps but instead select Turn Live Tile On.

Show the Apps Screen Instead of the Start Screen

Because not all apps automatically appear on the Start screen, many users will find the Apps screen (that displays all installed apps) more useful. You can configure Windows to display the Apps screen instead of the Start screen when you click the Start button.

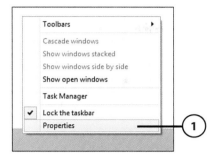

1. Open the Windows desktop, right-click the taskbar, and click Properties to display the Taskbar and Navigation Properties dialog box.

2. Click the Navigation tab.

3. Go to the Start Screen section and check Show the Apps View Automatically When I Go to Start.

4. Click the OK button.

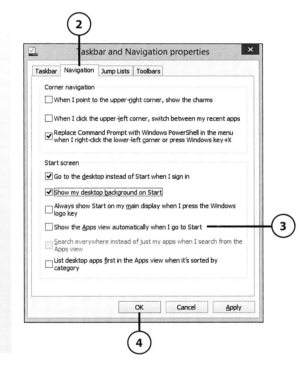

Personalizing the Lock Screen

You can also personalize the lock screen, which you see when you first start or begin to log into Windows. You can change the background picture of the lock screen, turn the lock screen into a photo slideshow, and add informational apps to the screen.

Change the Lock Screen Background

You can choose from several stock images for the background of your Lock screen, or you can upload your own photo to use as the background.

Lock Screen

The lock screen appears when you first power on your PC and any time you log off from your personal account or switch users. It also appears when you awaken your computer from Sleep mode.

1. From the Start screen, press Windows+C to display the Charms Bar and then click or tap Settings to display the Settings panel.

2. Click or tap Change PC Settings to display the PC Settings page.

3. Click or tap PC & Devices in the left column.

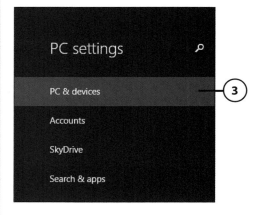

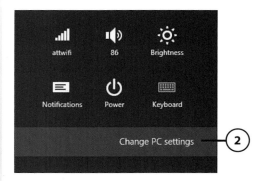

4 Click or tap Lock Screen.

5 Go to the Background section and click or tap the thumbnail for the picture you want to use.

6 Alternatively, click the Browse button to use your own picture as the background.

7 Navigate to and click or tap the picture you want to use.

8 Click or tap the Choose Image button.

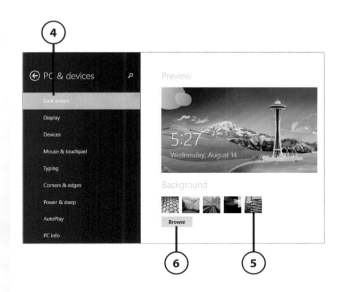

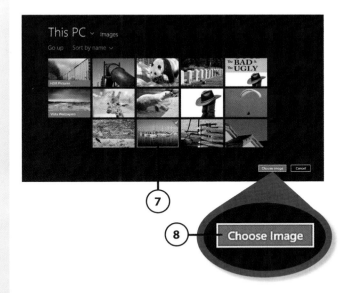

Display a Slideshow on the Lock Screen

Windows 8.1 lets you turn your computer into a kind of digital picture frame by displaying a slide show of your photos on the lock screen while your PC isn't being used.

New to Windows 8.1
The ability to display a picture slide show on the lock screen is new to Windows 8.1.

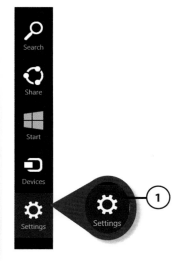

1. From the Start screen, press Windows+C to display the Charms Bar and then click or tap Settings to display the Settings panel.

2. Click or tap Change PC Settings to display the PC Settings page.

3. Click or tap PC & Devices in the left column.

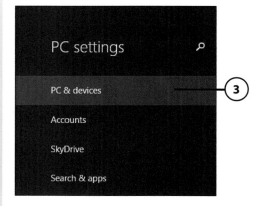

4 Click or tap Lock Screen.

5 Click "on" the Play a Slide Show on the Lock Screen switch.

6 Click or tap Add a Folder to select the picture folder you want to display in your slide show.

7 Alternatively, if you'd rather let Windows pick your slide show pictures, click "on" the Let Windows Choose Pictures for My Slide Show switch.

8 Use the Turn Off Screen After Slide Show Has Play For control to have Windows turn off the slide show (and dim the screen) after a set period of time. Select a time period—30 minutes, 1 hour, or 3 hours. To keep the slide show playing indefinitely, select Don't Turn Off.

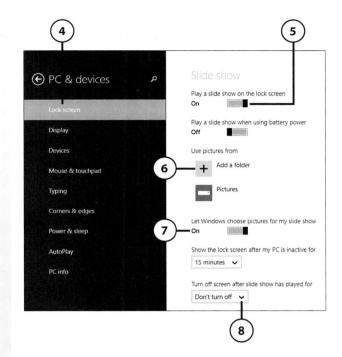

>>>Go Further

DISPLAY THE LOCK SCREEN

You can display the lock screen (and your photo slide show) at any time by going to the Start screen, clicking your profile picture at the top right, and selecting Lock. You can also have Windows display the lock screen after a selected period of inactivity by selecting that option on the lock screen customization screen.

Add Apps to the Lock Screen

The lock screen can display up to seven apps that run in the background and display useful or interesting information, even while your computer is locked. By default, you see the date/time, power status, and connection status, but it's easy to add other apps and information (such as weather conditions and unread email messages) to the lock screen.

(1)   From the Start menu, press Windows+C to display the Charms Bar and then click or tap Settings to display the Settings panel.

(2)   Click or tap Change PC Settings to display the PC Settings page.

(3)   Click or tap PC & Devices in the left column.

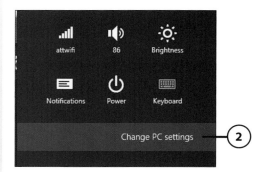

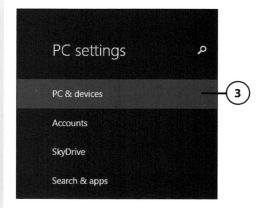

4 Click or tap Lock Screen.

5 Scroll down the Lock Screen panel to the Lock Screen Apps section and then click or tap a + button to display the Choose an App panel.

6 Click or tap the app you want to add.

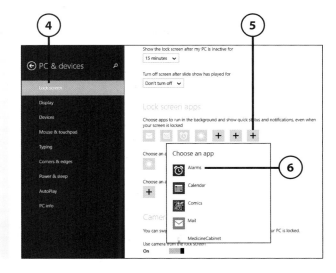

LIVE INFORMATION

You can also opt for one of the apps on the lock screen to display detailed live information. For example, you might want the lock screen to display current weather conditions from the Weather app or upcoming appointments from the Calendar app.

To select which app displays detailed information, click or tap the app button in the Choose an App to Display Detailed Status section.

Change Your Account Picture

Windows displays a small thumbnail image next to your account name when you log into Windows from the lock screen; this same image displays next to your name on the Windows Start screen. Instead of using Windows' default image, you can change this account picture to something more to your liking.

(1) From the Start screen, click or tap your account name in the top-right corner to display the pop-up menu.

(2) Click or tap Change Account Picture to display the Your Account page.

(3) Go to the Account Picture section and click one of the images displayed there, *or...*

(4) Click or tap the Browse button to display the Files screen.

(5) Navigate to and click or tap the picture you want.

(6) Click or tap the Choose Image button.

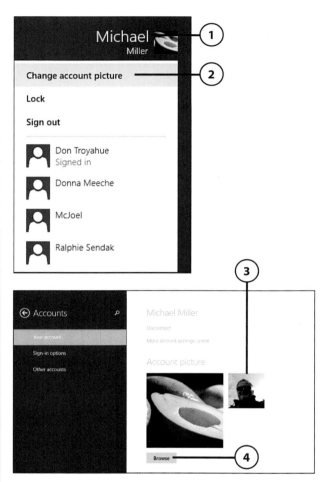

>>>Go Further

WEBCAM PICTURE

If your computer has a webcam, you can take a picture with your webcam to use for your account picture. From the Account Picture page, click or tap the Camera button and follow the onscreen directions from there.

Configuring Other Windows Settings

There are many other Windows system settings that you can configure. In most cases, the default settings work fine and you don't need to change a thing. However, you *can* change these settings, if you want to or need to.

Configure Settings from the PC Settings Screen

You configure the most common Windows 8/8.1 settings from the PC Settings screen. This screen consists of a series of tabs, accessible from the left side of the screen, that present different types of settings.

(**1**) From the Start screen, press Windows+C to display the Charms Bar and then click or tap Settings to display the Settings panel.

(2) Click or tap Change PC Settings to display the PC Settings screen.

(3) Select PC & Devices from the left column to configure the Windows lock screen, determine your computer's display settings, add and remove devices from your system, configure your mouse and keyboard, turn on and off autocorrect and highlighting for misspelled words, enable and disable edge and corner functionality, configure your PC's screen and sleep settings, determine how AutoPlay responds when you attach certain types of devices, and display information about your PC.

(**4**) Select the Accounts tab to change your account sign-in options and add new users to your computer.

(**5**) Select the SkyDrive tab to manage your cloud-based storage space on Microsoft's SkyDrive service.

6 Select the Search & Apps tab to manage Windows' search functionality, determine which apps can be shared with other users, configure Windows' system notifications, view installed apps by file size, and choose which apps open which types of files by default.

7 Select the Privacy tab to configure various privacy options, including which apps can use your location information, webcam, and microphone.

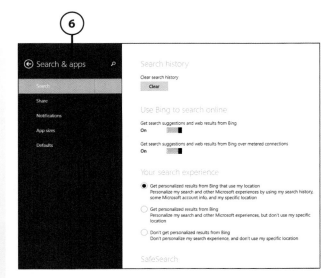

8 Select the Network tab to configure various settings for your
home network, HomeGroup,
and workplace network.

9 Select the Time & Language tab
to change your computer's date,
time, region, and language settings.

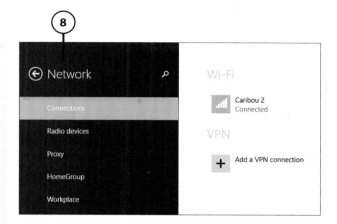

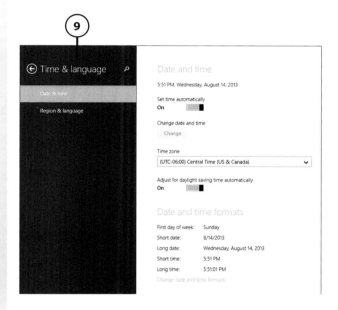

(**10**) Select the Ease of Access tab to configure accessibility options. (Learn more about accessibility options in Chapter 19, "Making Windows Easier to Use by Seniors."

(**11**) Select the Update & Recovery tab to configure automatic downloading of necessary system updates, enable or disable File History backup, and access Windows' Refresh and Restore functions.

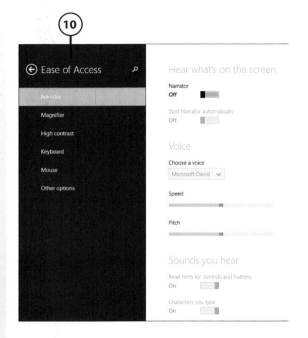

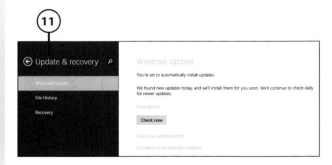

Configure Settings from the Traditional Control Panel

You can find even more configuration settings in the Windows Control Panel. The Control Panel is a holdover from older versions of Windows, and operates from the Windows Desktop. It's a good way to access a more complete set of system settings—even if most of those settings duplicate those found on Windows' PC Settings page.

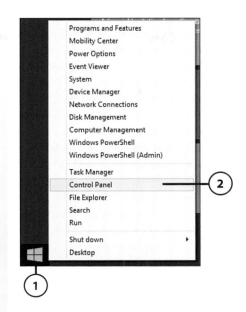

1 Right-click on the Start button to display the Quick Access menu.

2 Click Control Panel to open the Control Panel on the Windows desktop.

3 Click the link for the type of setting you want to configure.

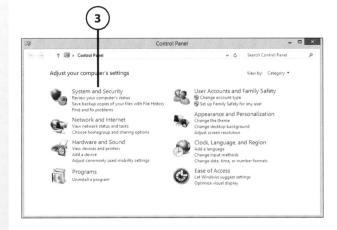

Windows Store

6

Using New Windows Apps

When you want to do something on your computer, you need to use the appropriate programs or applications. Applications—more commonly called apps—are software programs that perform one or more functions. Some apps are for work; others provide useful information; still others are more entertaining in nature. But whatever it is you want to do, you need to launch the right app.

With Windows 8.1, you can run two different kinds of apps. Traditional software programs, such as Microsoft Office, run in individual windows on the Windows desktop, whereas newer Windows 8/8.1 apps, dubbed Modern apps, run full-screen from the Windows Start screen. Day to day, most people use a mix of traditional and Modern apps.

Finding Apps in Windows 8.1

Traditional software programs and newer Modern apps have a lot in common, especially in how you find them, launch them, and switch between them. It's a matter of knowing the right commands and operations.

Search for Apps Installed on Your PC

When it comes to finding the app you want, you can scroll through the various pages of the Start screen, but not all apps are necessarily tiled there. For example, you might have removed little-used apps from the Start screen to make things a little less cluttered. And even if an app is on the Start screen, if there are too many tiles there, you might not be able to quickly find it. For this reason, Windows 8.1 enables you to search for apps by name.

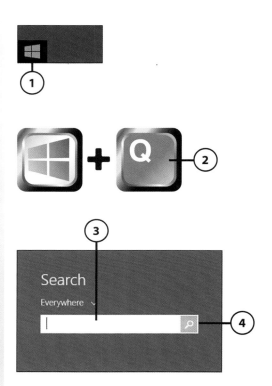

(1) Click the Start button or press the Windows key to go to the Start screen.

(2) Press Windows+Q or Windows+S to display the Search panel.

(3) Enter the full or partial name of the app you're looking for into the search box.

(4) Press the Enter key or click or tap the magnifying glass button to start the search. Windows displays apps and files that match your query.

(5) Click or tap the See All link to see more matching apps.

(6) Click or tap an app to launch it.

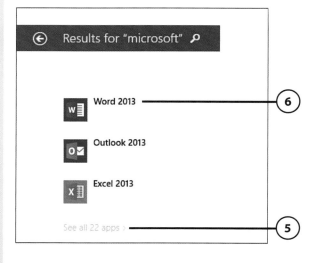

AUTOMATIC SEARCHING

Windows automatically opens the Search pane when you start typing within any Modern app—or on the Start screen itself. Just type a few letters on your computer keyboard, and the Search pane appears with your new query in the Search box. (This does not work from the Windows desktop, however.)

Display All Your Apps

You can also display all apps and utilities that are installed on your computer—and then launch any app from this screen.

(1) From the Start screen, click the Apps (down arrow) to display the Apps screen. All of the apps installed on your PC are displayed.

(2) Click the down arrow at the top left-corner to sort your apps by name, date installed, most used, or category.

(3) Click or tap an app to launch it.

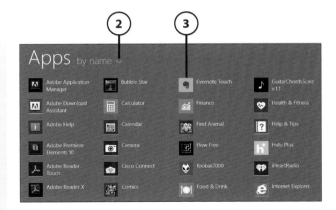

Pin an App to the Start Screen

You might find that it's easier to launch a frequently used app by adding it to the Windows Start screen. This is known as "pinning" the app. When you pin an app to the Start screen, you create a tile for the app; you can click or tap the tile to launch the app.

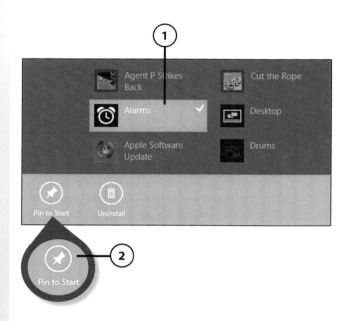

(1) From the Apps screen, right-click the app you'd like to pin. This selects the app and displays the Options bar at the bottom of the screen.

(2) Click or tap Pin to Start.

Unpin an App

You can also unpin any apps you've previously pinned to the Start screen. Learn how in Chapter 5, "Personalizing Windows."

Working with New Modern Apps

Most full-screen Modern apps are fairly intuitive to use. Most of what you need to do is right up front, not hidden behind pull-down menus and toolbars. There are, however, a few common operations you should become familiar with.

Configure App Options

Many Modern apps have options you can or need to configure. For example, the Weather app needs to know where you live so it can deliver the proper weather reports. You configure these options from the app's Options bar, which typically slides up from the bottom of the screen.

App Options

Every application has its own unique options. Some even have two Options bars, at the top and the bottom of the screen.

(**1**) From within the app, right-click the screen (or, on a touchscreen device, swipe up from the bottom) to display the Options bar.

(**2**) Click or tap the options you want to configure.

Switch Between Apps

If you have more than one app open, it's easy to switch between them. In fact, there are several ways to do this.

(**1**) Press Alt+Tab on your keyboard to display a box in the center of the screen, with the current app highlighted. Continue pressing Tab (while holding down the Alt button) to cycle through all open apps. *Or...*

From Desktop

2 ...press Windows+Tab on your keyboard. This displays a switcher panel at the left side of the screen, with the current app highlighted. Continue pressing Tab (while holding down the Windows button) to cycle through all open apps; release the Tab key to switch to a given app. *Or...*

3 ...mouse over the top-left corner of the screen and then drag the mouse down to display the switcher panel. Click the app you want to switch to. *Or...*

4 ...on a touchscreen device, touch the left edge of the screen, drag your finger to the right, and then quickly drag it back to the left. This also displays the switcher panel; you can then tap any app thumbnail to switch to that app. *Or...*

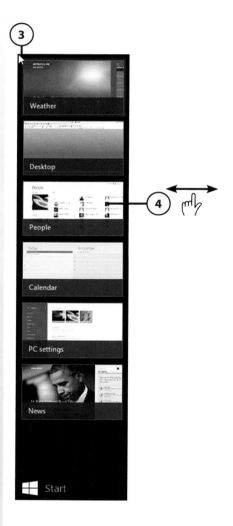

Snap Two or More Apps on the Same Screen

By default, all Modern apps display across your entire computer screen; they're designed for full-screen use. You can, however, display two or more Modern apps side-by-side. This is called snapping the apps. The wider your display, the more apps you can snap; you can snap up to eight apps side-by-side, if your display is wide enough.

New to Windows 8.1

The ability to resize snapped apps is new to Windows 8.1. In Windows 8, the two snapped apps were positioned at a fixed 70/30 ratio.

1 Display the first app in full screen mode, then bump your mouse against the top-left corner of the screen and drag it downward (without pressing the mouse button) to display the Switcher panel.

(2) Click and drag the other app you want to display to the right.

(3) When the shaded vertical bar appears in the middle of the screen, drop the second app into the blank area. The two apps are now displayed side by side.

Snap More Apps

If your screen is wide enough, you can snap more than two apps side by side. Just repeat steps 1 through 3 to snap additional apps.

(4) To change the width of the displayed apps, click and drag the vertical bar to one side or another.

(5) To revert to a single app onscreen, click and drag the vertical bar all the way to the other side of the screen from that app.

Close an Open App

In older versions of Windows, you needed to close open apps when you were done with them. That's not the case in Windows 8 and 8.1; you can leave any Modern app running as long as you like without using valuable system resources. You can still, however, close open apps, if you'd like. There are two ways to do this.

Paused Apps

An open but unused app is essentially paused until you return to it.

(1) From the open app, move the mouse cursor to the top of the screen until it changes to a hand shape.

(2) Click and drag the top of the screen downward to the bottom of the screen.

Swipe to Close

On a touchscreen display, use your finger to swipe the top of the open app downward to close.

Using Popular Windows 8.1 Apps

Windows 8.1 comes with numerous useful apps preinstalled, including News, Weather, Sports, Finance, and Calendar apps. You launch these apps by clicking or tapping their tiles on the Windows Start or Apps screen.

News

When you want to read the latest headlines, use Windows 8.1's News app. The first thing you see when you launch the app is the Top Story page. This is indeed the top story of the day, at least as selected by Microsoft's Bing News. Click or tap anywhere on this page to open the full story for in-depth reading.

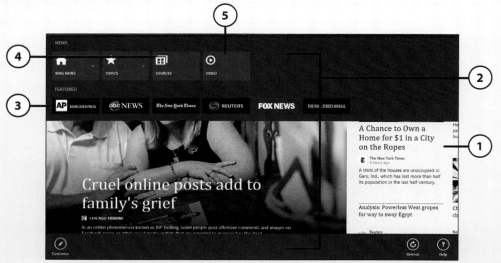

1. Scroll right to view stories organized by topic: U.S., World, Technology, Business, Entertainment, Politics, Sports, and Health.

2. Right-click anywhere in the app to display the Options bars at the top and bottom of the screen.

3. Click any news source to view stories from that newspaper or news service.

4. Click Sources to view additional news sources.

5. Click Video to view today's top news videos.

Weather

Windows 8.1's Weather app is one of the better looking and most useful apps available. The background image represents current conditions; for example, a sunny spring day is represented by a beautiful image of fresh leaves in the sunlight. Current conditions are on the left—temperature, wind, humidity, and the like. The rest of the screen is devoted to a five-day forecast.

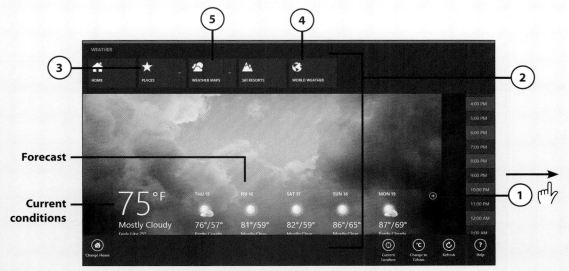

1. Scroll right to view hourly forecast and maps.
2. Right-click anywhere in the app to display the top and bottom Options bars.
3. Click Places to switch to different locations.
4. Click World Weather to view weather reports from around the globe.
5. Click Weather Maps to see real-time satellite and radar weather maps.

ADD YOUR LOCATION

Before the Weather app can deliver your weather, it has to know where you're located. To do this, right-click to display the Options bars and then click Places in the top bar to see a list of places already added. Click or tap the + tile and then enter a new location.

Sports

You can use the Sports app to read the latest headlines from the world of sports, as well as follow your favorite sports and teams. When you launch the app, you see the top story of the day; click to read the complete story.

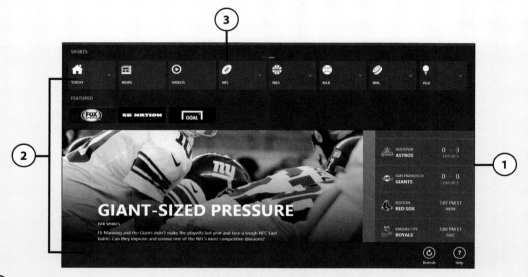

(1) Scroll to the right to view more stories, headlines, and videos.

(2) Right-click in the app to display the top and bottom Options bars.

(3) Click the tile for any given sport or league (NFL, NBA, MLB, NHA, and so forth) to view news, standings, scores, and stats for that league.

Finance

Windows 8.1's Finance app is the perfect way to stay up-to-date on the latest financial news, as well as keep track of your personal investments. Scroll past the top story of the day to view current market information and then scroll further right to view your own Watch List—those stocks you want to track.

1 Scroll to the right to view your stock Watch List.

2 Click a stock tile to view more information about that stock.

3 Click the + tile to add a stock to your Watch List; when the Add to Watchlist panel appears, enter the name or symbol of the stock and then click Add.

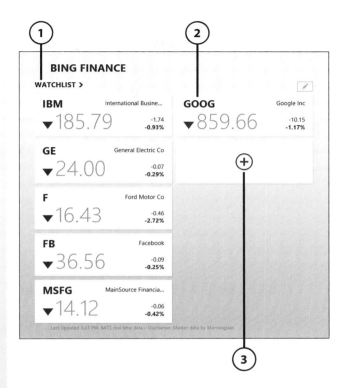

Travel

The Travel app is a mini-guidebook to popular travel destinations. It also lets you search for flights and hotels online.

1 Scroll right to the Featured Destinations section and then click a destination tile to learn more about that location.

2 To search for flights, scroll to the Tools and Tasks section and click the Search Flights tile.

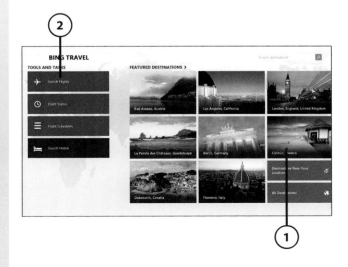

(3) Enter information about your trip (departure and arrival locations and dates) on the Flights page and then click Search Flights to view available flights.

(4) To search for hotels, return to the Travel app, scroll to the Tools and Tasks section, and click the Search Hotels tile.

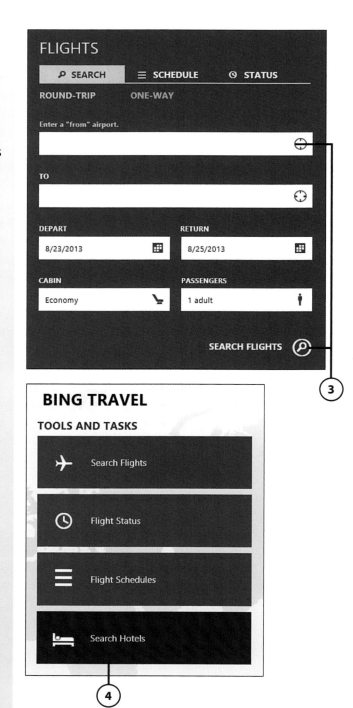

(5) Enter your destination and
check-in/check-out dates on the
Hotels page; click Search Hotels
to view available rooms and
rates.

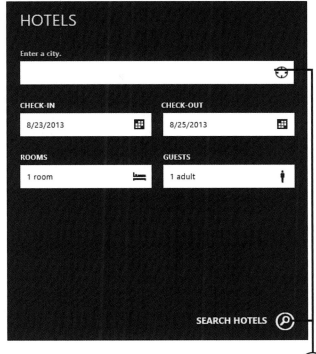

Maps

The Windows 8.1 Maps app lets you create street maps and driving directions. It's based on Bing Maps, which is Microsoft's web-based mapping service.

You can click and drag your mouse to move the map in any direction—or, if you have a touchscreen device, just drag or swipe your finger to move the map. You can zoom in and out of the map by using the +/- zoom controls at the lower right. On a touchscreen device, you can zoom out by pinching the screen with your fingers, or you can zoom in by expanding your fingers on the screen.

(1) Right-click anywhere on the map to display the Options bar.

(2) Click My Location to display your current location, click My Location.

(3) To switch to another location, click Find and then enter the street address, city, state, or ZIP code.

(4) To display current traffic conditions or change to satellite view, click Map Style and make a selection.

(5) To generate driving directions, click Directions to display the Directions pane.

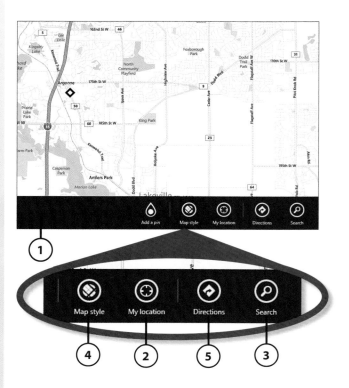

6 Enter your current location into the A box.

7 Enter your destination into the B box.

8 Click the right arrow to generate step-by-step driving directions and a map of your route.

9 Click any individual step to view a close-up map of that location.

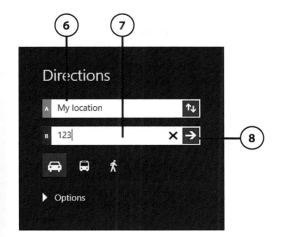

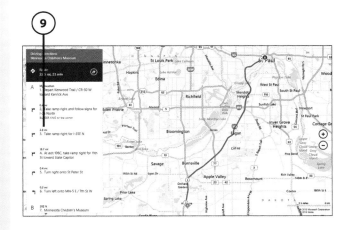

Calendar

The Calendar app lets you keep track of appointments and to-do lists. When you launch the app you see a monthly calendar, with all your scheduled appointments listed. To scroll back or forward through the months, use your keyboard's left and right arrow keys, or swipe the screen (on a touchscreen device).

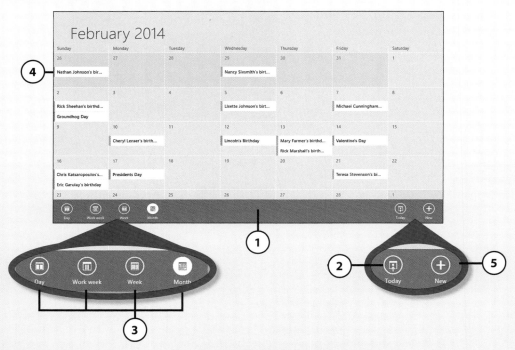

1. Right-click anywhere on the calendar to display the Options bar.

2. Click Today to re-center the calendar on the current day.

3. Click Day, Work Week, Week, or Month to switch to another view.

4. Click or tap an item on the calendar to view more details about that appointment.

5. To create a new appointment, click or tap the day of the appointment, or click New in the Options bar to display the appointment screen.

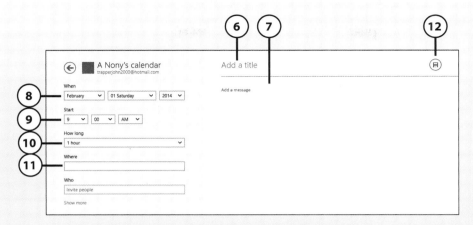

6 Enter the name of the appointment into the top-right section of the screen.

7 Enter details about the appointment into the Add a Message section.

8 Enter or change the date of the appointment with the When controls.

9 Enter the start time of the event with the Start controls.

10 Enter the length of the event with the How Long control.

11 Enter the location of the event into the Where box.

12 Click or tap the Save button to save the new appointment.

Alarms

The Alarms app turns your computer into a digital alarm clock, and it also includes timer and stopwatch functions.

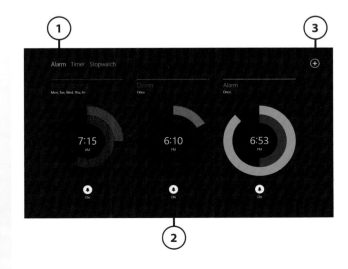

1 Click or tap Alarm to enter the alarm function.

2 Click the bell icon beneath an existing alarm to turn it on or off.

3 Click or tap the + button to set a new alarm.

4 Click and drag the outer circle to set the minutes.

5 Click and drag the inner circle to set the hour.

6 Click or tap AM or PM.

7 Click or tap Once to make this a one-time only alarm. To have this alarm repeat, click or tap Repeats and check those days you want the alarm to go off.

8 Click or tap the down arrow in the Sound section to set the sound for this alarm.

9 Click or tap the Alarm header to enter a new name for this alarm.

10 Click or tap the Save button to save this alarm.

11 Click or tap Timer to enter the timer function.

12 Click or tap the + button to create a new timer.

13 Click or tap Stopwatch to enter the stopwatch function.

14 Click or tap the Play (arrow) button to start the stopwatch. The Play button changes to a Pause button. Click or tap the Pause button to stop the stopwatch.

15 Click or tap the Reset button to reset the stopwatch to zero.

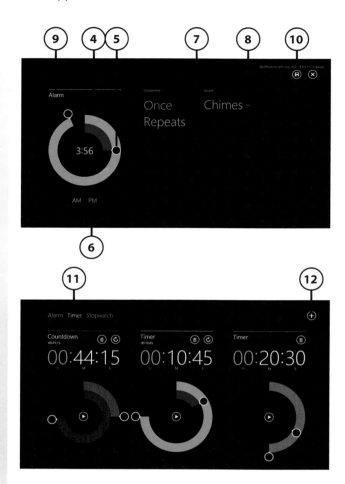

Calculator

The Calculator app functions as a standard or scientific calculator. It also lets you convert various measurements from one format to another (such as liters to teaspoons).

1. Click or tap Standard to use the standard calculator.

2. Click or tap Scientific to use the scientific calculator.

3. Use your mouse or (on a touchscreen display) your finger to tap the calculator keys, or use the numeric keypad on your computer keyboard.

4. Click or tap Converter to use the conversion function.

5. Click or tap the first down arrow to select the type of conversion—volume, length, weight, temperature, energy, area, speed, time, power, or data.

6. Click or tap the second down arrow to select the original unit of measurement.

7. Click or tap the third down arrow to select the converted unit of measurement.

8. Use the onscreen keypad or your computer's numeric keypad to enter the original unit you want converted; the conversion appears in the bottom box.

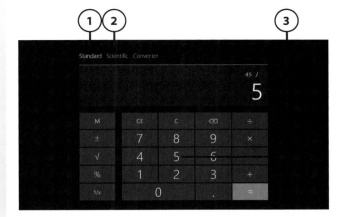

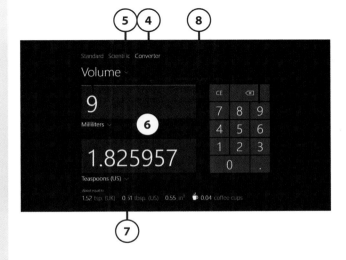

Food and Drink

The Bing Food & Drink app lets you search for recipes online, as well as create shopping lists based on the recipes you choose.

1. Click or tap Collections to create and view your collected recipes.

2. Click or tap Add a Recipe to create your own recipe.

3. Click or tap Shopping List to create a shopping list of items for a recipe.

4. Click or tap Today's Meal Plan to edit and view your daily meal planner.

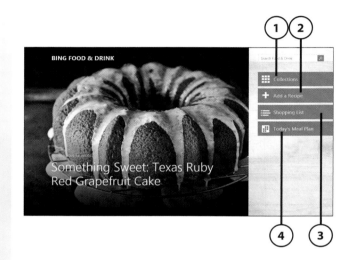

Health and Fitness

The Bing Health & Fitness app includes numerous tools to help you lead a healthier life, including a Diet Tracker, Exercise Tracker, and Health Tracker. It also includes online workouts and useful information about medical conditions and prescription drugs.

1. Click or tap an option in the Quick Access section to go directly to specific sections of the app—Diet Tracker, Nutrition and Calories, Exercise Tracker, Exercises, Health Tracker, Symptoms, Drugs, and Conditions.

2. Use the Search box to search for specific health-related information.

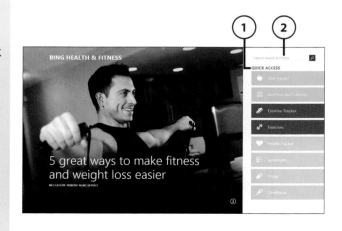

Finding New Apps in the Windows Store

Your new computer came with a bunch of programs preinstalled on its hard disk. Some of these are the apps that come with Windows 8.1, some are preview or limited-use versions provided by the PC manufacturer (included in the hope you'll purchase the full version if you like what you see), and some are real, honest-to-goodness fully functional applications.

As useful as some of these programs might be, at some point you're going to want to add something new. The best place (in fact, the only place) to find new Modern–style apps is in Microsoft's Windows Store. Many Windows Store apps are free, and all are easy to download and install on your new computer.

Browse the Windows Store

The Windows Store is accessible as if it were another app, from the Windows Start screen.

(1) Click or tap the Windows Store tile on the Start screen.

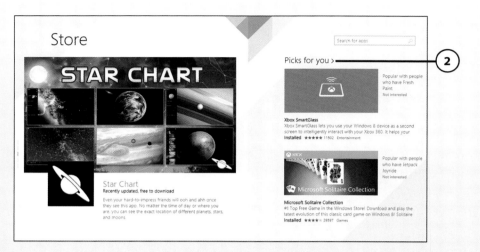

2 The Windows Store launches with a featured app. Scroll right to view Picks for You, Popular Now, New Releases, Top Paid, and Top Free apps.

3 Right-click to display the top options bar and view apps by category.

4 Click a category to view all apps in that category.

SEARCH THE STORE

Browsing is a good way to see everything that's available in the Windows Store. But if you have a specific app you're interested in, browsing might be inefficient.

In this instance, you can easily search for any given app. Just open the Windows Store and use the Search box in the top right corner. Enter the full or partial name of the app into the search box, and then press Enter. All matching apps are displayed.

Download and Install a New App

After you've browsed to a given category, it's easy to find apps you might like.

Pricing

Whereas a traditional computer software program can cost hundreds of dollars, most apps in the Windows Store cost $10 or less—and many are available for free.

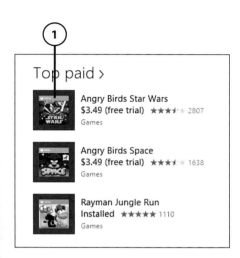

1. Click or tap the app in which you're interested to display the app's information page.

2. If you're looking at a paid app, you can often try it out for free by clicking the Try button. (Not all apps offer this "try" option, however.)

3. Click the Buy button to purchase the app; when prompted to confirm your purchase, click the Confirm button.

First-Time Purchase

The first time you purchase an app from the Windows Store (or music or videos from the Xbox Music and Xbox Videos stores), you're prompted to set up a payment method. Do so and Microsoft will remember this information for future purchases.

4 If the app is free, click the Install
button to download it to your
computer.

Updating Modern Apps

In Windows 8, you had to manually
update any installed apps. In Windows
8.1, updating is automatic. If an app
has been updated, that update is
downloaded and installed automatically the next time you connect your
computer to the Internet.

Piano8

Install ──────────────────── **4**

Free ★★★★☆ 7739

When you install an app, you agree to the Terms of Use
and any additional terms.

Description
Piano8 is a great acoustic piano for your
Windows 8 device. Simply select your octave
with arrows and play with real sounds of
piano!

Features
• Free real grand piano in your device with 31
  simultaneous notes
• Stereo HQ sounds for real music production

Desktop
shortcuts

Open
windows

Desktop

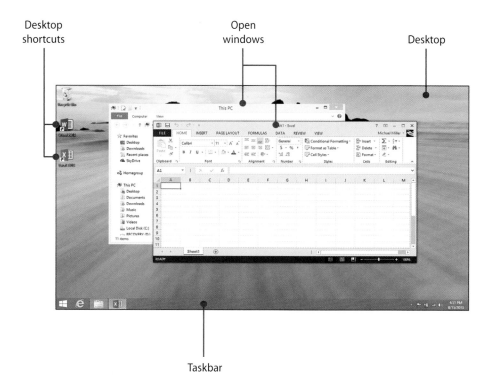

Taskbar

In this chapter you discover how to use the Windows desktop and traditional desktop software programs.

→ Personalizing the Windows Desktop
→ Launching Your Favorite Programs
→ Working with Traditional Software Programs

7

Using Traditional Apps on the Desktop

Microsoft would like you to use all Modern–style full-screen apps on your new PC. But there are lots of existing, traditional programs that you're probably accustomed to using and still find helpful. Fortunately, you can use all your existing programs in Windows 8.1. All you have to do is access the Windows desktop—which is pretty much like the desktop in previous versions of Windows.

Personalizing the Windows Desktop

As I said, the Windows 8.1 desktop is pretty much like the desktop that you might be familiar with from Windows 7 or Windows Vista. (Or even Windows XP!) As with previous versions of Windows, you can personalize the new Windows 8.1 desktop in a number of ways. You can change the color scheme, the desktop background, and even "pin" your favorite programs to the Taskbar or directly to the desktop itself.

A DIFFERENT DESKTOP

When comparing the Windows 8/8.1 desktop to previous versions of Windows, the operative phrase is "pretty much." As you learned in Chapter 3, "Using Windows 8.1—If You've Used Windows Before," Windows 8 introduced some key changes to the desktop, and most of these changes carry through to Windows 8.1.

Chief among these changes is the removal of the Start menu. This means you need to go to the Modern-style Start screen to launch new apps; you can do so directly from the desktop.

Windows 8 removed the Start button as well as the Start menu, but Windows 8.1 returns the Start button to the desktop. (It's at the far left side of the taskbar, just where you'd expect it to be.) This isn't the old Start button you learned to love, however. When you click the new Windows 8.1 Start button, you don't see the old Start menu; clicking the new Start button displays the Start screen, instead. But it's better than not having any Start button, I suppose.

The other big difference in the Windows 8/8.1 desktop is that it no longer displays the translucent window frames (what Microsoft called the Aero interface) you remember from Windows 7 and Windows Vista. That's strictly a cosmetic thing, however, and doesn't much affect how things operate.

Display the Desktop

Unlike previous versions of Windows, Windows 8.1 does not automatically open into the desktop. Instead, you have to launch the desktop as you would any Windows 8.1 app.

1. Click the Start button or press the Windows key to display the Start screen.

2. Click or tap the Desktop tile.

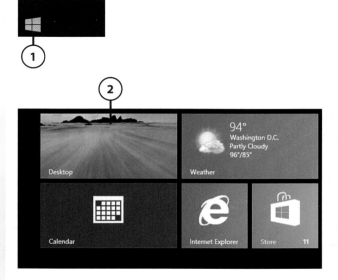

Change the Desktop Background

The Windows desktop displays across your entire computer screen. Now it's time to start personalizing the desktop—and one of the most popular ways to do so is to use a favorite picture or color as the background for your desktop.

1. Right-click in any open area of the desktop and select Personalize from the pop-up menu. The Personalization window displays.

2. Click Desktop Background to display the Choose Your Desktop Background page.

3. Pull down the Picture Location list and select the type of background image you want—Windows Desktop Backgrounds (stock background images that come with Windows), Pictures Library (your own pictures stored on your PC), Top Rated Photos (your favorite photos on your PC), Solid Colors (to display a solid-color background with no image), or Computer (to browse your entire hard drive for pictures).

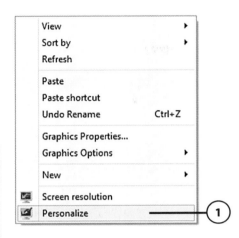

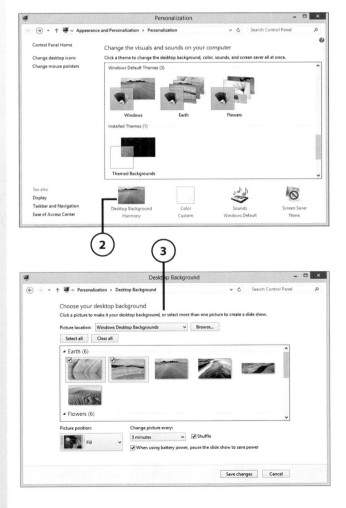

4 Browse for and then check the image or color you want to use for the desktop background.

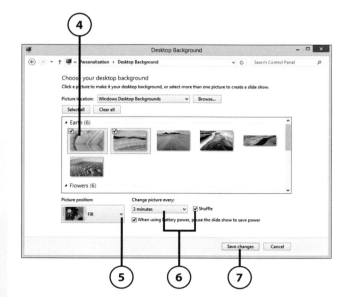

5 If the image is a different size from your Windows desktop, pull down the Picture Position list and select a display option— Fill (zooms into the picture to fill the screen), Fit (fits the image to fill the screen horizontally—but might leave black bars above and below the image), Stretch (distorts the picture to fill the screen), Tile (displays multiple instances of a smaller image), or Center (displays a smaller image in the center of the screen, with black space around it).

6 To display more than one image in a changing desktop slide- show, check more than one image. Pull down the Change Picture Every list to determine how quickly images change; check the Shuffle box to display images in a random order.

7 Click the Save Changes button when done.

Change the Color Scheme

You can select any color for the title bar and frame that surrounds open windows on the desktop.

(1) Right-click in any open area of the desktop and select Personalize from the pop-up menu. The Personalization window displays.

(2) Click Color to display the available color schemes.

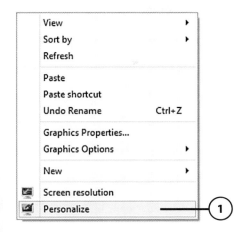

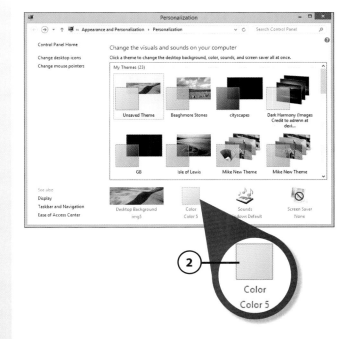

(**3**) Click the color you want to use for various window elements.

(**4**) To change the window color automatically based on the color of the current background image, click the first color tile (color swatch icon).

(**5**) To choose a custom color, click Show Color Mixer and adjust the Hue, Saturation, and Brightness controls. Click Hide Color Mixer to hide these controls.

(**6**) To change the saturation of the chosen color, adjust the Color Intensity slider.

(**7**) Click the Save Changes button when done.

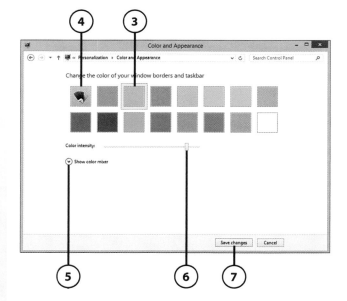

Choose a Screen Saver

You can opt to display a screen saver when your computer is inactive for a set amount of time. Although this isn't necessary, some people find it entertaining.

Burn In

On older computers with old-fashioned tube-type monitors, a screen saver was necessary to prevent "burn in" of static screen elements. With newer liquid crystal display (LCD) monitors (which are just like the LCD screen on your living room television set), burn in isn't an issue—which means you don't have to use a screen saver if you don't want to.

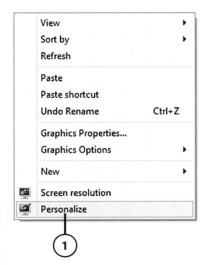

1. Right-click in any open area of the desktop and select Personalize from the pop-up menu. The personalization window displays.

2. Click Screen Saver to display the Screen Saver Settings window.

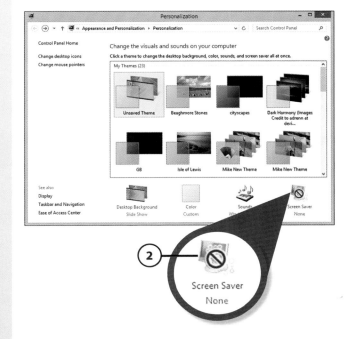

3 Pull down the Screen Saver list to select the type of screen saver to use—3D Text, Blank, Bubbles, Mystify, Photos, Ribbons, or None. (Your computer manufacturer might have installed additional screen savers, as well.)

4 Click the Settings button to adjust the settings for the selected screen saver; each screen saver has its own unique settings.

5 Use the Wait control to select how long your computer must remain inactive before displaying the screen saver.

6 If you want Windows to display the Lock screen when you resume work from screen saver mode, check the On Resume, Display Logon Screen option.

7 To preview the selected screensaver, click the Preview button.

8 Click OK when done.

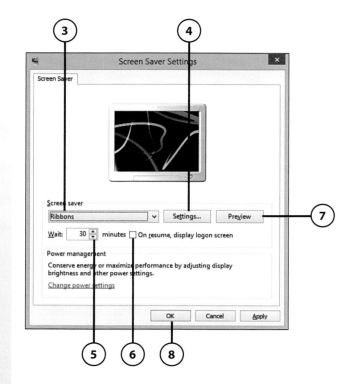

DESKTOP THEMES

The tasks in this section show you how to personalize individual elements of your Windows desktop. You can also choose predesigned *themes* that change multiple elements together. A given theme combines background images, color schemes, system sounds, and a screen saver to present a unified look and feel; some themes change the color scheme to match the current background picture.

To select a theme, right-click the desktop and select Personalize to open the Personalization window. All available themes are now displayed; click a theme to begin using it.

Launching Your Favorite Programs

All the applications installed on your PC—including traditional desktop programs—should be tiled somewhere on the Start or Apps screen. But you don't have to exit to the Start screen to launch a desktop program; you can "pin" shortcuts to the program to your desktop taskbar or to the desktop itself.

Create a Shortcut on the Desktop

If you frequently use a particular desktop program or file, you don't want to exit to the Start screen every time you want to launch that item. Instead, you can create a shortcut to that program or file on the desktop.

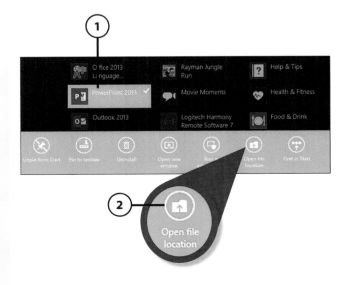

1. Display the Windows Start or Apps screen and right-click the tile for the particular program to select the tile and open the Options bar for that program.

2. Click Open File Location to open File Explorer with the file selected.

3 Right-click the file and select Create Shortcut.

4 Close the File Explorer window.

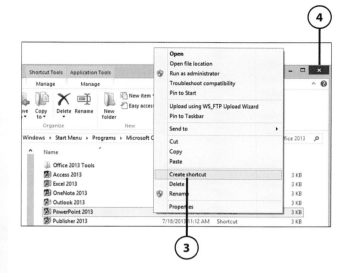

Pin a Program to the Taskbar

You can also pin a shortcut to any desktop program to the taskbar—that strip of icons that appears at the bottom of the desktop screen.

1 Display the Windows Start or Apps screen and right-click the tile for the particular program to select the tile and open the Options bar for that program.

2 Click Pin to Taskbar.

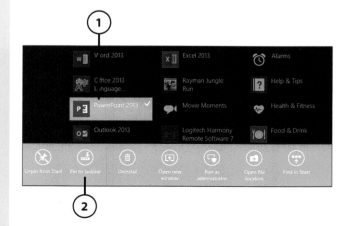

Open a Program

How you open a desktop program depends on where the shortcut to that program is.

(1) From the Windows Start or Apps screen, click or tap the tile for the program. *Or…*

(2) …from the Windows Desktop, double-click the shortcut for the program. *Or…*

(3) …from the taskbar, single-click the icon for the program.

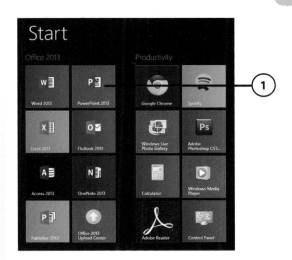

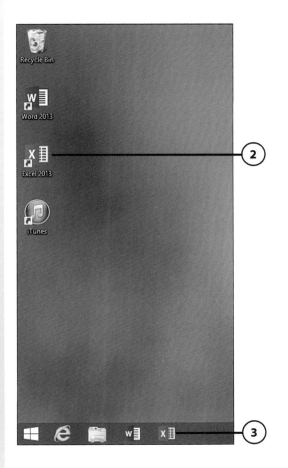

Working with Traditional Software Programs

Most traditional desktop software programs have different onscreen elements than do newer Modern-style apps. Let's examine how to use those traditional programs.

Manage Windows

Every desktop program opens in its own individual window on the Windows desktop. You can easily change the size of a window to better fit multiple windows on the desktop.

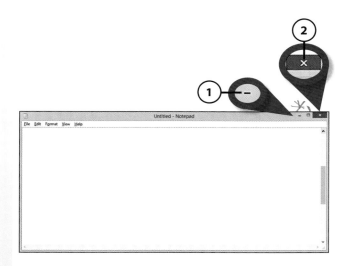

1. To minimize an open window, click the Minimize button in the top-right corner. The window shrinks to an icon on the Taskbar; to restore the window to its original size, click the window's icon on the Taskbar.

2. To maximize a window to appear full-screen, click the Maximize button in the top-right corner. When the window is maximized, the Maximize button turns into a Restore Down button; click this button to return the window to its original size.

3 To resize a window, use your mouse to click any side or corner of the window; the cursor should turn into a double-sided arrow. Keep the mouse button pressed and then drag the edge of the window to a new position.

4 To move a window to another position on the desktop, click and drag the window's title area.

5 To close a window (and shut down the program or document inside), click Close (the X) at the top-right corner.

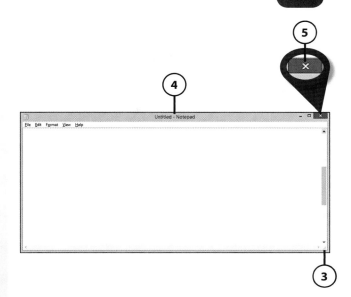

SNAP A WINDOW

Any open window can be "snapped" to the left or right side of the desktop, filling half the screen. This enables you to easily display two windows side-by-side.

Snapping windows on the desktop isn't the same as snapping Modern apps, however. With Modern app snapping, discussed in Chapter 6, "Using New Windows Apps," you can snap more than two apps if you have a big enough display. Although you can tile as many windows as you want on the desktop, you can only snap two at a time—one to the left and one to the right.

To snap a window to the left side of the desktop, click and drag the window to the left edge. To snap a window to the right side of the desktop, click and drag the window to the right edge.

Scroll Through a Window

Many programs, documents, and web pages are longer than the containing window is high. To read the full page or document, you need to scroll through the window.

(1) Click the up arrow on the window's scrollbar to scroll up one line at a time.

(2) Click the down arrow on the window's scrollbar to scroll down one line at a time.

(3) Click and drag the scroll box (slider) to scroll up or down in a smooth motion.

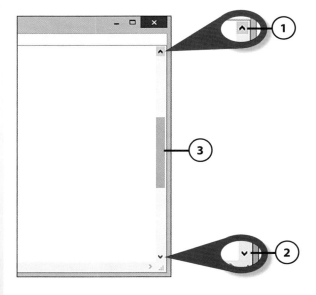

Other Ways to Scroll

You can also scroll up or down a window by pressing the PageUp and PageDn keys on your keyboard. In addition, if your mouse has a scroll wheel, you can use it to scroll through a window.

Use Pull-Down Menus

Many software programs use a set of pull-down *menus* to store all the commands and operations you can perform. The menus are aligned across the top of the window, just below the title bar, in what is called a *menu bar*.

(1) Click the menu's name to pull down the menu.

(2) A little black arrow to the right of the label indicates that additional choices are available, displayed on a *submenu*. Click the menu item or the arrow to display the submenu.

(3) Three little dots (called an ellipsis) to the right of a menu item's label indicates that additional choices are available, displayed in a dialog box. Click the menu item to display the dialog box.

(4) Click the menu item to select it.

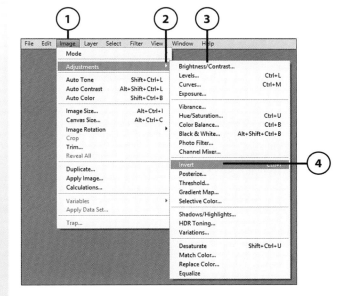

Use Toolbars and Ribbons

Some Windows programs put the most frequently used operations on one or more *toolbars* or *ribbons*, usually located just below the menu bar. A toolbar looks like a row of buttons, each with a small picture (called an *icon*) and maybe a bit of text. You activate the associated command or operation by clicking the button with your mouse.

Long Toolbars

If the toolbar is too long to display fully on your screen, you see a right arrow at the far-right side of the toolbar. Click this arrow to display the buttons that aren't currently visible.

1. Click a tab to select that particular ribbon.

2. Click a ribbon/toolbar button to select that operation.

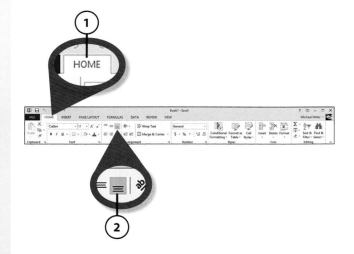

Internet Explorer
(Modern version)

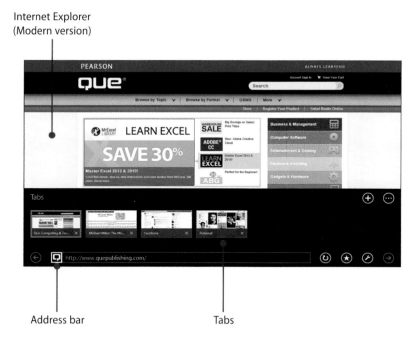

Address bar

Tabs

Address box

Tabs

Internet
Explorer
(desktop
version)

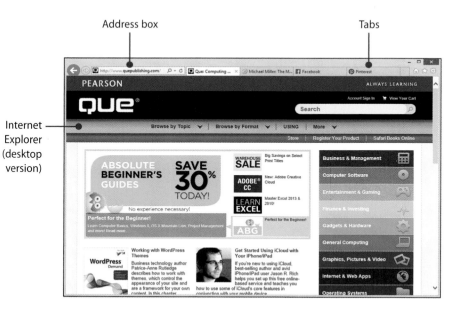

In this chapter you find out how to connect to the Internet to browse and search pages on the World Wide Web.

→ Connecting to the Internet—and Your Home Network
→ Connecting to the Internet at a Wi-Fi Hotspot
→ Using Internet Explorer (Modern Version)
→ Using Internet Explorer (Desktop Version)
→ Searching the Internet

8

Browsing and Searching the Web

Much of what you want to do with your new computer is found on the Internet. The Internet is a source of information, a conduit for shopping and other useful activities, a place to play games, and a tool for communicating with friends and family.

To get full use out of your new PC, then, you need to connect it to the Internet. You can connect to the Internet at home or away. All you need is access to a home network or, outside of your house, a Wi-Fi hotspot.

Connecting to the Internet—and Your Home Network

To get Internet in your home, you need to contract with an Internet Service Provider (ISP). You can typically get Internet service from your cable company, or from your phone company. Expect to pay somewhere between $25 and $50 a month.

Your ISP should set you up with a broadband modem that connects to the incoming cable or phone line. The modem takes the digital signals coming through the incoming line and converts them into a format that your computer can use.

In most cases, you connect your broadband modem to a wireless router. A router is a device that takes a single Internet signal and routes it to multiple devices; when you set up your router, following the manufacturer's instructions, you create a wireless home network. You connect your computer (as well your smartphone, tablet, and other wireless devices) wirelessly to your router via a technology called Wi-Fi.

Connect to Your Home Network

After your modem and wireless router are set up, you've created a wireless home network. You can then connect your PC to your wireless router—and access the Internet.

1. From the Start screen, press Windows+C to display the Charms bar.

2. Click or tap Settings to display the Settings panel.

3. Click or tap the Wi-Fi ("Available") icon to display a list of available networks. Your network should be listed here.

4. Click or tap your wireless network; the panel for this network expands.

5. Check the Connect Automatically box to connect automatically to this network in the future.

6. Click Connect.

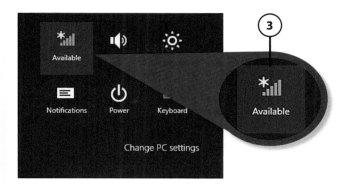

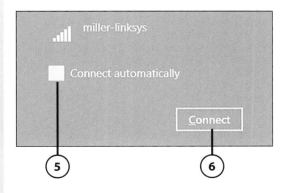

(7) Enter the password (called the *network security key*) for your network. You should have created this password when you first set up your wireless router.

(8) Click Next.

(9) When the next screen appears, click Yes to connect with other PCs and devices on your home network. (This lets you share pictures, music, and other files with other computers connected to your home network.) You're now connected to your wireless router, and should have access to the Internet.

One-Button Connect

If the wireless router on your network supports "one-button wireless setup" (based on the Wi-Fi Protected Setup technology), you might be prompted to press the "connect" button on the router to connect. This is much faster than going through the entire process outlined here.

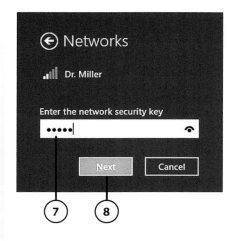

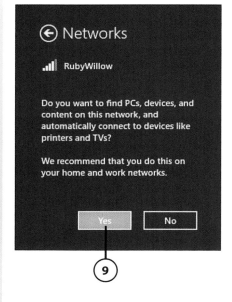

Connect to a HomeGroup

If you're just interested in connecting to your network, you're good to go as soon as you complete the steps in the preceding task. Just open Internet Explorer (discussed in the "Using Internet Explorer" sections, later in this chapter) and start browsing the Web.

If you're also interested in accessing music, photos, and other files stored on other computers in your home, you need to connect your PC to those other PCs via your home network. The easiest way to do this is to create a HomeGroup for your network. A HomeGroup is kind of a simplified network that enables you to automatically share files and printers between connected computers.

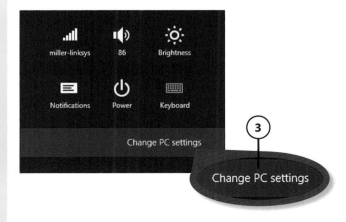

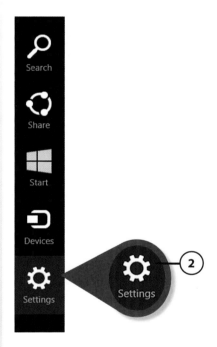

1. From the Start screen, press Windows+C to display the Charms bar.

2. Click or tap Settings to display the Settings pane.

3. Click or tap Change PC Settings to display the PC Settings screen.

Windows for HomeGroups

Only PCs running Windows 7, 8, and 8.1 can be part of a HomeGroup. PCs running older versions of Windows do not have the HomeGroup feature and must use the normal Windows networking functions instead, as discussed later in this section.

4 Scroll down the list on the left and select Network.

5 Click or tap HomeGroup.

6 Click or tap the Create button.

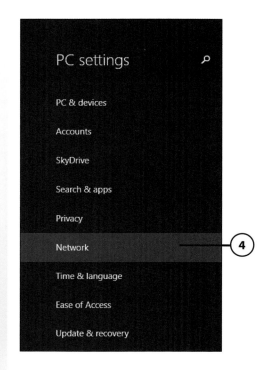

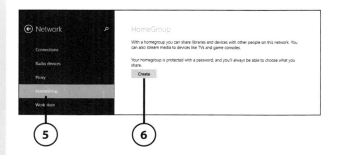

7 Click or tap "on" those items you want to share with other computers—Documents, Music, Pictures, Videos, and Printers.

8 If you want non-PC devices, such as network-connected TVs or videogame consoles, to be able to access the content on this computer, click or tap "on" the option for Let Devices on This Network (Like TVs and Game Consoles) Stream My Music and Videos.

9 Go to the Password section and write down the password that Windows generated. You'll need to provide this to users of other computers on your network who want to join your HomeGroup.

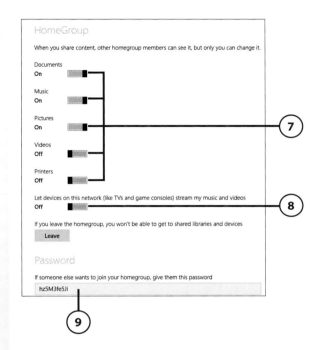

HomeGroup

When you share content, other homegroup members can see it, but only you can change it.

Documents
On

Music
On

Pictures
On

Videos
Off

Printers
Off

Let devices on this network (like TVs and game consoles) stream my music and videos
Off

If you leave the homegroup, you won't be able to get to shared libraries and devices

Leave

Password

If someone else wants to join your homegroup, give them this password

hz5M3fe5Ji

Configuring Other PCs

You'll need to configure each computer on your network to join your new HomeGroup. Enter the original HomeGroup password as instructed.

Access Other Computers in Your HomeGroup

After you have your home network set up, you can access shared content stored on other computers on your network. How you do so depends on whether the other computer is part of your HomeGroup. We'll look at HomeGroup access first.

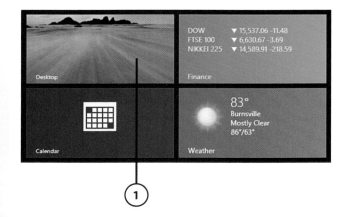

(1) Go to the Start screen and click or tap the Desktop tile to open the Windows desktop.

(2) Click the File Explorer icon on the taskbar to open File Explorer.

(3) Go to the HomeGroup section of the navigation pane and click the name of your HomeGroup.

(4) Windows displays the shared folders on all the computers in your HomeGroup. Double-click a folder to access that particular content.

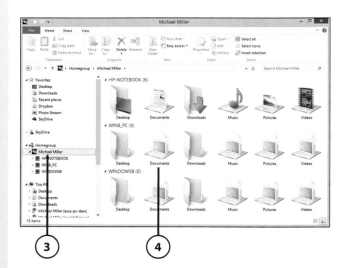

Access Non-HomeGroup Computers on Your Network

A computer doesn't have to be connected to your HomeGroup for you to access its content. Windows lets you access any computer connected to your home network—although you can only share content the computer's owner has configured as sharable.

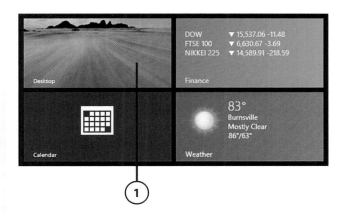

(1) Go to the Start screen and click or tap the Desktop tile to open the Windows desktop.

(2) Click the File Explorer icon on the taskbar to open File Explorer.

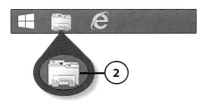

(3) Go to the Network section of the navigation pane and click the computer you want to access.

(4) Windows displays the shared folders on the selected computer. Double-click a folder to view that folder's content.

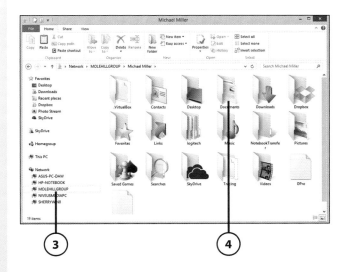

Look for the Public Folder

On many older computers, shared files are stored in the Public folder. Look in this folder first for the files you want.

Connecting to the Internet at a Wi-Fi Hotspot

The nice thing about the Internet is that it's virtually everywhere. This means you can connect to the Internet even when you're away from home. All you need to do is find a wireless connection, called a Wi-Fi hotspot. Fortunately, most coffeehouses, libraries, hotels, fast food restaurants, and public spaces offer Wi-Fi hotspots—often for free.

Connect to a Wi-Fi Hotspot

When you're near a Wi-Fi hotspot, your PC should automatically pick up the wireless signal. Just make sure that your computer's Wi-Fi adapter is turned on (it should be, by default), and then get ready to connect.

1. From the Start screen, press Windows + C to display the Charms bar.

2. Click or tap Settings to display the Settings panel.

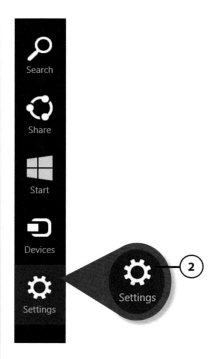

(**3**) Click or tap the Wi-Fi icon. (If there are Wi-Fi networks nearby, the icon should be labeled Available.) A list of available wireless networks displays.

(**4**) Click or tap the hotspot to which you want to connect to expand the panel.

(**5**) Click Connect to connect to the selected hotspot.

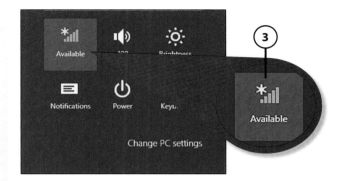

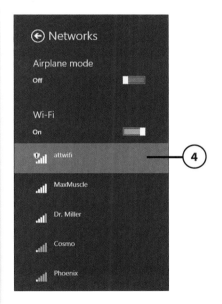

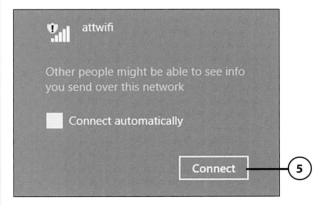

6 If the hotspot has free public access, you can now open Internet Explorer (from the Start screen) and surf normally.

7 If the hotspot requires a password, payment, or other logon procedure, Windows should open Internet Explorer and display the hotspot's login page. Enter the appropriate information to begin surfing.

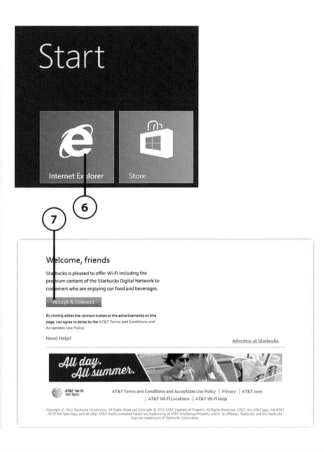

AIRPLANE MODE

>>>Go Further

If you're using a notebook PC on an airplane, you can switch to Window's special Airplane mode. This lets you use your computer while in the air, without turning on its Wi-Fi wireless receiver.

To switch into Airplane mode, go to the Start screen and display the Charms bar, click Settings, and then click the Wi-Fi icon. When the Networks pane appears, click "on" the Airplane Mode option. You can switch off Airplane mode when your plane lands.

If the plane you're on offers Wi-Fi service (many now do), you don't have to bother with Airplane mode. Instead, just connect to the plane's wireless network as you would to any Wi-Fi hotspot. You might have to pay for it, but it enables you to use the Internet while you're en route—which is a great way to spend long trips!

Using Internet Explorer (Modern Version)

Most of what's fun and useful on the Internet is found on the World Wide Web (WWW). The Web consists of millions of websites, each of which has its own collection of individual web pages. To access the Web, you use an application called a web browser. Windows 8.1 includes two versions of the Internet Explorer web browser—a Modern-style version and a traditional desktop version.

Launch Internet Explorer (Modern Version)

The Modern version of Internet Explorer is nice in that it lets you view web pages on your full computer screen. It's obviously the version you want to use if you primarily work within the Modern Windows environment.

New in Windows 8.1

Windows 8.1 includes Internet Explorer version 11 (IE11), which is vastly improved over the previous version 10—especially in the Modern, full-screen version. New to the Modern version of IE11 are the abilities to save Favorite sites and easily display different tabs.

1. Click the Start button or press the Windows key to return to the Windows Start screen.

2. Click or tap the Internet Explorer tile.

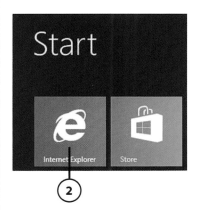

>>>Go Further

ZOOM INTO A WEB PAGE

If the text on a given web page is too small to read comfortably, you can "zoom" into the page to make it larger within Internet Explorer. This zooming does not affect how any other program looks in Windows; it only affects web pages in Internet Explorer.

The easiest way to do this is to press the Ctrl and plus sign (+) keys together. Each time you press the two keys, the page will be enlarged 25 percent. To zoom out (make the page smaller again), press the Ctrl and minus sign (–) keys together.

Web Page Addresses

The address for a web page is technically called a Universal Resource Locator, or URL. A typical website address starts with a www (for World Wide Web), has a com or org at the end, and the name of the website in the middle; all three parts are separated by dots or periods, like this: www.mywebsite.com. Individual pages within a larger website appear after a backslash (/) that follows the main site address, like this: www.mywebsite.com/page.

It's Not All Good

Different Types of Addresses

Don't confuse a web page address with an email address, or with a traditional street address. They're not the same.

As noted previously, a web page address has three parts, each separated by a period. A web page address typically starts with a **www** and ends with a **com** or **org**, and there are no spaces in it. You should only enter web page addresses into the Address box in Internet Explorer and other web browsers.

An email address consists of two parts, separated by an "at" sign (@). The first part of the address is your personal name, the last part your email provider's domain. A typical email address looks something like this: **yourname@email.com**. You use email addresses to send emails to your friends and family; you do *not* enter email addresses into the Address box in Internet Explorer.

Of course, you still have a street address that describes where you physically live. You don't use your street address for either web browsing or email online; it's solely for postal mail, and for putting on the front of your house or apartment.

Browse the Web

You can go directly to any page on the Web by entering its web address. Many web pages include links to other web pages; click a link to jump to the linked-to page.

1. When you first launch Internet Explorer, the Address bar should be displayed at the bottom of the screen. If you don't see the Address bar, right-click anywhere on the screen to display it.

2. Type the address for the page you want to go to into the Address box and then press Enter.

3. Click any underlined or bold link or picture on a web page to open the linked-to page. This lets you jump from one web page to another, via these page links.

4. To return to the last-viewed web page, click the Back button on the Address bar, or press the Backspace key on your keyboard.

5. If you've backed up several pages and want to return to the page you were on last, click the Forward button.

Open Multiple Pages in Tabs

If you're visiting more than one web page during a single session, you can display each page as a separate tab in the web browser. This use of tabs enables you to keep multiple web pages open simultaneously—which is great when you want to reference different pages or want to run web-based applications in the background.

(**1**) Right-click within the browser to open the Address bar at the bottom of the screen, the right-click again to display the row of tabs above the Address box.

(**2**) Click another open tab to switch to it.

(**3**) Click or tap the X by the tab to close it.

(**4**) To open a new tab, click or tap the New Tab (+) button to display the Frequent bar.

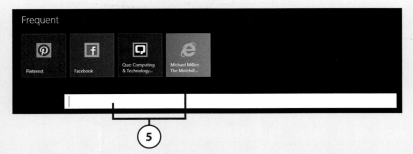

(**5**) Either click a tile on this screen or enter a new web page address in the Address box.

InPrivate Browsing

If you want to browse anonymously, without any traces of your history recorded, activate IE's InPrivate Browsing mode on a new tab. Display the Address bar and click the "three dot" (...) button, and then click New InPrivate Tab from the pop-up menu.

Save Your Favorite Web Pages

When you find a web page you like, you can save it in your Favorites list. Returning to a favorite page is as easy as clicking or tapping it in this list.

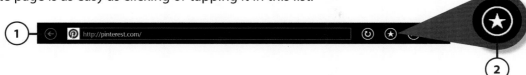

(1) Navigate to the web page you want to pin, and then right-click the page to display the Address bar.

(2) If the Favorites list is not displayed, click or tap the Favorites (star) button.

(3) Click or tap the Add to Favorites button to display the Pin panel

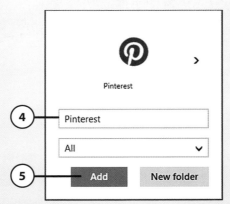

(4) Confirm or edit the name of the page.

(5) Click or tap the Add button.

Pin a Page

You can also pin a favorite page to the Windows Start screen. Display the Favorites list in the Address bar, then click or tap the Pin Site button on the far right.

Return to a Saved Page

To return to a page you've saved as a favorite, click or tap that page's tile in the Favorites list.

(1) Right-click the current page in Internet Explorer to display the Address bar.

(2) Click or tap within the Address box to display the Favorites bar.

(3) Click or tap the page you want to revisit.

Favorites Folders
You can organize favorite pages into folders in the Favorites list. To view favorites in a folder, click or tap the folder name. To return to the master Favorites list, click or tap All by the Favorites title.

Using Internet Explorer (Desktop Version)

If you've used a version of Windows prior to Windows 8/8.1, the desktop version of Internet Explorer 11 will be familiar to you. This web browser opens in its own window on the Windows desktop, and features an address bar and row of tabs that are always visible.

Launch Internet Explorer on the Desktop

The desktop version of Internet Explorer is launched, not surprisingly, from the taskbar on the Windows desktop.

(1) From the Start menu, click the Desktop tile to display the Windows desktop.

(2) Click the Internet Explorer icon on the taskbar to open the browser.

Browse the Web

Browsing the Web with the desktop version of Internet Explorer is similar to using the Modern version. The big difference is that all the navigational elements are always visible in the browser.

Blue

(1) To go to a specific web page, enter that page's address into the Address box and then press Enter.

(2) To return to the previous web page, click the Back (left arrow button) beside the Address box. *Must be blue.*

(3) To reload or refresh the current page, click the Refresh button.

(4) To jump to a linked-to page, click the hyperlink on the current page.

Going Forward

If you've backed up several pages and want to return to the page you were on last, click the Forward button.

>>>Go Further

REVISIT HISTORY

What do you do if you remember visiting a page earlier in the day, or even in the past few days, but can't get there by clicking the Back button? There are actually a few different ways to revisit your browsing history in Internet Explorer.

The first thing to try is clicking and holding the Back button. This displays a list of pages you've recently visited; click a page to revisit it.

To see even older pages, click and hold the Back button and then click History. This displays a full history list of pages you've visited.

If you want to delete your browsing history—say you've visited a web page you don't want anyone to know you visited—you can do that, too. Click the Tools (gear) button in the Internet Explorer browser and select Internet Options. When the Internet options dialog box appears, select the General tab, go the Browsing History section, and then click the Delete button. All the pages you've visited will be purged from the history list.

Open Multiple Pages in Tabs

Just as the Modern version of Internet Explorer features tabbed browsing, so does the desktop version. You can display web pages as separate tabs in the browser, and thus easily switch between web pages—which is great when you want to reference different pages or want to run web-based applications in the background.

(1) To switch to another open tab, click that tab.

(2) To close an open tab, click the X on that tab.

(3) To open a new tab, click the New Tab tab next to the last open tab.

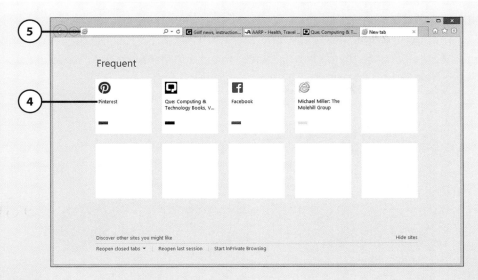

4 Click a tile on the new tab page *or...*

5 ...enter a new web page address into the Address box.

Save Your Favorite Pages

The desktop version of Internet Explorer also lets you save your favorite pages in the Favorites list.

1 Navigate to the web page you want to pin, and then click or tap the Favorites (star) button on the toolbar.

2 Click the Add to Favorites button to display the Add a Favorite dialog box.

3 Confirm or enter a name for this page.

4 Click the Add button.

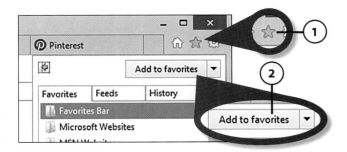

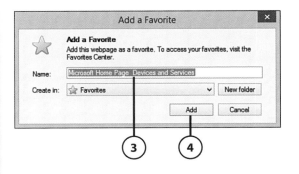

Favorites Folders

You can organize your favorite pages into separate folders in the Favorites list. When the Add a Favorite dialog box appears, select a folder from the Create In list or click the New Folder button to create a new folder.

Return to a Saved Page

To return to a page you've saved as a favorite, open the Favorites list and make a selection.

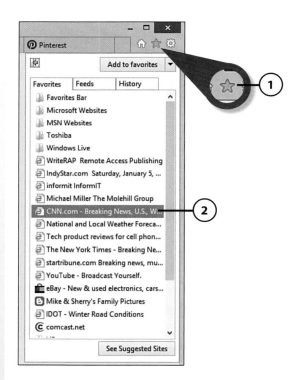

(1) Click the Favorites (star) button to display the Favorites list.

(2) Click or tap the page you want to revisit.

Favorites Bar

For even faster access to your favorite pages, display the Favorites Bar at the top of the browser window, beneath the Address bar. Right-click any open area at the top of the browser and then select Favorites Bar from the pop-up menu.

Set Your Home Page

The desktop version of Internet Explorer lets you set a home page that automatically opens whenever you launch the browser.

① Navigate to the page you want to use as your home page.

② Click the Options (gear) button.

③ Click Internet Options to display the Internet Options dialog box.

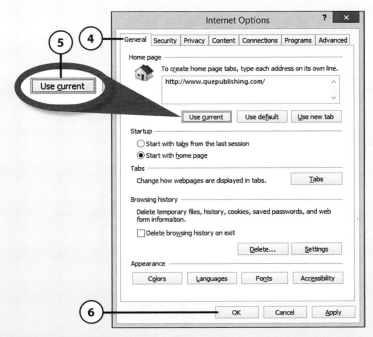

④ Click the General tab.

⑤ Go to the Home Page section and click the Use Current button.

⑥ Click OK.

>>>Go Further

USING OTHER WEB BROWSERS

You're not limited to using just Internet Explorer on the Windows desktop. There are several other third-party web browsers available, and some users prefer them for their simplicity and speed. The most popular of these non-Microsoft web browsers include Google Chrome (www.google.com/chrome/), Mozilla Firefox (www.mozilla.org/firefox/), and Apple Safari (www.apple.com/safari/).

Note, however, that all these web browsers do the same thing—take you to and display sites and pages on the Web. In terms of performances, there's not much difference from one to the next, and they all work by entering web page addresses into an Address box, and by clicking links on web pages. Most Windows users will use one of the two versions of Internet Explorer that come built into the operating system, but any of these alternative browsers will do the same job just as well. Which you use is up to you.

Searching the Internet

There is so much information on the Web—so many web pages—that it's sometimes difficult to find exactly what you're looking for. The best way to find just about anything on the Internet is to search for it, using a web search engine.

Search Google

The most popular search engine today is Google (www.google.com), which indexes billions of individual web pages. Google is easy to use and returns extremely accurate results.

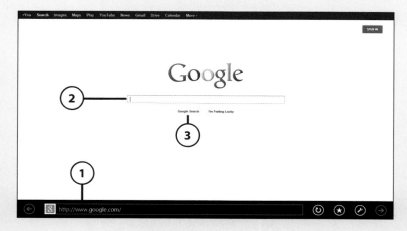

(**1**) From within Internet Explorer, enter **www.google.com** into the Address box and press Enter. This opens Google's main search page.

(**2**) Enter one or more keywords into the Search box.

(**3**) Press Enter or click the Google Search button.

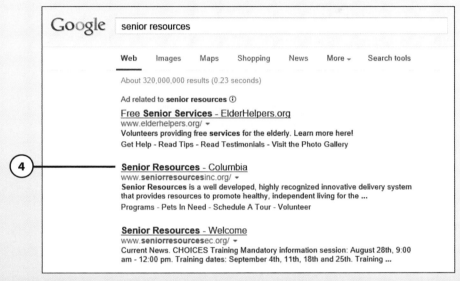

(**4**) When the results are displayed, go to the result you want to view, then click the link for that result. This displays the selected web page within Internet Explorer.

>>>Go Further

FINE-TUNE YOUR SEARCH RESULTS

Google lets you fine-tune your search results to display only certain types of results. Use the links at the top of Google's search results page to display only Images, Maps, Shopping, or News results—or click Search Tools for further refinements.

Search Bing

Microsoft's search engine is called Bing (www.bing.com). It works pretty much like Google, and Microsoft would very much like you to use it.

1. From within Internet Explorer, enter **www.bing.com** into the Address box and press Enter. This opens Bing's main search page.

2. Enter one or more keywords into the Search box.

3. Press Enter or click the Search (magnifying glass) button.

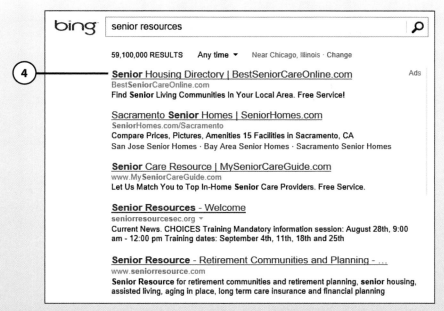

4) When the results are displayed, click any page link to view that page.

SEARCHING FOR SENIOR-RELATED INFORMATION

No doubt you'll be using Google or Bing to search for various senior-related information. You want to see results tailored to your age-specific needs, not general results of less interest and value to you.

In some cases, the topic itself defines age-appropriate results. For example, if you search for **retirement communities**, the results you see should link to pages that contain the information for which you're looking.

In other instances, your search query might be more general, and so it will return more general (and less age-specific) results. For example, searching for **Florida vacations** is going to bring up a lot of Mickey Mouse stuff of interest to youngsters and families, but not necessarily the snowbird-related information you were looking for.

In these instances, you can narrow your search results by including the word "seniors" in your query. In the vacation instance, change your query to search for **Florida vacations for seniors** and you'll be much more satisfied with the results. Same thing if you're searching for quilting clubs (**quilting clubs for seniors**), life insurance (**life insurance for seniors**), or comfortable clothing (**comfortable clothing for seniors**); adding a word or two to your main query makes all the difference.

Smart Search from Within Windows

Windows 8.1, like previous versions of Windows, lets you search your computer for files and apps. New to Windows 8.1, however, is the ability to expand this internal search to the Web, and use Bing to provide integrated web-based search results. This new global search is dubbed Smart Search, and it can make your searching more effective and efficient.

New to Windows 8.1
The Smart Search feature, incorporating Bing web search results, is new to Windows 8.1.

1. Press Windows + C to display the Charms bar.

2. Click or tap Search to display the search pane.

(3) Enter your query into the search box then press Enter.

(4) You now see a list of files and apps on your computer that match your query. Click or tap an item to open it.

(5) Depending on your query, you may also see web results from Bing. Scroll to the right to see additional results, then click an item to view that web page.

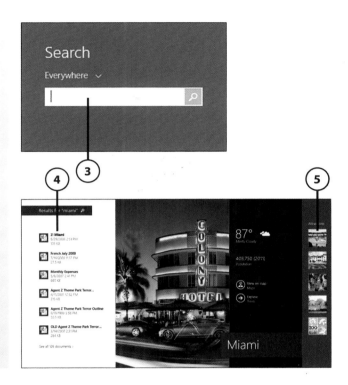

HERO RESULTS

Some web-based Smart Searches return what Microsoft calls "hero" results, where information about the subject is preassembled from data on the Web. For example, if you search for **Miami**, Windows displays the city's current weather conditions, population, and attractions, as well as a dining guide, images, current news, and more—along with traditional web search results.

>>>Go Further

Windows Defender
anti-malware utility

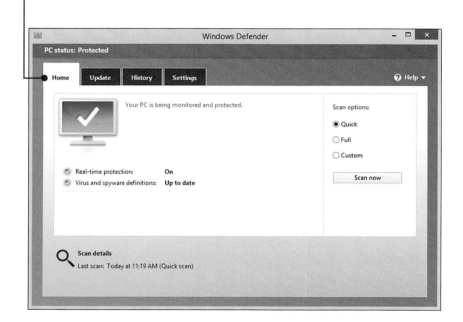

In this chapter you become familiar with the most common online threats and find out how to protect yourself against them.

→ Protecting Against Identity Theft and Phishing Schemes
→ Protecting Against Online Fraud
→ Protecting Against Computer Viruses and Other Malware
→ Protecting Against Online Attacks and Intrusions

Protecting Yourself from Online Threats

The Internet can be a scary place, especially for seniors. There are certain predators who target seniors online, and for good reasons. Many older computer users are more trusting than younger users, and they're also less tech savvy. In addition, seniors often have large nest eggs that are attractive to online predators, and older computer users are often ashamed to report being taken advantage of.

It all adds up to a potentially dangerous environment for seniors—which means you need to learn how to protect yourself when you're on-line. You need to be able to identify the most common online threats and scams, and know how to avoid becoming a victim.

Protecting Against Identity Theft and Phishing Schemes

Online predators want your personal information—your real name, address, online usernames and passwords, bank account numbers, and the like. It's called *identity theft*, and it's a way for a con artist to impersonate you—both online and in the real world. If your personal data falls into the hands of identity thieves, it can be used to hack into your online accounts, make unauthorized charges on your credit card, and maybe even drain your bank account.

Identity theft is a major issue. According to Javelin Strategy and Research, more than 11 million American adults became victims of identity theft in 2012. A typical case of identity theft costs the average victim more than $5,000.

There are many ways for criminals to obtain your personal information. Almost all involved tricking you, in some way or another, into providing this information of your own free will. Your challenge is to avoid being tricked.

It's Not All Good

Phishing Means Phony

A phishing scam typically starts with a phony email message that appears to be from a legitimate source, such as your bank, the postal service, PayPal, or other official institution. This email purports to contain important information that you can see if you click the enclosed link. That's where the bad stuff starts.

If you click the link in the phishing email, you're taken to a fake website masquerading as the real site, complete with logos and official-looking text. You're encouraged to enter your personal information into the forms on this fake web page; when you do so, your information is sent to the scammer, and you're now a victim of identity theft.

Avoiding Phishing Scams

Online, identity thieves often use a technique called *phishing* to trick you into disclosing valuable personal information. It's called that because the other party is "fishing" for your personal information, typically via fake email messages and websites.

How can you avoid falling victim to a phishing scam? There are several things you can do:

(1) Look at the sender's email address. Most phishing emails come from an address different from the one indicated by the (fake) sender. (In the example, note that the email address **619.RFX@jacksonville.com** doesn't seem to be one that would belong to FedEx; you'd expect an email from FedEx to look something like ***address*@fedex.com**.)

(2) Mouse over any links in the email. In a phishing email, the URL for the link will not match up with the link text or the (fake) sender's supposed website.

(3) Look for poor grammar and misspellings. Many phishing schemes come from outside the U.S. by scammers who don't speak English as their first language. As such, you're likely to find questionable phrasing and unprofessional text—not what you'd expect from your bank or other professional institution.

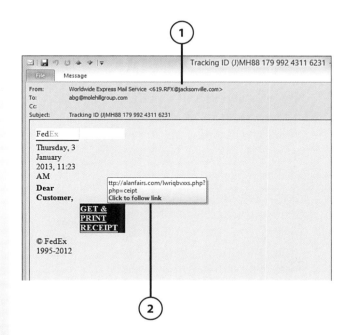

(4) If you receive an unexpected email, no matter the apparent source, do **not** click any of the links in the email. If you think there's a legitimate issue from a given website, go to that site manually in your web browser and access your account from there.

(5) Some phishing messages include attached files that you are urged to click to display a document or image. Do **not** click or open any of these attachments; they might contain malware that can steal personal information or damage your computer. (Read more about malware later in this chapter.)

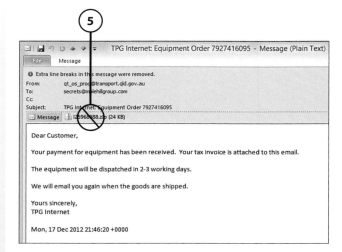

SmartScreen Filter

Windows 8.1 offers some built-in protection against phishing scams, in the form of a SmartScreen Filter that alerts you to potential phishing sites. If you click a bad link or attempt to visit a known or suspected phishing site, the web browser displays a warning message. Do not enter information into these suspected phishing sites—return to your home page, instead!

Keeping Your Private Information Private

Identity theft can happen any time you make private information public. This has become a special issue on social networks, such as Facebook, where users tend to forget that everything they post is publicly visible.

Many Facebook users not only post personal information in their status updates, but also include sensitive data in their personal profiles. Java Strategy and Research found that 68 percent of people with public social media profiles shared their birthday information, 63 percent shared the name of their high schools, 18 percent shared their phone numbers, and 12 percent shared their pet's names.

None of this might sound dangerous, until you realize that all of these items are the type of personal information many companies use for the "secret questions" their websites use to reset users' passwords. A fraudster armed with this publicly visible information could log onto your account on a banking website, for example, reset your password (to a new one he provides), and thus gain access to your banking accounts.

The solution to this problem, of course, is to enter as little personal information as possible when you're online. For example, you don't need to—and shouldn't—include your street address or phone number in a comment or reply to an online news article. Don't give the bad guys anything they can use against you!

(1) Unless absolutely necessary, do not enter your personal contact information (home address, phone number, and so on) into your social media profile.

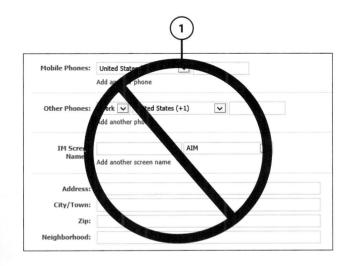

(2) Do not post or enter your birthdate, children's names, pet's
names, and the like—anything
that could be used to reset your
passwords at various websites.

(3) Do not post status updates that
indicate your current location—
especially if you're away from
home. That's grist for both physical stalkers and home burglars.

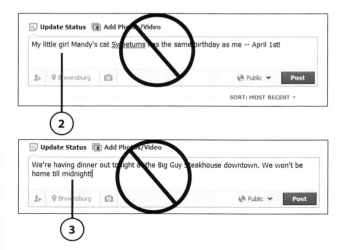

Hiding Personal
Information on Facebook

Too many Facebook users of all
ages make all their personal information totally public—visible to all users, friends or not. Fortunately, you
can configure Facebook's privacy settings to keep your private information private.

Facebook
Learn more about using the Facebook
social network in Chapter 13, "Connecting with Facebook and Other
Social Media."

(1) Click your name in the Facebook
toolbar to open your personal
Timeline page.

(2) Click the Update Info button.

3 Click the Edit button for the information you want to make private.

4 Click the Privacy button for the individual item you want to change.

5 Select Friends to make this information visible only to people on your friends list—or click Only Me to completely hide this information from others.

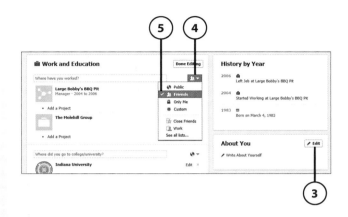

Keeping Your Facebook Posts Private

You can configure Facebook to hide your status updates from anyone not on your friends list. You can also configure the privacy settings for each individual post you make on Facebook. This way you can post more personal information only to select friends, and hide it from the general public

1 Click the Privacy Shortcuts button on the Facebook Toolbar to display the pull-down menu.

2 Select Who Can See My Stuff? to expand the pull-down menu.

3 Pull down the Who Can See My Future Posts? list and select Friends.

(4) To change who can see any individual status update, create a
new post, click the Privacy button, and make a new selection:
Public, Friends, or Only Me.

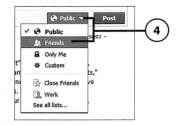

Custom Privacy
To hide posts from select individuals,
select Custom in the Privacy list and then
enter the names of people you don't
want to share with. Finish by clicking Save
Changes.

Protecting Against Online Fraud

Identity theft isn't the only kind of online fraud you might encounter. Con artists
are especially creative in concocting schemes that can defraud unsuspecting victims of thousands of dollars.

Most of these scams start with an email message that promises something for
nothing. Maybe the message tells you that you've won a lottery, or you are asked
to help someone in a foreign country deposit funds in a U.S. bank account. You
might even receive requests from people purporting to be far-off relatives who
need some cash to bail them out of some sort of trouble.

The common factor in these scams is that you're eventually asked to either send
money (typically via wire transfer) or provide your bank account information—
with which the scammers can drain your money faster than you can imagine. If
you're naïve or gullible enough, then the damage can be considerable.

Protecting yourself from the huge number of these online scams is both difficult
and simple. The difficulty comes from the sheer number of scams and their amaz-
ing variety. The simplicity comes from the fact that the best way to deal with any
such scam is to use common sense—and ignore it.

Scams Are Not Spam

You can't rely on your email program's spam filter to stop scam emails. Spam and scams are two different things, even if they're both unwanted. Although some scam messages will be stopped by spam filters, many messages will get through the filter and land in your inbox, just as if they were legitimate messages—which, of course, they aren't.

Identifying Online Scams

Most online fraud is easily detectible by the simple fact that it arrives in your email inbox out of the blue and seems too good to be true. So if you get an unsolicited offer that promises great riches, you know to press the Delete key—pronto.

Savvy Internet users train themselves to recognize scam emails at a glance. That's because most scam messages have one or more of the following characteristics in common:

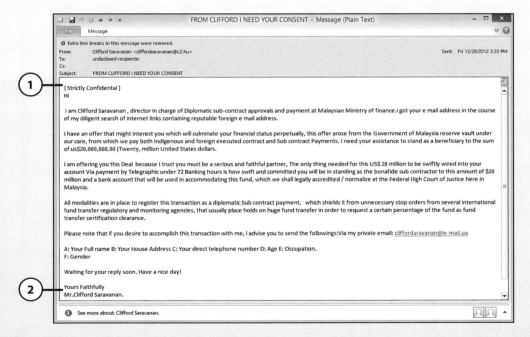

1. The email does not address you personally by name; your name doesn't appear any-where in the body of the message.

2. You don't know the person who sent you the message; the message was unsolicited.

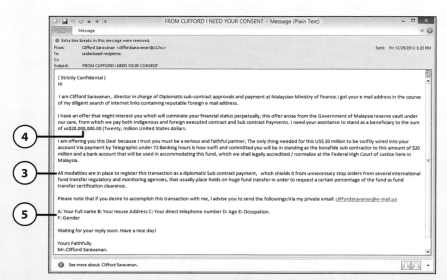

(3) The message is rife with spelling and grammatical errors. (Scammers frequently operate from foreign countries and do not use English as their first language.) Conversely, the text of the message might seem overly formal, as if written by someone not familiar with everyday English.

(4) You are promised large sums of money for little or no effort on your part.

(5) You are asked to provide your bank account number, credit card number, or other personal information—or are asked to provide money upfront for various fees, or to pay the cost of expediting the process.

Avoiding Online Fraud

Recognizing a scam email is just one way to reduce your risk of getting conned online. Here are some more tips you can employ:

- Familiarize yourself with the common types of online scams—and if a message in your inbox resembles any of these common scams, delete it.

- Ignore all unsolicited emails, of any type. No stranger will send you a legitimate offer via email; it just doesn't happen. When you receive an unsolicited offer via email, delete it.

- Don't give in to greed. If an offer sounds too good to be true, it is; there are no true "get rich quick" schemes.

• Never provide any personal information—including credit card numbers, your Social Security number, and the like—via email. If such information is legitimately needed, you can call the company yourself or visit their official website to provide the information directly.

WHAT TO DO IF YOU'VE BEEN SCAMMED

What should you do if you think you've been the victim of an email fraud? There are a few steps you can take to minimize the damage:

• If the fraud involved transmittal of your credit card information, contact your credit card company to put a halt to all unauthorized payments—and to limit your liability to the first $50.

• If you think your bank accounts have been compromised, contact your bank to put a freeze on your checking and savings accounts—and to open new accounts, if necessary.

• Contact one of the three major credit reporting bureaus to see if stolen personal information has been used to open new credit accounts—or max out your existing accounts.

• Contact your local law enforcement authorities—fraud is illegal, and it should be reported as a crime.

• Report the fraud to your state attorney general's office.

• File a complaint with the Federal Trade Commission (FTC) via the form located at www.ftccomplaintassistant.gov.

• Contact any or all of the following consumer-oriented websites: Better Business Bureau (www.bbb.org), Internet Crime Complaint Center (www.ic3.gov), National Consumers League (www.natlconsumersleague.org), and the NCL's Fraud Center (www.fraud.org).

Above all, don't provide any additional information or money to the scammers. As soon as you suspect you've been had, halt all contact and cut off all access to your bank and credit card accounts. Sometimes the best you can hope for is to minimize your losses.

Protecting Against Computer Viruses and Other Malware

Any malicious software installed on your computer is dubbed *malware*. There are two primary types of malware—*computer viruses* and *spyware*.

A computer virus is a malicious software program designed to do damage to your computer system by deleting files or even taking over your PC to launch attacks on other systems. A virus attacks your computer when you launch an infected software program, launching a "payload" that oftentimes is catastrophic.

Even more pernicious than computer viruses is the proliferation of *spyware*. A spyware program installs itself on your computer and then surreptitiously sends information about the way you use your PC to some interested third party. Spyware typically gets installed in the background when you're installing another program, and is almost as bad as being infected with a computer virus. Some spyware programs will even hijack your computer and launch pop-up windows and advertisements when you visit certain web pages. If there's spyware on your computer, you definitely want to get rid of it.

Protecting Against Malware

There are several things you can do to avoid having your PC infected with malware. It's all about smart and safe computing.

(1) Don't open email attachments from people you don't know—or even from people you do know, if you aren't expecting them. That's because some malware can hijack the address book on an infected PC, thus sending out infected email that the owner isn't even aware of. Just looking at an email message won't harm anything; the damage comes when you open a file attached to the email.

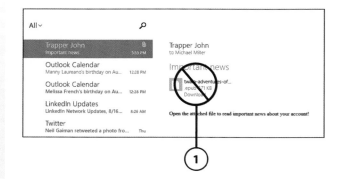

(**2**) Download files only from reliable file archive websites, such as Download.com (download.cnet.com) and Tucows (www.tucows.com/downloads/). Do not download files you find on sites you don't know.

(**3**) Don't access or download files from music and video file-sharing and BitTorrent networks, which are notoriously virus- and spyware-ridden. Instead, download music and movies from legitimate sites, such as the iTunes Store and Amazon MP3 Store.

BitTorrent

BitTorrent is a technology that enables the sharing of large files between individual computers on the Internet. Today, BitTorrent is typically used to illegally share pirated music and movie files.

(**4**) Because viruses and spyware can also be transmitted via physical storage media, share USB drives, CDs, DVDs, and files only with users you know and trust.

(**5**) Use anti-malware software, such as Windows Defender, to identify and remove viruses and spyware from your system.

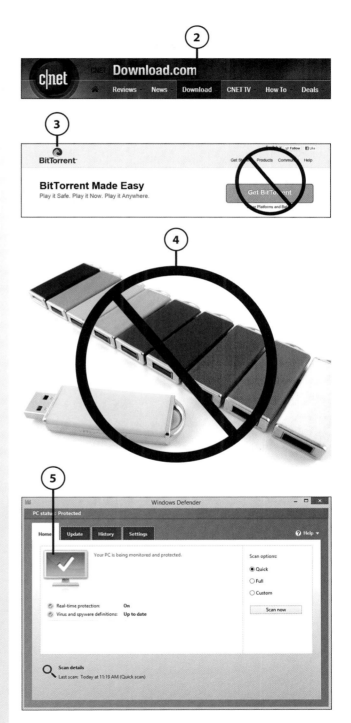

>>Go Further

ANTI-MALWARE SOFTWARE

Windows 8.1 comes with its own antivirus utility built in. It's called Windows Defender, and you can see it in action by going to the All Apps page, scrolling to the Apps section, and clicking or tapping Windows Defender.

Of course, you're not locked into using Microsoft's anti-malware solution. There are several third-party antivirus programs available, including the following:

- AVG Internet Security (www.avg.com)
- Avira Antivirus (www.avira.com)
- Kaspersky Internet Security (www.kaspersky.com)
- McAfee Internet Security (www.mcafee.com)
- Norton Internet Security (us.norton.com)
- Trend Micro Titanium (www.trendmicro.com)

If you just purchased a new PC, it might come with a trial version of one of these third-party antivirus programs preinstalled. That's fine, but know that you'll be nagged to pay for the full version after the 90-day trial. You can do this if you want, but you don't need to; remember, you have Windows Defender built into Windows, and it's both free and very effective.

(By the way, if you want to get rid of the trial version of one of these antivirus programs, right-click the Start button and select Programs and Features. When the Programs and Features window opens, select the program you want to get rid of and then click Uninstall. This will get rid of all the "upgrade" nagging from the program in question.)

Whichever anti-malware solution you employ, make sure you update it on a regular basis. These updates include information on the very latest viruses and spyware, and are invaluable for protecting your system from new threats. (You'll be happy to know that Windows Defender is configured to update itself automatically—so there's nothing you have to do manually.)

Protecting Against Online Attacks and Intrusions

Connecting to the Internet is a two-way street—not only can your PC access other computers online, but other computers can also access your PC. So, unless you take proper precautions, malicious hackers can read your private data, damage your system hardware and software, and even use your system (via remote control) to cause damage to other computers.

Zombie Computers

When a computer is controlled by remote control to attack other computers or send out reams of spam, that computer is said to be a *zombie*. A collection of zombie computers is called a *botnet*.

Employing a Firewall

You protect your system against outside attack by blocking the path of attack with a *firewall*. A firewall is a software program that forms a virtual barrier between your computer and the Internet. The firewall selectively filters the data that is passed between both ends of the connection and protects your system against outside attack.

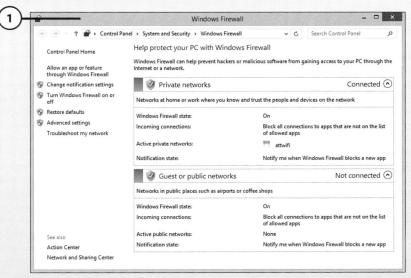

1 Windows 8.1 includes a built-in firewall utility. The Windows Firewall is activated by default and is, for most users, more than enough protection against computer attacks.

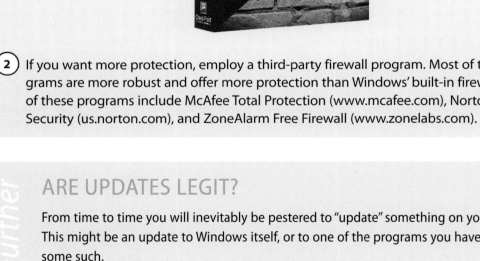

2 If you want more protection, employ a third-party firewall program. Most of these programs are more robust and offer more protection than Windows' built-in firewall. The best
of these programs include McAfee Total Protection (www.mcafee.com), Norton Internet
Security (us.norton.com), and ZoneAlarm Free Firewall (www.zonelabs.com).

>>>Go Further

ARE UPDATES LEGIT?

From time to time you will inevitably be pestered to "update" something on your computer.
This might be an update to Windows itself, or to one of the programs you have installed, or
some such.

Should you click "yes" when asked to install one of these updates? Or is this just another way
to install malware on your system?

Although most updates are legitimate and necessary (they typically contain important bug
fixes), some are just another way for the bad guys to install bad stuff on your system. This is
especially so if the "update" notice is for a program or service you've never heard about and
don't even have installed on your PC.

That said, if it's Windows that's asking you to approve the update, you should do it. Microsoft beams out updates to Windows over the Internet on a regular basis, and these *patches* (as they're called) help keep your system in tip-top running condition. The same thing with updates to legitimate software programs; these updates sometimes add new functionality to the apps you use day-to-day.

(This includes updates to Java and Flash, two behind-the-scenes technologies that help power the web pages you visit. They're both legitimate and need periodic updating.)

You can manage how Windows handles updates via the aptly named Windows Update utility. Open the Charms bar, click Settings, click Change PC Settings, and then select Update & Recovery. Click Choose How Updates Get Installed to change from the automatic installation (default) to another option with more manual control.

So here's the rule. If it's an update to Windows or a program that you know and use on a regular basis, approve it. If it's an update to a program you don't use or don't know, then don't approve it. When in doubt, play it safe.

Senior Corps
(www.seniorcorps.org)

NIH Senior Health
(www.nihseniorhealth.gov)

AARP
(www.aarp.org)

AMAC
(www.amac.us)

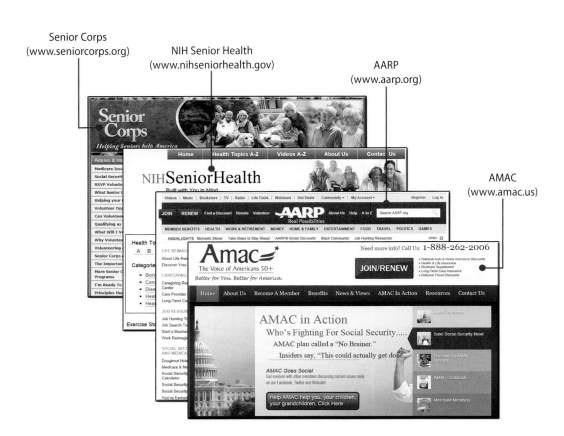

In this chapter you discover tons of useful online resources of interest to seniors.

→ Reading Local and Community News Online
→ Exploring Travel Opportunities Online
→ Discovering Recipes Online
→ Finding Healthcare Information Online
→ Obtaining Legal Advice Online
→ Managing Your Finances Online
→ Shopping Online

10

Senior Living Online

The Internet offers a ton of useful and interesting resources for people of all ages, and especially for seniors. Whether you're looking for community news, healthcare information, or shopping bargains, you can find it online—using your Windows PC.

Reading Local and Community News Online

The Internet has become a primary source of news in today's digital world. We might have grown up reading newspapers and magazines, but readers today are more likely to get their news and information online. In fact, most newspapers and magazines have their own online editions—often readable for free.

Find Local News

There are numerous sources of local news online, from your local newspaper to websites devoted solely to community news.

1. One of the best sources of local news is your local newspaper. Use Google or Bing to search for your local newspaper online, or go to the US Newspaper List (www.usnpl.com) for a list of newspapers nationwide.

2. Many local television and radio stations also have websites with up-to-date local news, sports, and weather information. Search Google or Bing for radio and TV station sites in your area. (For example, to search for TV stations in Orlando, query **Orlando tv stations**.)

3. Patch (www.patch.com) is a consortium of neighborhood news websites, aggregated by AOL. Enter your ZIP Code to view news and information gathered locally by neighborhood correspondents.

Online Subscriptions

Most local newspapers have free online editions, although some charge for online access. You might get free or discounted online access as part of your print subscription, however, so ask about available options. Some paid newspaper sites also let you view a limited number of articles at no charge, even without a subscription.

KEEPING IN TOUCH WHEREVER YOU ARE

You're not limited to reading the local news from where you currently reside. If you're vacationing elsewhere, doing the snowbird thing during the winter, or just curious about what's happening where you grew up, then you can use the Internet to access those local news sites from wherever you happen to be.

For example, if your current home is in Minnesota but you winter in Florida, use Google to search for your local Minneapolis newspaper or television station and then read your northern news while you're sunning in the south. Likewise, if you grew up in Indiana but now live in Arizona, there's nothing stopping you from reading the *Indianapolis Star* online in your web browser.

You can even read news from other countries online. If your family has Irish roots, for example, just search Google for newspapers in Ireland, and keep in touch from around the globe.

Find Local Weather

Many local news sites also provide local weather reports. There are also several national weather sites that provide local forecasts.

(1) The Weather Channel's website (www.weather.com) is one of the most detailed in terms of local weather forecasts and conditions. You can view hourly, daily, weekly, and long-term forecasts, as well as view current conditions on an interactive radar map.

2. AccuWeather (www.accuweather.com) is another popular general weather website. Enter your location for local conditions and forecasts.

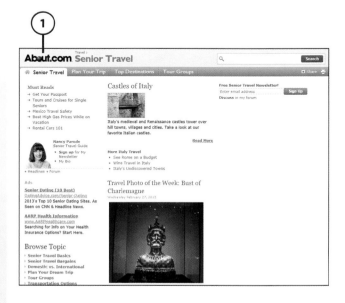

Exploring Travel Opportunities Online

Many seniors like to travel, and there is a ton of travel-related information and services online you can use to plan your next trip.

Research a Destination

Before you make a trip, find out more about where you're going. The Internet has pretty much replaced traditional travel guidebooks as a source for information about key destinations.

1. About.com has a great Senior Travel section (http://seniortravel.about.com), complete with information about planning a trip, top destinations, and tour groups.

(2) Most of the traditional printed guidebooks have travel-oriented websites, with lots of free information. Check out the sites for Fodor's (www.fodors.com), Frommer's (www.frommers. com), and Lonely Planet (www. lonelyplanet.com).

(3) When you want reviews of hotels, restaurants, and other destinations, check out TripAdvisor (www.tripadvisor. com). You can link directly from the site's user reviews to make reservations, if you like.

(4) Virtual Tourist (www. virtualtourist.com) is another good site for user reviews of popular destinations. You can even share your own experiences with other users.

Travel App

The Windows Travel app is another good source of travel information and reservation services. Learn more in Chapter 6, "Using New Windows Apps."

(2)

(3)

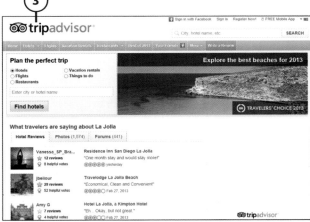

(4)

Make Reservations

You can't beat the Internet for making flight and hotel reservations, from the comfort of your living room. Just log on, enter the required information, and reserve away!

1 You can make flight reservations directly from the websites of major carriers. Some of the most popular airline sites include American Airlines (www.aa.com), Delta (www.delta.com), Southwest (www.southwest.com), United (www.united.com), and US Airways (www.usairways.com).

2 You can make hotel reservations directly at the websites of most big hotel chains. Some of the most popular chains include Choice Hotels (www.choicehotels.com for Comfort Inn, Quality Inn, Clarion, and EconoLodge), Hilton (www.hilton.com for Doubletree, Embassy Suites, Hampton Inn, Homewood Suites, and Hilton), Hyatt (www.hyatt.com for Hyatt and Hyatt Place), and Marriott (www.marriott.com for Courtyard, Fairfield Inn and Suites, Marriott, Residence Inn, Springhill Suites, and TownPlace Suites); use Google to search for other hotels you like.

(3) There are several general travel sites you can use to research destinations and book hotel rooms, rental cars, cruises, and flights. These sites include Expedia (www.expedia.com), Orbitz (www.orbitz.com), and Travelocity (www.travelocity.com).

Discovering Recipes Online

The Internet is a great resource for home cooks. It's easy to search Google for your favorite recipes, or browse sites that contain nothing but recipes.

Find Tasty Recipes

Can't remember the ingredients you need for a particular dish? Want to explore new tastes? Then check out some of the most popular recipe sites online; great food is just a click away!

(1) My Recipes (www.myrecipes.com) offers more than 50,000 recipes for all kinds of meals. Search or browse for what you want.

2 All Recipes (www.allrecipes.com) is another general recipe site. It also offers how-to videos that lead you step-by-step through your favorite recipes and cooking techniques.

3 Epicurious (www.epicurious.com) is a community for serious home cooks. Browse this site for recipes, food-related articles, and cooking guides.

4 Want to cook like the famous chefs you see on TV? Then check out the all-star recipes on the Food Networks' website (www.foodnetwork.com). Whether you're into Guy Fieri, Bobby Flay, or Rachel Ray, you'll find their recipes here.

Food & Drink App

You can find even more recipes via the Bing Food & Drink app included with Windows 8.1. Learn more in Chapter 6.

Finding Healthcare Information Online

Health is a big concern for most seniors. Fortunately, the Internet is a great source of healthcare information and services. Whether you need to research a particular medical condition, make a doctor's appointment, or fill prescription, you can do it online.

Research Medical Conditions

Have a new ache or pain? Stubborn cough? Just not feeling right? Turn to these websites to research all sorts of medical conditions, before you call your doctor.

(1) WebMD (www.webmd.com) is one of the most popular websites for researching all sorts of ailments and conditions. The site features sections for specific health conditions, drugs and supplements, and living healthy.

(2) MedicineNet.com (www.medicinenet.com) features health news and information, including a huge database of diseases and conditions, along with an online symptom checker.

(3) The National Institutes of Health offers the SeniorHealth website (www.nihseniorhealth.gov), with stories, videos, and other information specifically geared for a senior audience.

Health & Fitness App

The Bing Health & Fitness app, included with Windows 8.1, offers a ton of useful medical information and advice, including an interactive Symptom Checker (just answer the onscreen questions and get diagnosed), comprehensive drug database (enter the name of a drug to learn all about it), and conditions database (learn risk factors, symptoms, diagnosis, and treatment). Learn more in Chapter 6.

Find a Doctor

Looking for a new doctor? You can find one online.

(1) Find a Doctor (www.findadoctor. com) lets you search for physicians by specialty and location, and then schedule an appointment—all online.

(2) The American Medical Association maintains a comprehensive database on more than 814,000 licensed doctors nationwide. The AMA's DoctorFinder site (https:// extapps.ama-assn.org/doctor-finder/) lets you search this database for a doctor near you.

(3) When you're looking for physicians and healthcare professionals who are enrolled in the Medicare program, use Medicare's official Physician Compare site (www.medicare.gov/find-a-doctor/).

APPOINTMENTS AND RECORDS ONLINE

Many (but not all) doctors and clinics let you schedule future appointments online. Some even let you access your medical records via secure websites.

Check with your doctor or clinic to see what web-based services they offer. You'll probably need to set up a secure account, complete with username and password, so that only you can access your records. After you've set up an account, it's then easy to track your readings and progress via your computer and the Internet.

>>>Go Further

Order Prescription Drugs

You can fill your prescriptions at your local pharmacy or using one of a number of online prescription services. And your local pharmacy probably has a website that makes ordering easier!

1 The big national pharmacy chains have their own websites for filling your prescriptions so that you can pick them up at your local store. You can order online from CVS (www.cvs.com), Rite Aid (www.riteaid.com), and Walgreens (www.walgreens.com); you can also access the pharmacy departments of Target (www.target.com/pharmacy/) and Walmart (www.walmart.com/pharmacy/) on the Web.

2 There are several "virtual pharmacies" on the Web that let you order prescription drugs and have them delivered to your door, via the mail. The most popular include Express Scripts (www.express-scripts.com), Familymeds (www.familymeds.com), HealthWarehouse (www.healthwarehouse.com), and RXdirect (www.rxdirect.com). You need to have your doctor fax or email your prescriptions to get started.

1

2

Insurance Plans

Check with your health insurance company to see which online pharmacies are covered under your specific insurance plan.

Obtaining Legal Advice Online

The Internet will never replace a licensed attorney, but you can still find lots of legal advice online. Whether you need help with estate planning or anticipate a nasty guardianship fight, the Web is a great place to start.

Find Legal Advice and Services

When you need legal advice, there are a few general sites to start with. You can also search Google for legal services in your state or city.

(1) With LawHelp.org (www.lawhelp.org) you can search for legal advice and services by state. There's a special section just for seniors, covering wills and trusts, guardianship and conservatorship, nursing homes and assisted living, elder abuse and exploitation, and other issues of interest to older Americans.

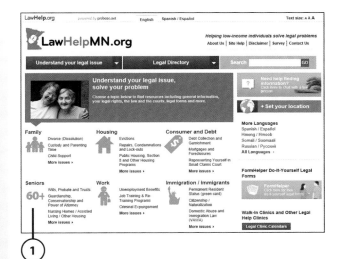

(2) LegalAdvice.com (www. legaladvice.com) enables you to ask questions of legal professionals, as well as search past answers.

(3) The National Senior Citizens Law Center (www.nsclc.org) is an advocacy organization providing legal services to low-income seniors nationwide. Although the site does not provide specific legal advice, it does include links to several organizations that do.

Managing Your Finances Online

As you get older, it becomes more difficult to get out and about to do your daily banking activities. Thanks to the Internet, however, you can do your banking and bill paying online—as well as manage all your other financial activities, too.

Do Your Banking and Pay Your Bills

When it comes to managing your banking activities, you have two choices. You can use your bank's website or an online financial management site, such as Mint.

① Most banks have their own websites, from which you can view and reconcile your checking and saving accounts, transfer funds between accounts, and even pay your bills online. You typically need your bank account numbers, personal identification numbers (PINs), and other personal data to create your account; after you log on, each activity is no more than a few clicks away.

② Your credit card companies also have their own websites. After you sign up and sign in, you can review past transactions, make payments, and more.

③ If you want to manage all your financial transactions in one place, consider signing up for Mint (www.mint.com). Mint is a personal finance site where you can enter all your online accounts (banking, credit cards— you name it) and view your daily activities online. You can use Mint to pay bills, transfer funds, and perform other essential tasks—as well as review your income and expenditures over time.

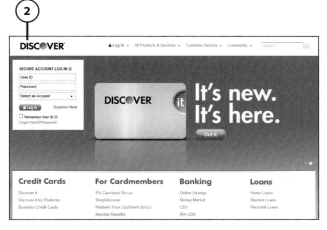

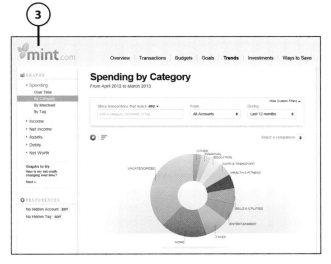

It's Not All Good

Sign Out

When you're dealing with websites that contain sensitive information, such as banks and other financial sites, make sure you sign out of the site when you're done using it. You don't want some other user of your computer to be able to access your personal information just because you left the site open on your PC.

Track Your Investments

If you have a number of investments—in stocks, mutual funds, IRAs, or 401(k) plans—you can track their performance online, in real time. There are a number of websites that offer both investment tracking and financial news and advice.

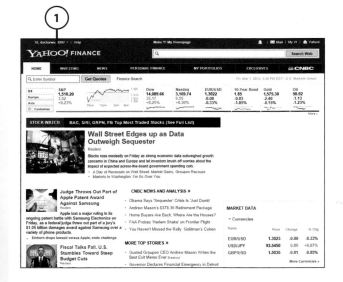

1. Yahoo! Finance (finance.yahoo.com) is the most popular financial website today. It's loaded with tons of financial news and opinion, and lets you track your own portfolio online.

2. CNN Money (money.cnn.com) is the online home of both *Fortune* and *Money* magazines. In addition to some of the best financial news and opinion on the Web, you can also use the site to create a Watch List of your own personal investments, and then track your investments over time.

(3) The Motley Fool (www.fool.com) has more opinion and advice than competing financial sites, and is both fun and useful. Plus, of course, you can create your own Watchlist to track your investments.

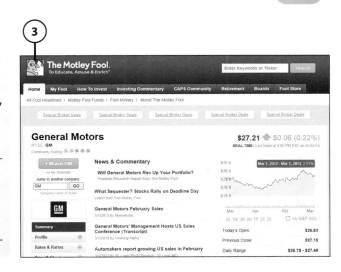

Finance App

The Windows 8 Finance app is another good way to track your investments and read financial news. Learn more in Chapter 6.

Shopping Online

Online shopping is a practical alternative for older shoppers for whom real-world shopping can be inconvenient, at best. Almost every brick-and-mortar store has an online storefront, offering a similar, if not expanded, selection. And there are plenty of bargains to be had online, too—if you know where to look.

Find a Bargain

When it comes to shopping online, you have lots of choices. You can shop at the sites of established retailers, or use a price comparison site to compare prices from multiple retailers. Many of these sites include customer reviews of both the products and the available merchants; some even let you perform side-by-side comparisons of multiple products, which is great if you haven't yet made up your mind as to what you want to buy.

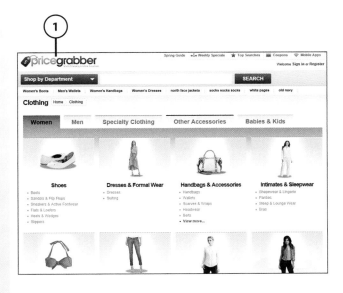

(1) PriceGrabber (www.pricegrabber. com) lets you shop by department or search for specific products.

(2) Shopping.com (www.shopping.com) not only compares pricing but also offers customer reviews of individual retailers.

(3) Google Shopping (www.google.com/shopping) differs from the other sites in that it searches retailer sites with its own search engine, and doesn't rely on paid listings for its results.

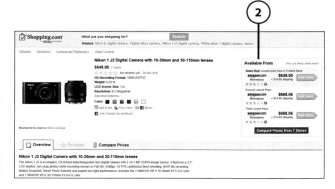

RETAILERS ONLINE

Most physical retailers have their own online shopping sites. For example, Kohl's (www.kohls.com), Macy's (www.macys.com), and Sears (www.sears.com) all have online store-fronts, as do Target (www.target.com) and Walmart (www.walmart.com).

You can also shop at online-only retailers, such as Amazon.com (www.amazon.com) and Overstock.com (www.overstock.com). These are retailers without physical stores that conduct all their business online and then ship merchandise direct to buyers.

Purchase an Item

Shopping at most online retailers is an easy and intuitive process—much like shopping at a real store, but in your web browser. This example uses Amazon.com.

(**1**) Browse for merchandise by category. *Or…*

(**2**) …search for a specific product by name or model number.

(**3**) Read the product specifics and then click to add the item to your shopping cart.

(**4**) Go to your shopping cart to check out and pay for your item(s), typically via credit card.

Shop Safely

Some consumers are wary about buying items online, but online shopping can be every bit as safe as shopping at a traditional brick-and-mortar retailer—as long as you take the proper precautions. The big online retailers are just as trustworthy as traditional retailers, offering safe payment, fast shipping, and responsive service.

(**1**) Make sure the online retailer prominently displays its contact information, and offers multiple ways to connect. You want to be able to call the retailer if something goes wrong—and not rely solely on email communication.

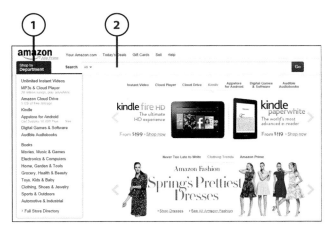

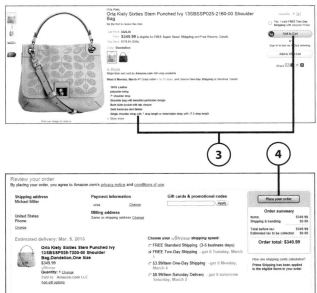

2 Look for the site's returns policy and satisfaction guarantee. You want to be assured that you'll be taken care of if you don't like whatever you ordered.

3 A reputable site should tell you whether an item is in stock and how long it will take to ship—before you place your order.

4 For the best protection, pay by major credit card.

Returns or Exchanges by Mail in Two Easy Steps

1. **Complete a Return and Exchange Form**

   Download and complete the online form, or use the form printed on the packing slip that came with your order.

   ‣ **Print a Return and Exchange Form** (PDF)

2. **Print a Prepaid Return Label**

   Please note: **L.L.Bean Visa Cardmembers receive free returns** when using our prepaid return labels: **for all others, your refund will be reduced by $6.50.**

   ‣ **Prepaid label for US or Puerto Rico** (opens in a new window)
   Ship your return via UPS (our preferred method) or US Postal Service.

   ‣ **Prepaid label for APO/FPO or US Territories** (PDF)
   Returns from these locations must be sent via US Postal Service.

   If you choose not to use our prepaid label, you will be responsible for paying all return shipping costs up front. Please ship your return to:

   L.L.Bean Returns
   3 Campus Dr.
   Freeport, ME 04034

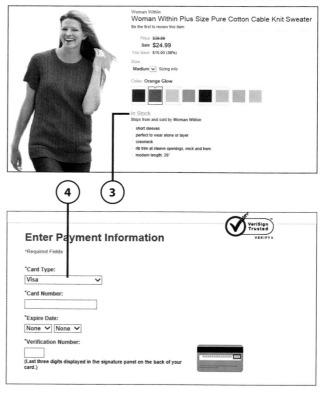

Woman Within
Woman Within Plus Size Pure Cotton Cable Knit Sweater
Be the first to review this item

Price: $39.99
Sale: $24.99
You Save: $15.00 (38%)

Size
Medium ▾ Sizing info

Color: Orange Glow

In Stock
Ships from and sold by Woman Within
· short sleeves
· perfect to wear alone or layer
· crewneck
· rib trim at sleeve openings, neck and hem
· modern length: 26"

Enter Payment Information
*Required Fields

*Card Type:
Visa ▾

*Card Number:

*Expire Date:
None ▾ None ▾

*Verification Number:

(Last three digits displayed in the signature panel on the back of your card.)

5 Make sure that the retailer uses a secure server for its checkout process. Look in the Address box for the letters **https:** (not the normal http:\\) before the URL, and the "lock" symbol after. If the checkout process is not secure, do not proceed with payment.

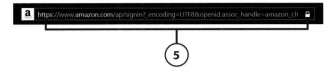

Credit Card Protection

In the U.S., credit card purchases are protected by the Fair Credit Billing Act, which gives you the right to dispute certain charges and limits your liability for unauthorized transactions to $50. In addition, some card issuers offer a supplemental guarantee that says you're not responsible for any unauthorized charges made online.

>>>Go Further

SENIORS ORGANIZATIONS ONLINE

Many prominent organizations for seniors have sites on the Web. These websites typically offer news for members, as well as useful advice, services, and the like.

The most popular organizations for seniors on the Web include the following:

- AARP (www.aarp.org)
- American Seniors (www.americanseniors.org)
- American Seniors Housing Association (www.seniorshousing.org)
- Association of Mature American Citizens (AMAC) (www.amac.us)
- Canadian Snowbird Association (CSA) (www.snowbird.org)
- Senior Corps (www.seniorcorps.org)
- Senior Job Bank (www.seniorjobbank.com)

Obviously, there are many more resources for seniors online than I can list here in this chapter. Remember to search Google or Bing for whatever it is you're looking for.

Folder
pane   Mail app   Message pane   Content pane

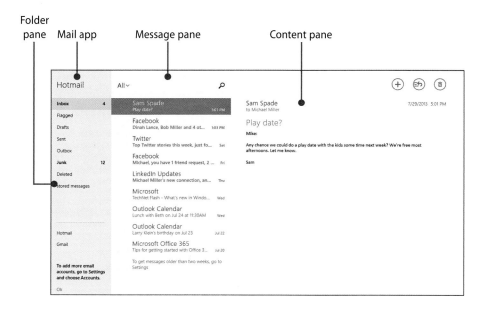

In this chapter you find out how to send and receive private messages via email.

→ Using the Windows Mail App
→ Using Web-Based Email
→ Managing Your Contacts with the People App

Emailing Friends and Family

When it comes to keeping in touch with the people you know and love, the easiest way to do so is via electronic mail, otherwise known as email. An email message is like a regular letter, except that it's composed electronically and delivered almost immediately via the Internet. You can use email to send both text messages and computer files (such as digital photos) to pretty much anyone with an Internet connection.

One of the easiest ways to send and receive email from your new PC is to use the Windows Mail app. You can also send and receive email with Internet Explorer, using a web-based email service such as Gmail or Yahoo! Mail. Either approach is good and lets you create, send, and read email messages from all your friends and family.

Using the Windows Mail App

Windows 8.1 includes a built-in Mail app for sending and receiving email messages. By default, the Mail app manages email from any Microsoft email service linked to your Microsoft Account, including Outlook.com and the older Hotmail. This means you'll see Outlook and Hotmail messages in your Mail Inbox, and be able to easily send emails from your Hotmail or Outlook account.

Set Up Your Email Account

By default, the Mail app sends and receives messages from the email account associated with your Microsoft account. You can, however, configure Mail to work with other email accounts, if you have them.

Account Types

The Mail app lets you add Outlook. com (including Hotmail addresses), Google (Gmail), AOL, and Yahoo! Mail accounts.

(1) From the Windows Start screen, click or tap the Mail tile to open the Mail app.

(2) Press Windows+C to display the Charms bar and then click or tap Settings to display the Settings pane.

(3) Click or tap Accounts to display the Accounts pane.

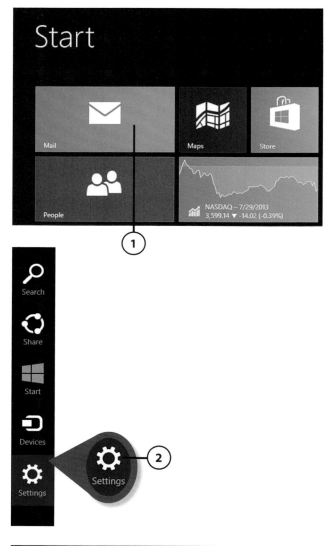

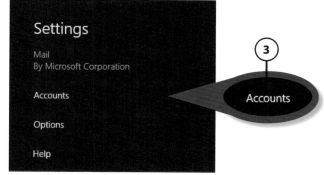

(4) Click or tap Add an Account.

(5) Click the type of account you want to add.

(6) Enter your email address and password in the Add Your Account pane.

(7) Click the Connect button.

Switching Accounts

To view the Inbox of another email account, right-click to display the Options bar and then click Accounts. When the Accounts pane appears, click or tap the name of the other email account.

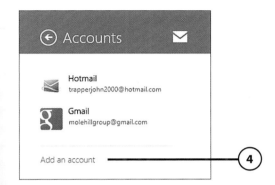

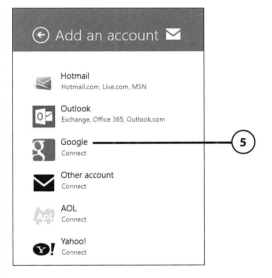

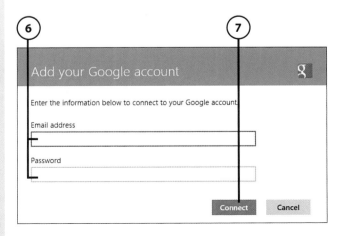

View Incoming Messages

All email messages sent to you from others are stored in the Inbox of the Mail app. From there you can read any and all email messages you receive.

1 From the Windows Start screen, click or tap the Mail tile to open the Mail app.

Tile Info

On the Start screen, the Mail app is a "live" tile; your most recent unread messages scroll across the face of the tile, and the number at the bottom right indicates how many unread messages you have.

2 Select Inbox from the Mail pane to display a list of all your incoming email messages.

3 Tap a message to view it in the content pane on the right.

4 If the message has a file attached, click Download to download the file to your computer.

It's Not All Good

Downloading Attachments

Be cautious when downloading and opening files attached to email messages. This type of file attachment is how computer viruses are often spread; opening a file that contains a virus automatically infects your computer.

You should only download attachments that you're expecting from people you know. Never open an attachment from a stranger. Never open an attachment you're not expecting. When in doubt, just ignore the attachment. That's the safest way to proceed.

Reply to a Message

Replying to an email message is as easy as clicking a button and typing your reply. The bottom of your reply "quotes" the text of the original message.

(1) From an open message, click or tap the Respond button at the top of screen.

(2) Select Reply from the pop-up menu to display the Reply screen.

(3) Enter your reply at the top of the message; the bottom of the message "quotes" the original message.

(4) Click or tap the Send button when you're ready to send the message.

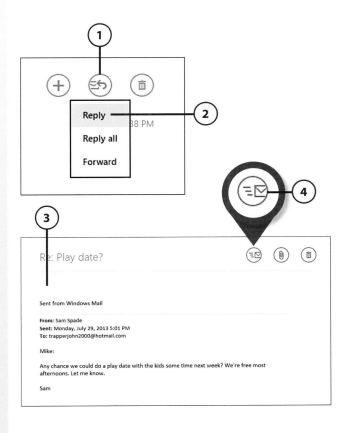

Send a New Message

Composing a new message is similar to replying to a message. The big difference is that you have to manually enter the recipient's email address.

(**1**) Click the New (+) button at the top of any Mail screen to display the new message screen.

(**2**) Click or tap the Add a Subject area and type a subject for this message.

(**3**) Click or tap within the To box and begin entering the name or email address of the message's recipient.

(**4**) Mail displays a list of matching names from your contact list; select the person you want to email.

(**5**) Click or tap within the main body of the message area and type your message.

COPYING OTHER RECIPIENTS

You can also send carbon copies (Cc) to additional recipients. Just enter one or more email addresses into the Cc box.

In addition, you can "blind" carbon copy (Bcc) additional recipients, who then remain invisible to your other recipients. Click the See More link to display the Bcc box, then enter the addresses of the intended recipients.

Formatting Your Message

Right-click anywhere on the screen to open the Options bar and then use the Font, Bold, Italic, Underline, Text Color and other buttons to format your message.

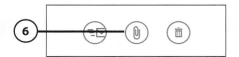

6 To send a file, such as a digital photo, along with this message, click the Attachments (paperclip) button to display the Files screen.

7 Navigate to and select the file you want to attach. Click the Attach button.

8 When you're ready to send the email, click the Send button at the top of the message.

Large Files

Be careful when sending extra-large files (2 MB or more) via email. Files of this size, such as large digital photos or home videos, can take a long time to upload—and just as long for the recipient to download when received.

Move a Message to Another Folder

New messages are stored in the Mail app's Inbox, which is actually a folder. Mail uses other folders, too; there are folders for Flagged mail, Drafts, Sent Items, Outbox (messages waiting to be sent), Junk (spam), Deleted messages, and Stored messages. For better organization, you can easily move messages from one folder to another.

Flagged Mail
A "flagged" message is one you've singled out for attention at a later date by clicking the Flag button in the Options bar. It typically appears with a small flag icon in the message list.

(1) From within the Mail app, click or tap any folder to view the contents of that folder.

(2) Right-click the message you want to move; this displays the Options bar.

(3) Click Move.

(4) Click the destination folder (where you want to move the message).

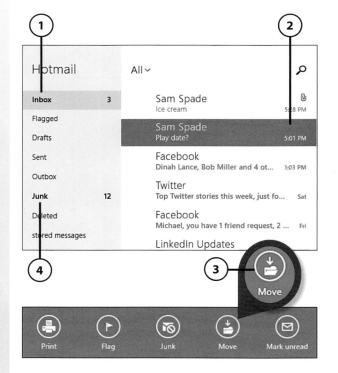

>>>Go Further

CREATING A NEW FOLDER

You're not limited to the Mail app's default folders; you can create additional custom folders at any time. To create a new folder, right-click in the navigation pane to display the options bar and then click Folder Options, New Folder. When the next dialog box appears, give the new folder a name, then click the Create Folder button. That's it; your new folder is created and awaiting messages.

Using Web-Based Email

In addition to the email account you were given when you signed up for your home Internet service, you can create additional email accounts with various web-based email services. These services, such as Yahoo! Mail and Gmail, let you send and receive email from any computer connected to the Internet, via your web browser. They're ideal if you travel a lot, or maintain two homes in different locations. (Snowbirds rejoice!!)

Send and Receive Messages with Yahoo! Mail

Many Internet service providers offer email service through Yahoo! Mail. You can then check and send email from within Internet Explorer or any other web browser just by going to the Yahoo! Mail web page (mail.yahoo.com).

You can also use the Yahoo! Mail app to receive and send email from your Yahoo! Mail account. To download and install the Yahoo! Mail app from the Windows Store, click the Store tile on the Start screen and search for yahoo mail. The Yahoo! Mail app is free.

Free Email

All of the web-based email services discussed in this section are totally free to use. All you need to do is sign up for an account.

(1) From the Windows Start screen, click the Yahoo! Mail tile to open the Yahoo! Mail app.

Signing In/Signing Up

The first time you launch the Yahoo! Mail app, you'll be prompted to enter your Yahoo! ID and password, then log into your account. If you don't yet have a Yahoo! Mail account, click the Sign Up button.

(2) Click Inbox in the left-hand pane to display all incoming messages.

(3) Click the message you want to read; this displays the text of that message in the reading pane on the right.

(4) To reply to an open message, click Reply to open the Reply screen.

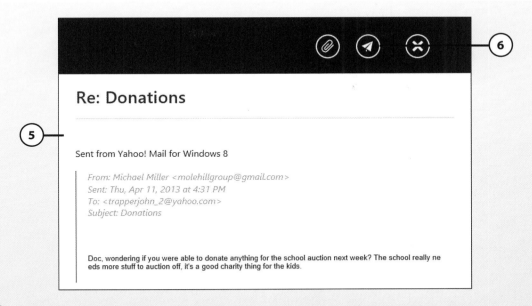

5 Enter your reply text in the message window, above the "quoted" original text.

6 Click the Send button when you're done and ready to send your message.

7 Return to the Inbox screen and click Compose to send a new email message.

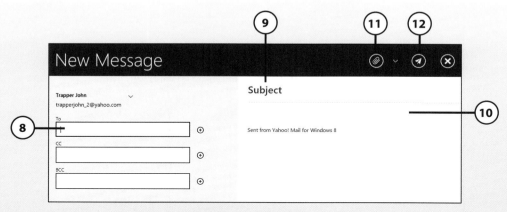

(8) Enter the email address of the recipient(s) in the To box.

(9) Enter a subject in the Subject area.

(10) Move your cursor to the main message area and type your message.

(11) Attach a file to a message by clicking the Attach (paperclip) icon, navigating to and selecting the file you want to attach, and then clicking the Open button.

(12) Click the Send button.

Send and Receive Messages with Gmail

Google's Gmail is another popular free web mail service. Anyone can sign up for a free Gmail account and then access email from any computer with an Internet connection, using any web browser, such as Internet Explorer.

(1) Launch Internet Explorer, go to mail.google.com, and sign into your account.

2 Gmail organizes your email into three types, each with its own tab: Primary, Social (messages from Facebook, Google+, and similar social networks), and Promotions (advertising messages). Most of your messages will be the Primary tab, so click that or another tab you want to view.

3 Click the Inbox link to display all incoming messages.

4 Click the header for the message you want to view.

5 To reply to an open message, click Reply and then enter your reply text in the message window and click Send when done.

6 To send a new email message, click Compose from any Gmail page to display the New Message pane.

7 Enter the email address of the recipient(s) in the To box.

8 Enter a subject in the Subject box.

9 Move your cursor to the main message area and type your message.

10 To attach a file to a message, click the Attach Files (paperclip) icon, navigate to and select the file you want to attach, and then click the Open button.

11 Send the message by clicking the Send button.

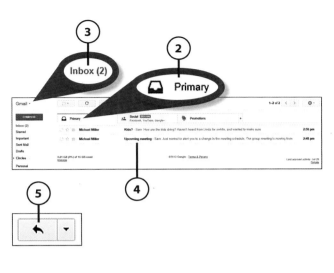

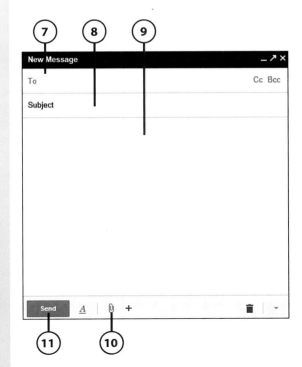

Send and Receive Messages with Outlook.com

Microsoft has its own web-based email service, dubbed Outlook.com. Outlook.com was formerly known as Hotmail and then the name changed to Windows Live Hotmail; it's now just Outlook. It works pretty much like Yahoo! Mail, Gmail, and other web-based email services.

(1) Launch Internet Explorer, go to www.outlook.com, and sign into your account.

(2) Click Inbox in the Folders list to display all incoming messages.

(3) Click the header for the message you want to view; the content of that message is displayed in the Content pane.

(4) To reply to an open message, click Reply, and then enter your reply text in the message window and click Send when done.

(5) To send a new email message, click New at the top of any page.

(6) Enter the email address of the recipient(s) in the To box.

(7) Enter a subject in the Add a Subject box.

(8) Move your cursor to the main message area and type your message.

(9) To attach a file to a message, click Attach Files, navigate to and select the file you want to attach, and then click the Open button.

(10) Send the message by clicking Send.

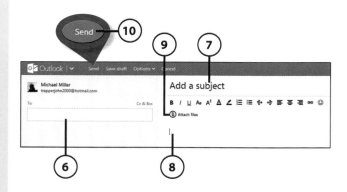

Managing Your Contacts with the People App

The people you email regularly are known as contacts. When someone is in your contacts list, it's easy to send her an email; all you have to do is pick her name from the list instead of entering her email address manually.

In Windows 8 and 8.1, all your contacts are managed from the People app. This app connects to the Microsoft Account you used to create your Windows account so that all the contacts from your main email account are automatically added.

You can also manually connect the People app to your Facebook, Google+, LinkedIn, and Twitter social network accounts, as well as your Gmail, Outlook. com, and Microsoft Exchange email accounts. The People app serves as the central hub for everyone you interact with online.

Social Media Updates

The People app also serves as a hub for updates from all your friends on Facebook and other social networks. Learn more in Chapter 13, "Connecting with Facebook and Other Social Media."

View Your Contacts

The People app centralizes all your contacts in one place, and it even combines a person's information from multiple sources. So if a given person is a Facebook friend and is also in your email contact list, his Facebook information and his email address appear in the People app.

1 From the Windows Start screen, click the People tile to open the People app.

(2) Scroll to the All section to view all your contacts in alphabetical order.

(3) Click or tap a person's name to view that person's contact information.

(4) Click Send Email to send this person an email.

(5) Click Map Address to view where this person lives.

(6) Click View Profile to view this person's social media profile.

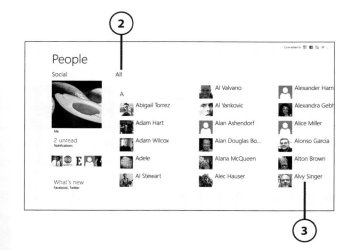

Add a New Contact

When you find someone you know online, you can add that person as a contact in the People app.

(1) From within the People app, right-click anywhere on the screen to display the Options bar.

(2) Click New Contact to display the New Contact screen

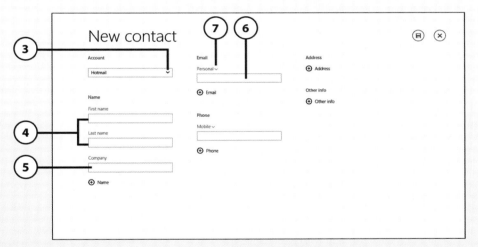

(3) If you have more than one email account connected to the People app, pull down the Account list and select which account you want to use to send email to this person.

(4) Enter the person's name into the First Name and Last Name boxes.

(5) Enter the person's employer into the Company box.

(6) Enter the person's email address into the Email box.

(7) Click the down arrow to select what type of email account this is (Personal, Work, or Other).

(8) Enter the person's phone number into the Phone box.

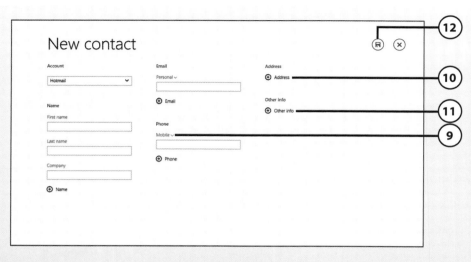

9) Click the down arrow to select what type of phone this is (Home, Work, Mobile, and so forth).

10) Click + Address to enter the person's address.

11) Click + Other Info to enter other information about this person.

12) Click Save when done.

>>>Go Further

OPTIONAL AND ADDITIONAL INFORMATION

Many of the fields available when you create a new contact are optional. For example, you don't have to enter a person's company information if you don't want to.

You can also add more information than is first apparent. For example, you can enter additional phone numbers (for work, home, mobile, and the like) by clicking the + under the Phone box. It's the same thing if you want to enter additional email addresses, street addresses, companies, and other information; just click the appropriate + sign and enter the necessary information.

Making a call with Skype

Person you're calling

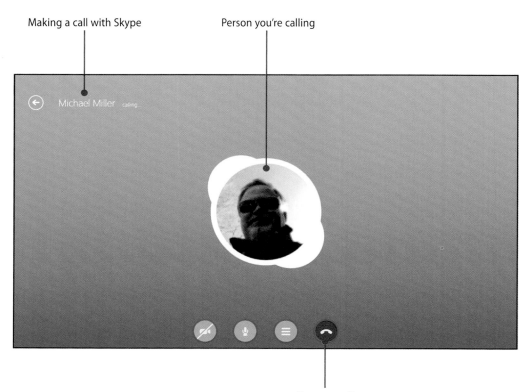

Michael Miller calling.

Hang up call

In this chapter you discover how to use Skype to talk one-on-one with friends and family members—via voice or video chat.

→ Setting Up Skype
→ Calling with Skype

12

Video Calling with Skype

If you travel a lot, or winter in warmer climes, you often find yourself far away from the people you love. Just because you're far away, however, doesn't mean that you can't stay in touch—on a face-to-face basis.

When you want to talk to your family members and other loved ones, nothing beats a video call. All you need is a webcam built into or connected to your PC and an app that lets you make face-to-face calls. Fortunately, just such an app is built into Windows 8.1; it's called Skype, and it's so easy even your grandkids can use it.

Setting Up Skype

Skype is a service that enables subscribers to connect with one another over the Internet, in real time. You can use Skype to conduct one-on-one text chats, audio conversations, and video chats. You can even use Skype to make Internet-based phone calls from your PC to landline or mobile phones (for a fee).

To use Skype for video calling, both you and the person you want to talk to must have webcams built into or connected to your PCs. In addition, you both must be connected to the Internet for the duration of the call.

If you log into Windows with your Microsoft Account, Skype connects to and uses information from that account. You have the same username and password, and you can access your full list of contacts. To log into Skype with a different user account, you must first switch to that user within Windows.

Skype and Microsoft

Formerly an independent company, Skype was acquired by eBay in 2005 and then by Microsoft in 2011. Skype currently has more than 650 million users worldwide.

Launch the Skype App

The Skype app in Windows 8.1 is a full-screen app. Although you can also use Skype's desktop application (available from www.skype.com), the full-screen app takes full advantage of Windows 8.1's Modern interface.

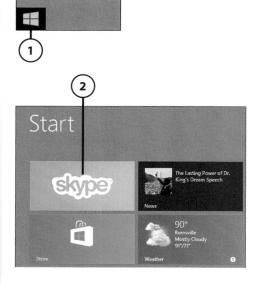

1. Click the Windows button or press the Windows key to go to the Windows Start screen.

2. Click or tap the Skype tile to launch the Skype app.

Configure Your Skype Account

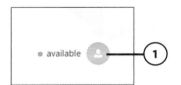

You can, at any time, configure the various details of your Skype account.

(1) From within the Skype app, click the Available icon in the top-right corner to display the Options pane.

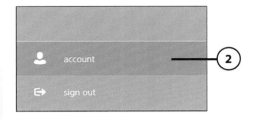

(2) Click Account to launch Internet Explorer and open Skype's My Account page.

(3) Scroll to the Account Details section of the My Account page and click Profile.

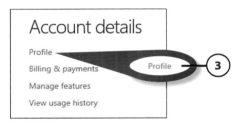

(4) Scroll to the Personal Information section and click Edit to open all the fields for editing.

(5) Enter the necessary information, as you deem fit.

(6) Click the Save button when done.

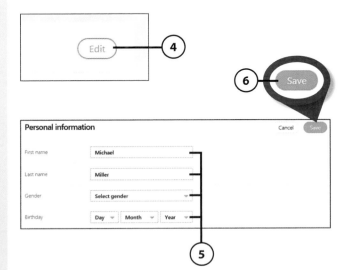

Skype Premium

The basic Skype service is free, and lets you make one-on-one voice and video calls to other Skype users. Skype also offers a Premium service, from $4.99/month, that offers the capability of group video chats with up to ten participants. You can also use Skype to call landline and mobile (non-Skype) phones, for 2.3 cents/minute; monthly subscriptions are also available if you do a lot of non-Skype calling.

Add a Contact

Before you call someone with Skype, you have to add that person to your Skype contacts list.

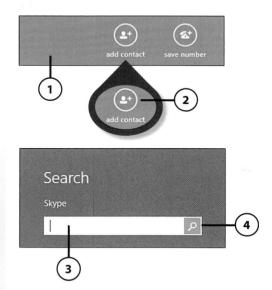

1. From within the Skype app, right-click anywhere on the screen to display the Options bar.

2. Click Add Contact to display the Search pane.

3. Enter into the Search box the actual name or Skype username of the person you want to add.

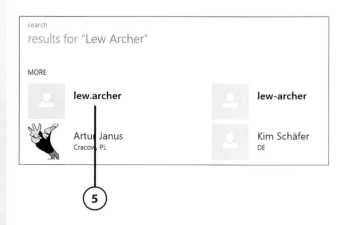

4. Press Enter or click the Search (magnifying glass) button.

5. When the search results appear, click the name of the person you want to add.

6. Click the Add to Contacts button.

7 You now have to send a contact request to this person; if he accepts your request, you'll be added to each other's contact lists. Enter a short message into the text box, or accept the default message.

8 Click Send.

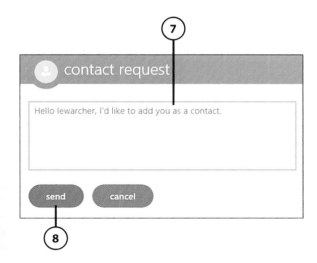

Calling with Skype

The whole point of Skype is to let you talk to absent friends and family. You can use Skype to make voice-only calls or to make video calls—which are great for seeing your loved ones, face-to-face.

Make a Video Call

If both you and the person you want to talk to have webcams built into or attached to your PCs, and if you're both online at the same time, it's easy to use Skype to initiate a one-to-one video call.

1 From within the Skype app, scroll to the People section and click the tile for the person you want to call. (People who are online and ready to chat have green dots next to their names.)

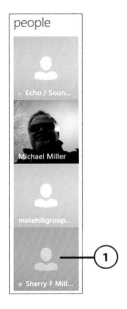

(2) Click the Camera button at the left side of the screen; Skype calls this person.

(3) When the other person answers the call, her live picture appears in the main part of the screen; your live picture appears smaller, in the lower-right corner. Start talking!

(4) Click the red "hang up" button to end the call.

WEBCAMS

Most notebook PCs have webcams built in. You can use your notebook's built-in webcam to make video calls with Skype. Because the webcam includes a built-in microphone, you can also use it to make voice calls.

If your PC doesn't have a built-in webcam, you can purchase and connect an external webcam to make Skype video calls. Webcams are manufactured and sold by Logitech and other companies, and connect to your PC via USB. They're inexpensive (as low as $30 or so) and sit on top of your monitor. After you've connected it, just smile into the webcam and start talking.

Make a Voice Call

If you don't have a webcam attached to your computer, or if you'd rather talk to a person without seeing him, you can use Skype to make a voice call. To do this, you both need microphones and speakers attached to your PC, or you can use a USB headset with built-in microphone.

1. From within the Skype app, scroll to the People section and click the tile for the person you want to call.

(**2**) Click the Telephone button at the left side of the screen; Skype calls this person.

(**3**) When the other person answers the call, you're ready to start talking.

(**4**) Click the red "hang up" button to end the call.

Facebook

Post a new
status update

Toolbar

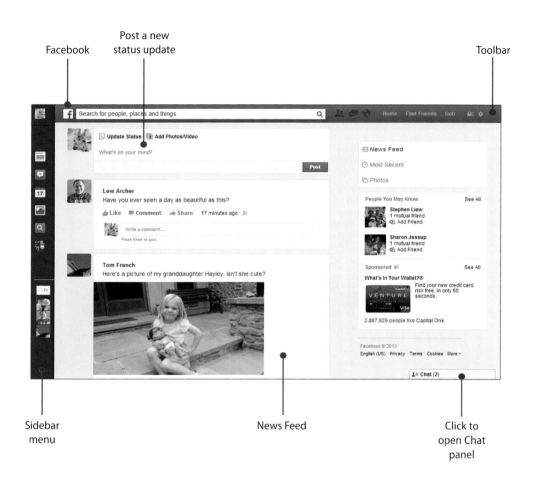

Sidebar
menu

News Feed

Click to
open Chat
panel

In this chapter you find out how to use Facebook and other social networks to connect with friends and family.

→ Sharing with Friends and Family on Facebook
→ Pinning Items of Interest to Pinterest
→ Managing Your Social Media with the People App

13

Connecting with Facebook and Other Social Media

When you want to keep track of what old friends and family are up to and keep them up-to-date on your activities, there's no better place to do it than Facebook. Facebook is a *social network*, which is a website that lets you easily share your activities with people you know. Write one post and it's seen by hundreds of your online "friends." It's the easiest way I know to connect with almost everyone you know.

Facebook isn't the only social network on the Internet, however. Other social media, such as Pinterest and Twitter, target particular types of users. You might find yourself using social media other than Facebook to keep in touch with friends and family of various ages.

Sharing with Friends and Family on Facebook

A social network is a website community that enables users to connect with and share their thoughts and activities with one another. Think of it as an online network of friends and family, including former schoolmates, co-workers, and neighbors.

The largest and most popular social network today is Facebook, with more than 1 billion active users worldwide. Although Facebook started life as a social network for college students, it has since expanded its membership lists, and it is now the preferred social network for seniors. (In fact, the fastest growing segment of Facebook users are those aged 45 and older.)

Seniors use Facebook to connect with current family members and re-connect with friends from the past. If you want to know what your friends from high school or the old neighborhood have been up to over the past several decades, chances are you can find them on Facebook.

Sign Up for Facebook

To use Facebook, you have to sign up for an account and enter some personal information. Fortunately, signing up for an account is both easy and free.

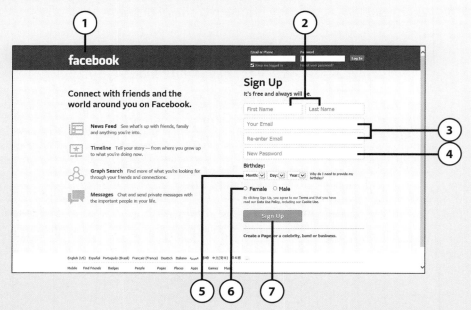

(1) Launch Internet Explorer and go to the Facebook home page at www.facebook.com.

(2) Go to the Sign Up section and enter your first and last name into the First Name and Last Name boxes.

(3) Enter your email address into the Your Email box, and re-enter it into the Re-enter Email box.

(4) Enter your desired password into the New Password box.

(5) Use the Birthday controls to enter your month, day, and year of birth.

(6) Check your gender (Female or Male).

(7) Click the Sign Up button. Facebook sends you an email message asking you to confirm your new Facebook account; when you receive this email, click the link to proceed.

Facebook App

Facebook has promised to deliver a Modern full-screen app for Windows 8.1, but as of Fall 2013 this app is not yet available. When it is available in the Windows Store, you'll be able to access Facebook directly from the app instead of using your web browser.

Additional Information

After you've created your Facebook account, you'll be prompted to enter additional personal information and then search for friends. You can do both of these things now or later, as you want.

Discover New—and Old—Friends on Facebook

To connect with someone on Facebook, you must become mutual *friends*. A Facebook friend can be a real friend, or a family member, colleague, acquaintance, you name it. When you add someone to your Facebook friends list, he sees everything you post—and you see everything he posts.

The easiest way to find friends on Facebook is to let Facebook find them for you—based on the information you provided for your personal profile. The more Facebook knows about you, especially in terms of where you've worked and gone to school, the more friends it can find.

(1) Log into your Facebook account and click the Friends button on the Facebook toolbar.

(2) The pull-down menu lists any friend requests you've received, and offers a number of friend suggestions from Facebook ("People You May Know"). To add one of these people to your friends list, click the Add Friend button.

Suggested Friends

The people Facebook suggests as friends are typically people who went to the same schools you did, worked at the same companies you did, or are friends of your current friends.

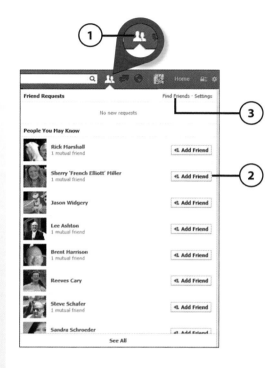

(3) To continue searching for friends, click Find Friends at the top of the menu to display your Friends page.

(4) Scroll down the page to view other suggested friends from Facebook in the People You May Know section. Click the Add Friend button for any person you'd like to add as a friend.

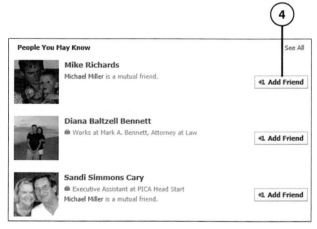

5 To find people in your email contacts list who are also members of Facebook, scroll to the top of the Friends page. Click the Find Friends link for the email service you use and then enter any requested information (typically your email address and password). Facebook lists all matching contacts.

6 Check the people you'd like to add as a friend and then click the Send Invites button.

7 To search directly for any old friends who might be on Facebook, enter a person's name into the search box in the Facebook toolbar.

8 Facebook displays a list of suggestions beneath the search box; click See More and then select the People Named item.

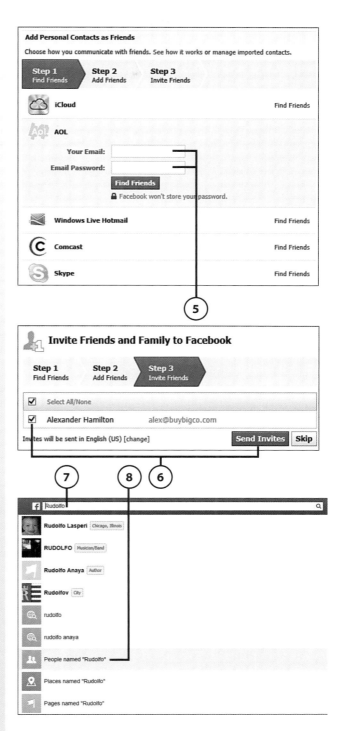

9 The next page displays the results of your search, which you can fine-tune by using the controls in the Refine This Search box. For example, you can filter the results by gender, current city, hometown, and school.

10 If your friend is listed, click the Add Friend button to send him a friend request.

Friend Requests

Facebook doesn't automatically add a person to your friends list. Instead, that person receives an invitation to be your friend; she can accept or reject the invitation. To accept or reject any friend requests you've received, click the Friend Request button on the Facebook toolbar. (And don't worry; if you reject a request, that person won't be notified.)

HOW MANY FRIENDS?

By the time you get to retirement age you've made the acquaintance of thousands of people through school, work, neighborhood activities, and the like—not to mention all the many members of your immediate and extended family. Do you really want to keep in touch with all these people via Facebook?

The answer is probably "no." Sure, there are some folks you're close to and want to stay close to, but there are others who you didn't like that much way back then, and probably won't like any better today. The reality is that you don't have to make everyone you've ever known a Facebook friend; you don't even have to put every member of your family on your friends list.

>>>Go Further

Facebook is great for getting back in touch with all the people you've cared about over the years—true friends and trusted family members. Not every acquaintance you've ever made falls into that category. So don't get carried away with adding more names to your Facebook friends list; the more "friends" you have, the more updates you have to keep track of in your News Feed. Too many friends can be overwhelming.

In particular, you might want to avoid having Facebook cull through your email contacts list for possible friends. Just because you've sent a few emails to someone in the past doesn't mean you want to be informed of all her thoughts and activities every blasted day on Facebook. Be proactive about making friends on Facebook, and choose only those you want to hear from on a regular basis.

Post a Status Update

To let your family and friends know what you've been up to, you need to post what Facebook calls a *status update*. Every status update you make is broadcast to everyone on your friends list, displayed in the News Feed on their home pages. A basic status update is text only, but you can also include photos, videos, and links to other web pages in your posts.

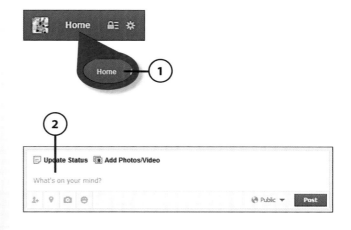

(**1**) Click Home on the Facebook toolbar to return to your home page.

(**2**) Type a short message into the Update Status box at the top of the page.

(**3**) If you're with someone else and want to mention them in the post, click the Who Are You With? button and enter that person's name.

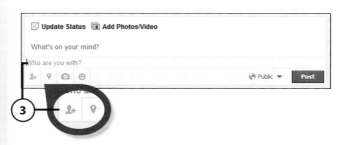

4 If you want to include your current location in your post, click the Where Are You? button and enter the city or place you're at.

5 To determine who can read this post, click the Privacy button and make a selection.

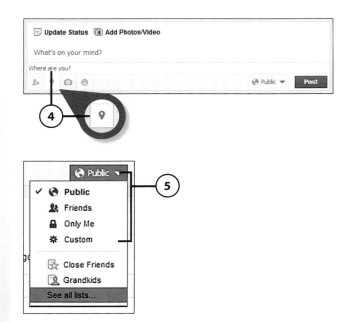

Who Sees Your Posts?

You can opt to make any post Public (meaning anyone can read it), visible only to your Friends, visible only to yourself (Only Me), or Custom (you select individuals who can and can't view it).

6 To include a link to another web page, enter that page's URL in your status update. Facebook should recognize the link and display a Link panel; select a thumbnail image from the web page to accompany the link, or check the No Thumbnail box.

7 To include a picture or video with your post, click Add Photos/Video. When the panel changes, click Upload Photos/Video to select the photos or videos to include.

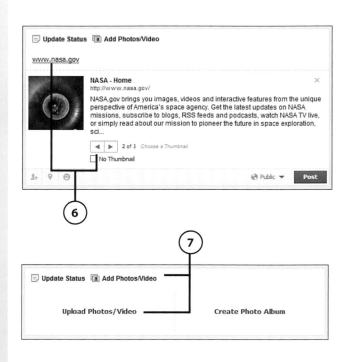

Sharing Photos

Facebook has become the Web's most popular site for sharing photos. To learn more about photo sharing on Facebook, see Chapter 14, "Storing and Sharing Photos with Loved Ones."

8. When you're ready to post your update, click the Post button.

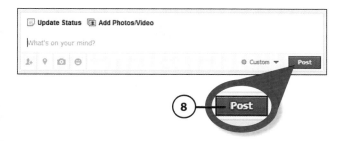

Find Out What Your Friends Are Up To

Your home page on Facebook displays a News Feed of all the status updates made by people on your friends list. The newest posts are at the top; scroll down through the list to read older posts.

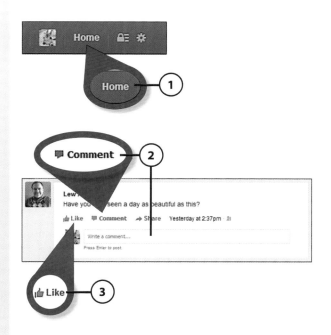

1. Click Home on the Facebook toolbar to return to your home page.

2. Your friends' posts are displayed in the News Feed in the middle of the page. To leave your own comments about a post, click Comment and then enter your text into the resulting text box.

3. To "like" a post, click Like.

4. If a post includes a link to another web page, that link appears beneath the post, along with a brief description of the page. Click the link to open the other page in your web browser.

5 If a post includes one or more photos, click the photo to view it in a larger onscreen lightbox.

6 If a post includes a video (which is indicated by a Play icon in the middle of the thumbnail), click the video thumbnail to begin playback.

Explore Your Friends' Timelines

If you want to know what an old friend has been up to over the years, you can do so by visiting that person's Facebook Timeline. As the name implies, this is a "timeline" of that person's posts and major life events. It also displays that person's personal information, photos and videos, upcoming events, and the like.

1 Click a person's name anywhere on the Facebook site to display his or her profile or Timeline page.

2 View key personal information by clicking About.

3 View a list of this person's friends by clicking Friends.

4 View your friend's photos by clicking Photos.

5 View a person's status updates in reverse chronological order (newest first) in the right-hand column on the Timeline.

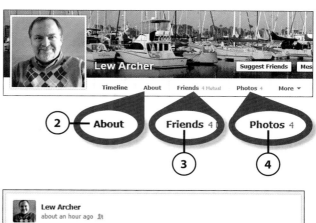

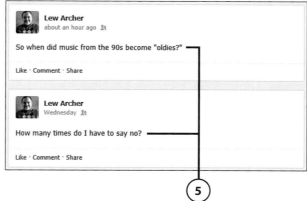

Pinning Items of Interest to Pinterest

Facebook isn't the only social network of interest to seniors. Pinterest (www. pinterest.com) is a newer social network with particular appeal to middle-aged and older women.

Unlike Facebook, which lets you post text-based status updates, Pinterest is all about images. The site consists of a collection of virtual online "pinboards" that people use to share pictures they find interesting. Users "pin" photos and other images to their personal message boards, and then they share their pins with online friends.

You can pin images of anything—clothing, furniture, recipes, do-it-yourself projects, and the like. Your Pinterest friends can then "repin" your images to their pinboards—and on and on.

Joining Pinterest

Like other social media sites, Pinterest is free to join and use. You can join with your email address or by using your Facebook account login.

Create New Pinboards

Pinterest lets you create any number of pinboards, each dedicated to specific topics. If you're into quilting, you can create a Quilting board; if you're into radio-controlled airplanes, you can create an RC Airplanes board with pictures of your favorite craft.

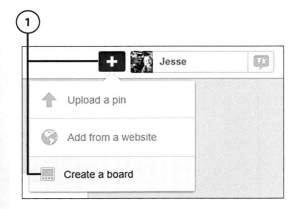

1. From the top of any Pinterest page, click the + button, and then click Create a Board to display the Create Board panel.

2. Enter the name for this board into the Name box.

3. Enter a short description of this board into the Description box.

4. Pull down the Category list and select a general category for this board.

5. Click the Create Board button.

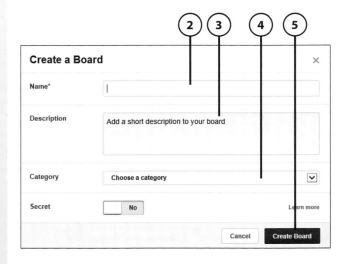

Find and Repin Interesting Items

Some people say that Pinterest is a little like a refrigerator covered with magnets holding up tons of photos and drawings. You can find lots of interesting items pinned from other users—and then "repin" them to your own personal pinboards.

(**1**) Enter the name of something you're interested in into the Search box at the top of any Pinterest page and then press Enter. Pinterest displays pins that match your query.

(**2**) Mouse over the item you want to repin and click the Pin It button. The Repin a Pin panel displays.

(**3**) Pull down the Board list and select which board you want to pin this item to.

(**4**) Accept the previous user's description or add your own in the Description box.

(**5**) Click the red Pin It button to repin the item.

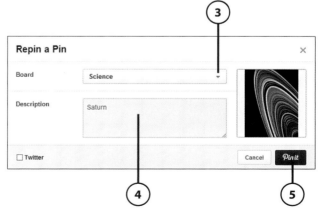

Pin an Item from a Web Page

You can also pin images you find on nearly any web page. It's as easy as copying and pasting the page's web address.

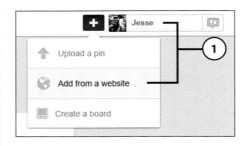

1. From any Pinterest page, click the + arrow at the top of the page and then click Add from a website.

2. Enter the web address (URL) of the page you want to pin into the bottom text box.

3. Click the Find Images button.

4. Pinterest now displays all images found on the selected web page. Mouse over the image you want to pin and click the Pin It button to open the Repin a Pin panel.

Images and Pins

Beneath the images found for a given web page are pins that others have made from this page. You can also repin one of these pins by mousing over the pin and clicking the Pin It button.

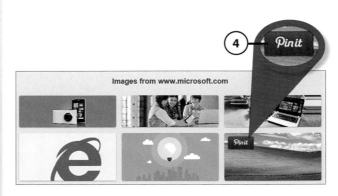

5 Pull down the Board list and select the board to which you want to pin this image.

6 Enter a short (500 characters or less) text description of or comment on this image into the Description box.

7 Click the red Pin It button when done.

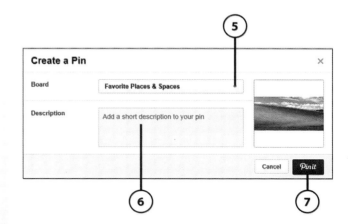

Pin It Button

Pinning a page is even easier if the page displays its own Pin it button. Just click the button, select an image from the page, and you're good to go.

Find People to Follow

When you find someone who posts a lot of things you're interested in, you can follow that person on Pinterest. Following a person means that all that person's new pins display on your Pinterest home page.

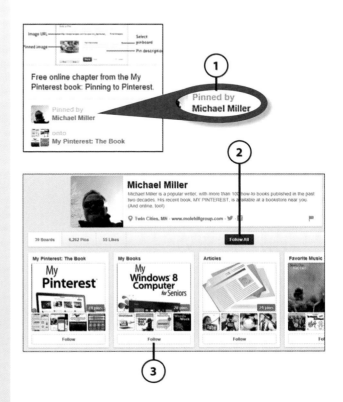

1 When you find a pin you like, click the name of the person who pinned it to see that person's personal page.

2 Click the Follow All button to follow all of this person's pins.

3 Alternatively, if you only want to follow pins to one of this person's boards, click the Follow button for the board you want to follow.

OTHER POPULAR SOCIAL MEDIA

Facebook and Pinterest are the two most popular social networks among older Americans, but they aren't the only social networks out there. Other social media cater to different demographic groups—and might be worth considering if you want to connect to younger friends or family members.

The most popular of these other social networks include the following:

- Google+ (plus.google.com), of particular appeal to young, technically savvy males

- LinkedIn (www.linkedin.com), which targets business professionals and is good for business networking and job hunting

- Twitter (www.twitter.com), the social medium of choice for the younger set—high school and college-aged users

All of these social networks are free to use, and work in much the same fashion as does Facebook. Don't expect to find a lot of your contemporaries on these networks, however; Facebook is still the social network of choice for middle-aged and senior users.

Managing Your Social Media with the People App

If you follow a lot of friends on multiple social networks, it can be quite time-consuming. Fortunately, the Windows People app consolidates messages from several major social networks and your email accounts. You can view the latest updates from your friends in one place, as well as comment on and repost those updates—without having to visit the social networking sites themselves.

In fact, you can use the People app to handle all of your Facebook activities. You can view your friends' status updates as well as post your own, directly from the People app. It's a convenient way to use Facebook from within the Windows 8.1 full-screen interface.

Connect to Your Social Network Accounts

The People app automatically connects to the Microsoft Account you used to create your Windows account. You can then manually connect the People app to your Facebook, Google+, LinkedIn, and Twitter social network accounts.

1 From the Windows Start screen, click the People tile to open the People app.

2 Click or press Connected To at the top-right corner of the screen to display the Accounts panel. All your current linked accounts are listed here.

3 Click Add an Account to display the Add an Account panel.

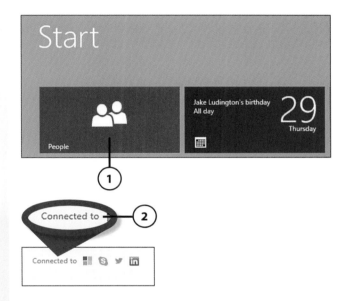

(4) Click the type of account you want to add and then follow the onscreen instructions specific to that type of account.

View Your Friends' Social Activity

The People app displays the most recent posts from your social media friends. You can then like or comment on any specific post.

(1) From the Windows Start screen, click the People tile to open the People app.

Live Tile

The People tile on the Start screen is a "live" tile, displaying the latest activity from your connected friends.

2 Click What's New to display the What's New screen.

3 The What's New screen displays status updates and tweets in their own panels. Scroll right to view additional posts.

4 To like a Facebook post, click the Like link.

5 To comment on a Facebook post, click the Comment link to display the Comments pane.

6 Enter your comment into the Add a Comment box.

7 Click Comment.

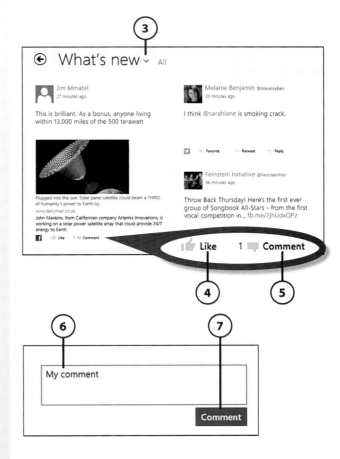

Post to Facebook

In addition to displaying the most recent posts from your Facebook (and other) friends, the People app also lets you post new status updates to your Facebook account.

1. From the Windows Start screen, click the People tile to open the People app.

2. Click the Me tile to display your personal People screen.

3. Go to the What's New section and enter your status update into the Facebook box and then press Enter. Your message is posted to your Facebook feed.

Post to Other Accounts

To post to Twitter or another social network, click the down arrow at the top of the Facebook box and select the social network from the list.

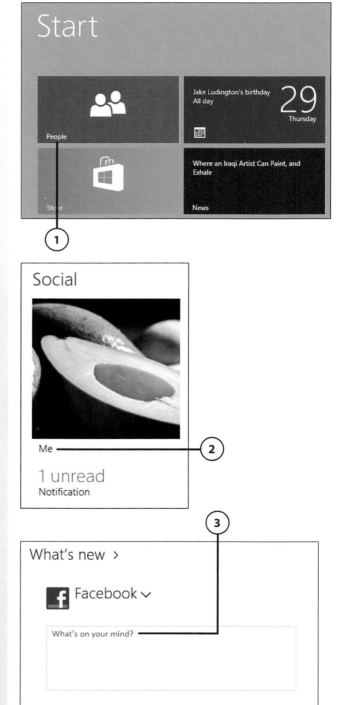

Windows Photos app   Click to view picture fullscreen

In this chapter you find out how to transfer photos from your digital camera to your Windows PC, how to edit those photos, and how to share them online with friends and family.

→ Using Your Digital Camera with Your Windows PC
→ Viewing Photos on Your PC
→ Touching Up Your Photos
→ Sharing Your Pictures Online

14

Storing and Sharing Pictures with Loved Ones

If you're like me, you take a lot of pictures with your digital camera—pictures of places you've been and people you've met—and lots and lots of pictures of your family, especially your grandkids. You need to store those photos someplace, and there's no place better than your Windows PC. Even better, you can use your computer to touch up your photos and share them with friends and family—online, over the Internet.

Using Your Digital Camera with Your Windows PC

The first step in managing all your digital photos is to transfer those pictures from your digital camera or smartphone to your computer. There are a number of ways to do this.

Transfer Photos from a Memory Card

Most digital cameras store the photos you take on removable memory cards. If your PC has a memory card reader (one or more slots somewhere on the front or side of the unit), you can easily transfer your image files from the memory card to your PC's hard drive.

Connecting Your Camera Directly

You can also transfer photos by connecting your digital camera to your computer via USB. Windows should recognize when your camera is connected and automatically download the pictures in your camera, while displaying a dialog box that notifies you of what it's doing.

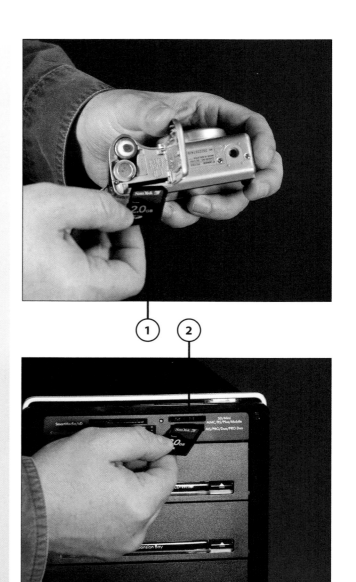

1. Turn off your digital camera and remove the flash memory card.

2. Insert the memory card from your digital camera into the memory card slot on your PC.

Copying Automatically

Windows might recognize that your memory card contains digital photos and start to download those photos automatically—no manual interaction necessary. Alternatively, you might get prompts from other apps, such as Photoshop Express or Picasa, to download your photos, depending on which programs you have installed on your computer.

(**3**) From the Start screen, click the Desktop tile to open the Windows Desktop.

(**4**) Click File Explorer on the Taskbar to open the File Explorer app.

(**5**) Click This PC in the navigation pane.

(**6**) Click the drive for your memory card reader, select the main folder (typically labeled DCIM), and then select the appropriate subfolder to see your photos.

Different Folder Names

Some cameras might use a name other than DCIM for the main folder.

(**7**) Hold down the Ctrl key and click each photo you want to transfer.

(**8**) Select the Home tab, click Copy To, and then select Pictures.

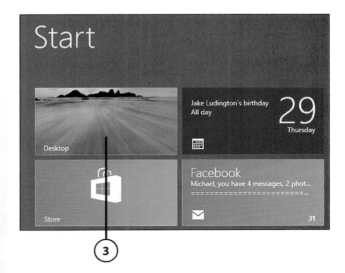

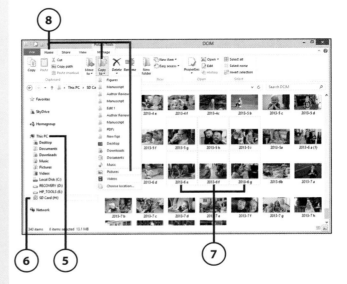

Transfer Photos from an iPhone or iPad

Many people are ditching dedicated digital cameras and instead taking pictures with the cameras built-into their iPhones or iPads. It's certainly more convenient to whip out your phone or tablet to take a quick picture than it is to lug around a digital camera everywhere you go.

If you have your iPhone or iPad configured to use iCloud to back up your photos and other data, the photos you take will automatically be transferred from your device to your home computer whenever your device is connected to your home Wi-Fi network. You can also manually transfer photos from your iPhone or iPad to your PC, using Apple's standard connection cable.

1. Connect one end of the supplied cable to your iPhone or iPad.

2. Connect the other end of the cable to a USB port on your PC.

iTunes

When you connect your iPhone or iPad to your computer, the iTunes software will probably open automatically. Close it or just ignore it; you don't use iTunes to copy photos.

3 From the Start screen, click the Desktop tile to open the Windows Desktop.

4 Click File Explorer on the Taskbar to open the File Explorer app.

5 Click the This PC icon in the navigation pane, select the iPhone or iPad icon, the Internal Storage folder, and then select the DCIM folder to display one or more subfolders that contain your device's pictures. Double-click each of these folders to display their contents.

6 Hold down the Ctrl key and click each photo you want to transfer.

7 Select the Home tab, click the Move To button, and then click Pictures.

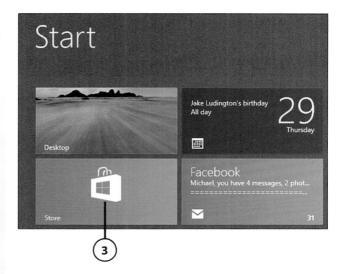

Viewing Photos on Your PC

Windows 8.1 includes a built-in Photos app for viewing and editing photos stored on your PC. It's the easiest way to look at your favorite pictures.

New to Windows 8.1

The Photos app underwent significant changes from Windows 8 to Windows 8.1. Whereas the Windows 8 version of the app let you view photos stored on Facebook, Flickr, and SkyDrive, the Windows 8.1 app is limited to viewing only photos stored on your PC. It does, however, add photo editing features not found in the Windows 8 version of the app.

View Your Photos

The Photos app is the hub for all your photo viewing and editing in Windows. It lets you navigate to and view all the photos stored on your PC.

(1) From the Windows Start screen, click or tap the Photos tile. This opens the Photos app and displays all the subfolders within your main Pictures folder.

(2) To view photos stored in a specific folder, click or tap the tile for that folder.

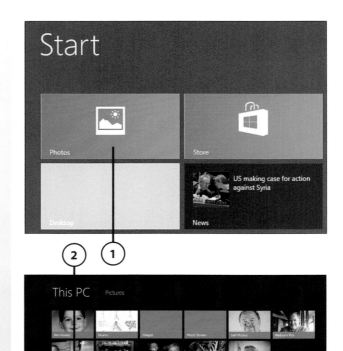

3 Click through the folders and subfolders until you find a photo you want to view, and then click that photo to view it full-screen.

4 To enlarge the picture, click the + button at the lower-right corner of the screen. To make a picture smaller, click the – button.

5 To move to the next picture in the folder, click the right arrow on screen or press the right arrow key on your keyboard. To return to the previous picture, click the left arrow on screen or press the left arrow key your keyboard.

6 To view a slide show of the pictures in this folder, starting with the current picture, right-click the open photo to display the options bar, and then click or tap Slide Show.

7 To delete the current picture, right-click the screen to display the options bar, and then click or tap Delete.

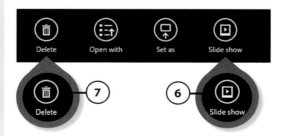

>>>Go Further

LOCK SCREEN PICTURE

To use the current picture as the image on the Windows Lock screen, display the photo full screen, and then right-click the screen to display the Options bar and click Set As, Lock Screen.

Touching Up Your Photos

Not all your pictures turn out perfect. Maybe you need to crop a picture to highlight the important area. Maybe you need to brighten a dark picture, or darken a bright one. Or maybe you need to adjust the tint or color saturation.

Fortunately, the Windows 8.1 Photos app lets you do this sort of basic photo editing. With Windows 8.1, a better-looking photo is only a click or a tap away!

Auto Fix a Photo

When you want to quickly touch up a photo, use the Photos app's Auto Fix command. Auto Fix delivers several possible variations of your original photo; just choose the one that looks best to you.

(1) From within the Photos app, navigate to and display the photo you want to edit.

(2) Right-click the photo to display the Options bar and then click Edit to display the editing screen.

3 Click the Auto Fix button on the left side of the screen.

4 Click the best suggested result on the right side of the screen.

Rotate a Photo

Is your picture sidewise? To turn a portrait into a landscape, or vice versa, use the Photos app's Rotate control.

1 From within the Photos app, navigate to and display the photo you want to edit.

2 Right-click the photo to display the Options bar,

3 Click Rotate to rotate the picture 90 degrees clockwise. Continue clicking to further rotate the picture.

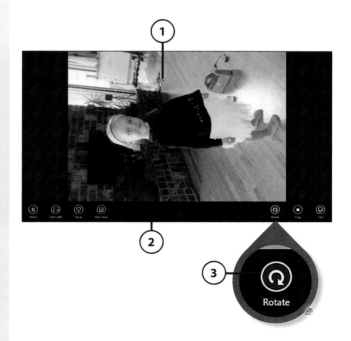

Crop a Photo

Sometimes you don't get close enough to the subject for the best effect. When you want to zoom in closer, use the Photos app's Crop control to crop out the edges you don't want.

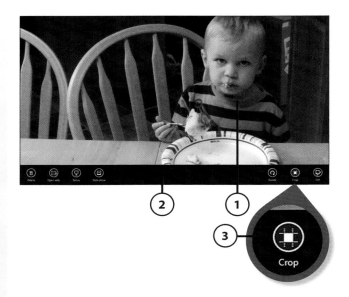

1. From within the Photos app, navigate to and display the photo you want to edit.

2. Right-click the photo to display the Options bar.

3. Click Crop to display the crop screen.

4. Use your mouse or fingers (on a touchscreen display) to drag the corners of the white border until the picture appears as you like.

5. Click Apply.

Aspect Ratio

By default, Windows maintains the original aspect ratio when you crop a photo. To crop to a different aspect ratio, click the Aspect Ratio button and make a new selection.

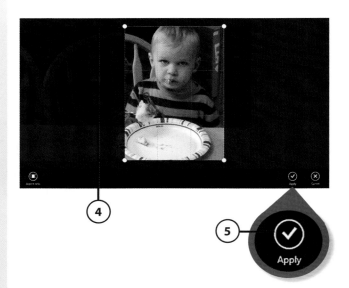

Remove Red Eye

Red eye is caused when a camera's flash causes the subject's eyes to appear a devilish red. The Photos app lets you remove the red eye effect by changing the red color to black in the edited photo.

(**1**) From within the Photos app, navigate to and display the photo you want to edit.

(**2**) Right-click the photo to display the Options bar; then click Edit to display the editing screen.

(**3**) Click Basic Fixes on the left side of the screen.

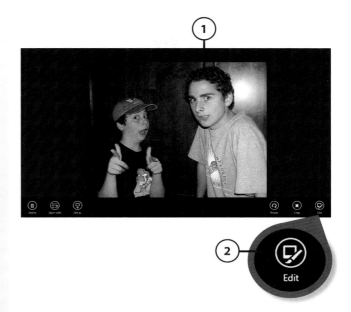

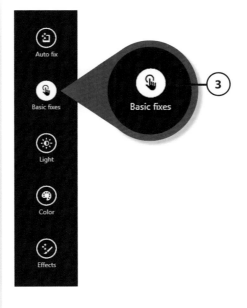

(4) Click Red Eye on the right side of the screen; the cursor changes to a blue circle.

(5) Move the circle to the eye(s) you want to fix and then click the mouse button to remove red eye.

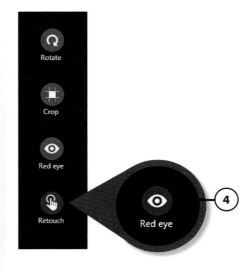

Retouch a Photo

Does someone in your photo have a blemish or a loose hair, or is there a rough or scratched area in the photo you want to get rid of? Use the Photos app's Retouch control to smooth out or remove blemishes from your photos.

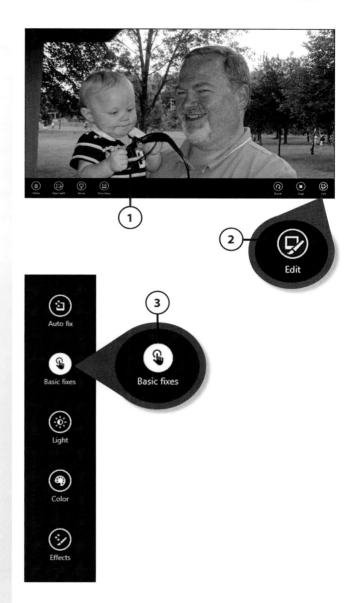

(**1**) From within the Photos app, navigate to and display the photo you want to edit.

(**2**) Right-click the photo to display the Options bar; then click Edit to display the editing screen.

(**3**) Click Basic Fixes on the left side of the screen.

4 Click Retouch on the right side of the screen; the cursor changes to a blue circle.

5 Move the circle to the area you want to repair; then click the mouse button to do so.

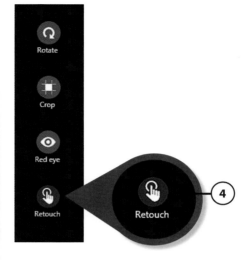

Adjust Brightness and Contrast

When a photo is too dark or too light, use the Photos app's Light controls. The Brightness control makes the picture lighter or darker. The Contrast control increases or decreases the difference between the photo's darkest and lightest areas. Use the Highlights control to bring out or hide detail in too-bright highlights; use the Shadows control to do the same in too-dark shadows.

1 From within the Photos app, navigate to and display the photo you want to edit.

2 Right-click the photo to display the Options bar; then click Edit to display the editing screen.

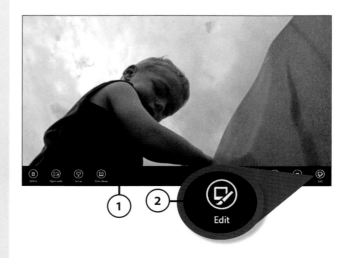

3 Click Light on the left side of the screen.

4 Click the control you want to adjust—Brightness, Contrast, Highlights, or Shadows.

5 The selected control changes to a circular control. Click/tap and drag the control clockwise to increase the effect, or counterclockwise to decrease the effect.

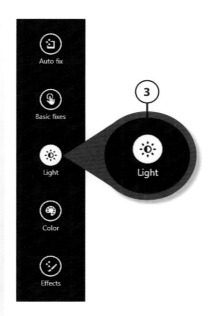

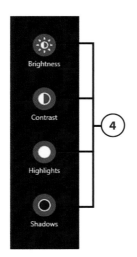

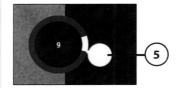

Adjust Color and Tint

The Photos app lets you adjust various color-related settings. The Temperature control affects the color characteristics of lighting; you can adjust a photo so that it looks warmer (reddish) or cooler (bluish). The Tint control affects the shade of the color. The Saturation control affects the amount of color in the photo; completely desaturating a photo makes it black and white. And the Color Enhance control lets you click an area of the photo to increase or decrease color saturation.

1. From within the Photos app, navigate to and display the photo you want to edit.

2. Right-click the photo to display the Options bar; then click Edit to display the editing screen.

3. Click Color on the left side of the screen.

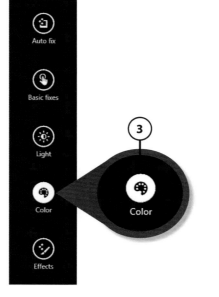

4 Click the control you want to adjust—Temperature, Tint, Saturation, or Color Enhance.

5 The selected control changes to a circular control. Click/tap and drag the control clockwise to increase the effect, or counter-clockwise to decrease the effect.

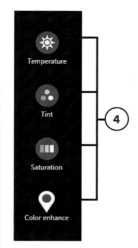

Cancel Changes

If, when you're editing a photo, you decide you don't want to keep the changes you've made, simply right-click to display the Options bar and select Cancel to return to the original version of the photo.

Apply Special Effects

You can also use the Photos app to apply various vignette and selective focus effects to a picture.

1 From within the Photos app, navigate to and display the photo you want to edit.

2 Right-click the photo to display the Options bar; then click Edit to display the editing screen.

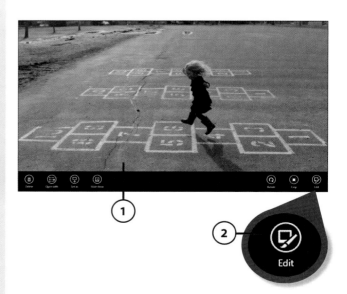

3 Click Effects on the left side of the screen.

4 To apply a vignette to your photo, click Vignette on the right side of the screen; then rotate the control clockwise for a dark (positive) vignette or counterclockwise for a light (negative) vignette.

5 To apply a selective focus effect, click Selective Focus.

6 On the next screen, use your mouse to move or resize the circle in the middle of the screen; the center of this circle will be in focus, while the area outside the circle will be blurred.

7 To change the strength of the selective focus effect, click Strength and select a new value, from Minimum to Maximum.

8 Click Apply to apply the effect.

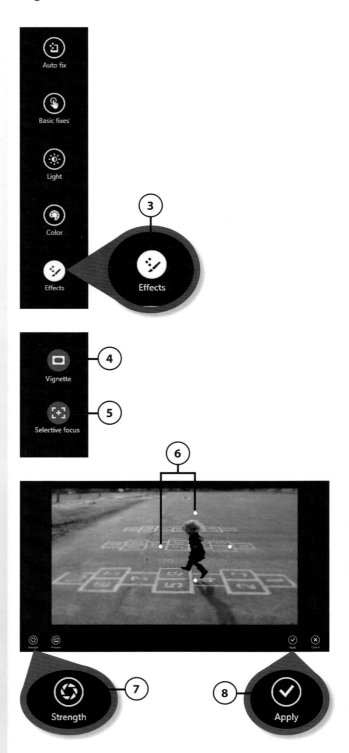

>>>Go Further

OTHER PHOTO EDITING PROGRAMS

If you need to further edit your photos beyond what you can do in the Photos app, you need to install and use a more full-featured photo editing program. These programs let you fix red eye, correct bad color and brightness, and perform additional touch-up functions.

Some of the more popular photo editing programs include Picasa (picasa.google.com) and Adobe Photoshop Elements (www.adobe.com). Picasa is free and is a good choice for most seniors; it's easy to use and offers the most popular touch-up options. If your photos need further touch up, Photoshop Elements runs $99.99 and will do almost anything you need it to do.

Sharing Your Pictures Online

It's fun to look at all the digital pictures you've stored on your PC, but it's even more fun to share those pictures with family and friends. Fortunately, the Internet makes it easy to share your favorite digital photos online, so everyone can view those cute photos of your grandkids.

Attach a Photo in Windows Mail

If you only have a picture or two to share, the easiest way to do so is probably via email. That is, you can attach a picture file to an email message and send that picture along with the message to your intended recipients. When a friend or family member opens your email, she can click to view the attached picture.

It's Not All Good

Resolution and Size

A photo's *resolution* measures how sharp a picture is, in terms of pixels. A pixel is a very small dot that represents a small piece of the picture; lots of dots work together to define the larger image. You can measure either total pixels (in *megapixels*, which stands for a million pixels) or the horizontal and vertical pixel counts.

Obviously, the more pixels in a photo, the higher the resolution and the sharper it looks. That said, higher-resolution photos result in larger files—and files that are too big are more difficult to share with others.

For example, some email programs and services put a limit on how large a file you can attach to a message. If you receive an error message when attaching a large picture file, use your photo editing program to reduce the resolution (and corresponding file size) of the photo.

All email programs and services let you attach image files to your messages. Let's look at how it's done in the Windows Mail app.

(1) Go to the Windows Start screen and click the Mail tile to open the Mail app.

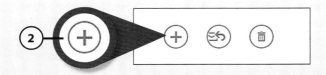

(2) Click the New (+) icon to open a new email message.

(3) Enter the recipient's name or email address into the To box.

(4) Type a subject line into the Add a Subject area.

(5) Enter any accompanying text into the message area.

(6) Click the Attachments (paper clip) icon to display the Files screen.

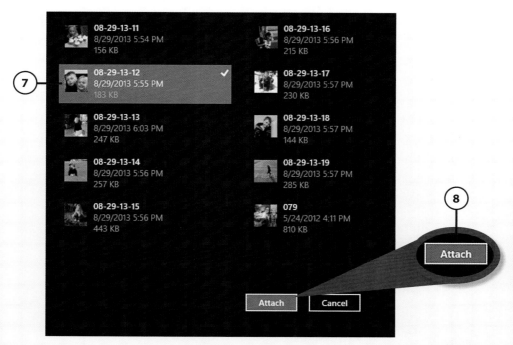

7 When the Files screen appears, navigate to and select the photo(s) you want to share.

8 Click Attach.

9 A thumbnail of the selected photo appears in your message; click Send to send the message to its recipients.

Other Email Programs

Other email programs and service, such as Gmail and Microsoft Outlook.com, also let you attach photos in a similar fashion.

View an Attached Photo

When you receive an email message with a photo attached, it's easy to view that picture. Here's how to do it from within the Windows Mail app.

1. An email message with an attachment appears in your inbox with a paper clip icon. Click the message to display it in the viewing pane. A link to the image file appears in the body of the open message.

2. Click the Download link to display a thumbnail of the photo.

3. To save this photo to your own PC, click the thumbnail and select Save. The Files screen opens.

4. Select a location to store the photo and then click the Save button.

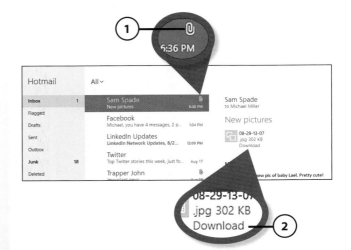

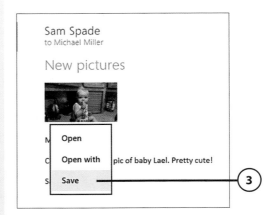

Upload Photos to a New Facebook Photo Album

Assuming that you and your friends and family are all on Facebook, you can use that social network as a photo sharing site. In fact, Facebook is the largest site for photo sharing on the Internet; you can easily upload photos that can then be viewed by all your Facebook friends.

Facebook

Learn more about Facebook in Chapter 13, "Connecting with Facebook and Other Social Media."

To share a photo on Facebook, you must first upload it to a photo album on the Facebook site. The uploaded photo appears as a status update in your friends' News Feeds.

Photo Requirements

Facebook lets you upload photos in the JPG, GIF, PNG, TIF, and BMP file formats. The maximum file size you can upload is 15MB. You're limited to 1,000 photos per album, but you can have an unlimited number of albums—which means you can upload an unlimited number of photos.

The photos you upload to Facebook are stored in virtual photo albums. These are file folders located on the Facebook site (not on your own PC) that function much like traditional photo albums, but with the image files you upload. You can upload photos to an existing album, or create a new album when uploading new photos.

(1) Click Photos in the navigation sidebar to display your Photos page.

(2) Click the Create Album button to display the Files page; then select the photos you want to upload. The Untitled Album page opens.

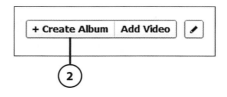

2

Selecting Multiple Photos

You can upload more than one photo at a time. Hold down the Ctrl key while clicking files to select multiple files.

(3) Click Untitled Album and enter the desired album title.

(4) Click Say Something About This Album and enter an album description.

(5) To enter a geographic location for all the photos in this album, go to the Where Were These Taken? box and enter a location.

(6) To add a date to all the photos in this album, click Add Date and select a date from the pop-up box.

Optional Information

All the information you can add to a photo album is entirely optional; you can add as much or as little as you like. You don't even have to add a title—if you don't, Facebook uses the title Untitled Album.

(7) To enter information about a specific picture, enter a description in the Say Something About This Photo box.

(8) To tag a person who appears in a given photo, click that person's face and enter his or her name when prompted.

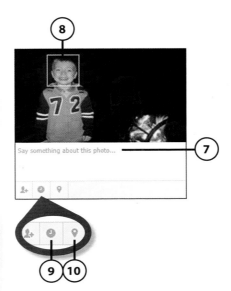

Photo Tagging

You identify people in your photos by tagging them. That is, you click on a person in the photo and then assign a friend's name to that part of the photo. You can then find photos where a given person appears by searching for that person's tag.

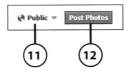

(9) To enter the date a photo was taken, click that photo's Date button and then select the year, month, and date.

(10) To enter the place a photo was taken, click that photo's Location button and then enter a location into the Where Was This? box.

(11) To determine who can view the photos in this album, click the Privacy button and make a selection—Public, Friends, Only Me, or Custom

(12) Click the Post Photos button when done.

High-Quality Photos

For the best possible picture for anyone downloading or printing your photos, check the High Quality option to upload and store your photos at their original resolution. Note, however, that it takes longer to upload high-quality photos than those in standard quality.

Upload Pictures to an Existing Facebook Photo Album

After you've created a photo album, you can easily upload more photos to that album; you don't have to create a new album every time you want to upload new photos.

(1) Click Photos in the navigation sidebar to display your Photos page.

(2) Click Albums to display your existing photo albums.

(3) Click to open the album to which you want to add new photos.

(4) Click the Add Photos button and select the photos to upload.

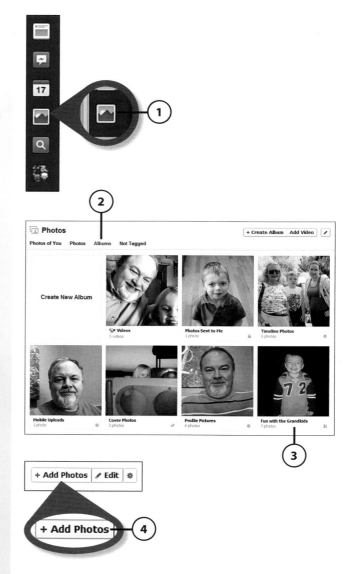

(5) The photos you selected are
added to the album page. Add
any information you want about
a given photo—location, date,
information, and the like. You
can also tag people in each
photo.

(6) Click the Post Photos button.

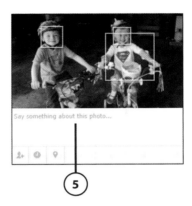

View Photos on Facebook

Facebook makes it easy to view photos that your friends post. You can
navigate through a friend's photo
albums to find and view the items
you like.

(1) Click your friend's name anywhere on Facebook to open his
Timeline page.

(2) Click Photos to display your
friend's Photos page.

Tom French
Hello, spring. Goodbye, winter.

👍 Like   💬 Comment   ➡ Share   38 minutes ago

(3) To view individual photos of your friend, click Photos of *Friend.*

(4) To view all photos posted by your friend, click Photos.

(5) To view photos as posted in her photo albums, click Albums and then click to open the selected album.

(6) Click the thumbnail of the picture you want to view. Facebook displays the selected picture in a *lightbox* superimposed on top of the previous page.

(7) To go to the next picture in the album, mouse over the current picture to display the navigational arrows and then click the right arrow. To go to the previous picture, mouse over the current picture to display the navigational arrows and then click the left arrow.

(8) Click the Like link to "like" a photo.

(9) To enter your comments on a photo, enter your comments into the Write a Comment box and then press Enter.

(10) Click the X at the top right of the lightbox to close the photo viewer.

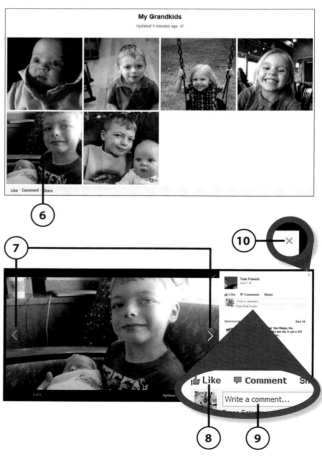

Barnes & Noble's NOOK bookstore

In this chapter you discover where to find eBooks online and how to read them on your Windows 8.1 PC.

→ Reading eBooks with Amazon's Kindle App
→ Reading eBooks with Barnes & Noble's NOOK App

Reading Books on Your PC

Whether your love is westerns or romance novels or historical nonfiction, it's likely that you're an avid book reader. But did you know that you can use your Windows 8.1 PC to read your favorite fiction and nonfiction books?

Most books today are available in digital format, what we call electronic books or eBooks. And eBooks can be read on any PC if you have the right apps installed. It's a great way to take your favorite books with you, all of them inside a single notebook PC.

Reading eBooks with Amazon's Kindle App

There are two major eBook formats in use today. Unfortunately, the two formats are incompatible, meaning you need separate eBook reader apps to read books in both formats.

Currently, the most popular seller of eBooks is Amazon, the online bookseller. Amazon sells both traditional printed books and electronic books in their own proprietary format. You can read Amazon's eBooks on Amazon's Kindle eBook reader devices and on any PC using Amazon's Kindle app.

After you have the Kindle app installed on your PC, you can purchase new eBooks from Amazon's online bookstore. Your eBooks are automatically downloaded to your PC, where you can read them using the Kindle app.

Download the Kindle App

To download the Kindle app, go to the Start screen and click the Store tile to open the Windows Store. Search for kindle and then click the Kindle tile in the search results. When the app screen appears, click the Install button. The app is free.

Purchase eBooks from Amazon

Kindle-compatible eBooks are available only from Amazon's online Kindle Store. When you purchase a new eBook, it's immediately available for reading on your computer.

1. From the Windows Start screen, click or tap the Kindle tile to open the Kindle app.

First Time

The first time you open the Kindle app you're prompted to either sign into your existing Amazon account, if you have one, or create a new account. Each subsequent time you open the app, it opens directly into your Amazon account.

2 The Kindle app displays all the eBooks you've previously purchased in the My Books section. To purchase new books, click Kindle Store to enter the online store.

3 This launches Internet Explorer and takes you to Amazon's Kindle Store website. To search for a specific book, enter that book's title or author into the top-of-screen search box and then click Go.

4 To browse books by category, click Kindle eBooks underneath the search box.

5 Click a category in the left-hand navigation column.

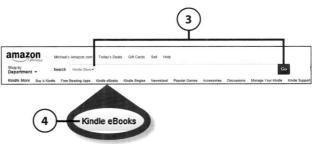
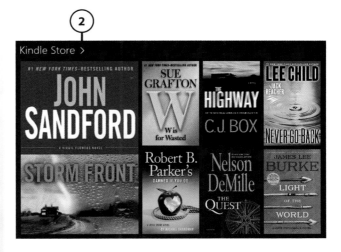

6 Click the book you want to purchase; this displays the book's Amazon page.

7 In the Buy Now box, pull down the Deliver To list and select *Yourname* Kindle for PC.

8 Click Buy Now with 1-Click. The book is now purchased and delivered electronically to your account.

Free Samples

Amazon offers free samples for many of the eBooks it sells. Look for the Try It Free box and then click the Send Sample Now button.

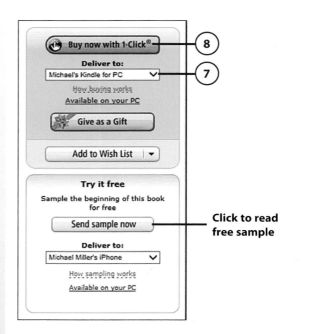

Click to read free sample

Read an eBook

All the eBooks you purchase from Amazon are automatically stored online, in what Amazon calls the cloud. You can use the Kindle app to open any book you've purchased and read it on your computer screen.

1 From the Windows Start screen, click or tap the Kindle tile to open the Kindle app.

2 Click My Books to all view the books you've purchased.

3 Click Cloud to view books you've purchased that are currently stored online. (These might be books that you're reading on other devices, such as your tablet or smartphone.)

4 Click On Device to view those books you've purchased that are stored on your PC.

5 Click a book cover to begin reading that book.

6 To turn the page, press the right arrow key on your keyboard or click the right side of the screen with your mouse.

7 To return to the previous page, press the left arrow key on your keyboard or click the left side of the screen with your mouse.

8 To bookmark the current page for future reference, click the Bookmark icon at the top-right corner of the screen.

9 To return to your eBook library, click the Library icon at the top-left corner of the screen.

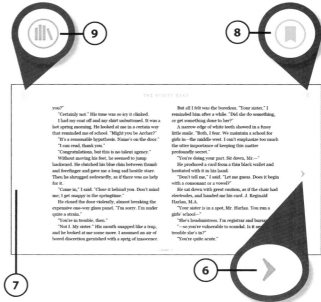

10 To view additional functions, right-click anywhere on screen to display the top and bottom Options bars.

11 To jump to another location in the book, click and drag the slider in the bottom Options bar.

Change How a Book Is Displayed Onscreen

One of the nice things about eBooks is that you can easily change how the text is displayed onscreen. You can make the text larger or smaller, change the page margins, and even change the color of the text and the page background.

1 From within the book, right-click to display the Options bar.

2 Click View to display the View Options pane.

3 To make the text larger or smaller for easier reading, drag the Font Size slider to a new position.

4 To change the white space on the sides of the screen, drag the margin slider to a new position.

5 To change the way the text appears onscreen, go to the Color Mode section and select White (black text on a white background), Sepia (black text on a sepia background), or Black (white text on a black background).

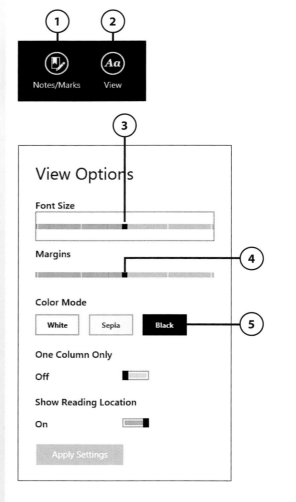

(6) To force the book to display only a single column at a time, go to the One Column Display section and click On.

(7) Click Apply Settings when done.

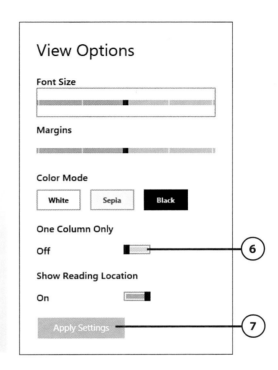

PDF FILES

Many eBooks are also available in Adobe's PDF format. The advantage of PDF files is that they appear exactly as designed by the publisher; a PDF file is an exact representation of the original printed book. (Kindle- and ePub-format books, on the other hand, can be formatted by the reader for easier reading on any given device.)

As such, many readers prefer the PDF format for visually oriented books, such as children's books or four-color "coffee table" titles. For this reason, many publishers make their books available in PDF format, as well as Kindle and ePub formats.

You can use either the Kindle or NOOK app to read PDF-format eBooks. You can also use Adobe's Acrobat Reader app for PDF files.

Reading eBooks with Barnes & Noble's NOOK App

Amazon's Kindle format is one of the two major eBook formats, and it's proprietary. That is, you can only read Kindle books on a Kindle eBook reader device or via the Kindle app.

The other major eBook format is called ePub, and it's more universal. Although you can't read ePub books in the Kindle app, you can read them in other eBook apps, and on other eBook reader devices.

The most popular ePub-compatible eBook reader is the Barnes & Noble NOOK. Barnes & Noble makes a NOOK app available for Windows 8.1, which enables you to read all ePub-format eBooks on your computer, no matter where you purchase them. Of course, Barnes & Noble operates its own eBook bookstore, so that's as good a place as any to purchase your ePub-format eBooks.

Download the Nook App

To download the Nook app, go to the Start screen and click the Store tile to open the Windows Store. Search for nook and then click the Nook tile in the search results. When the app screen appears, click the Install button. The app is free.

Purchase eBooks from Barnes & Noble

You can purchase ePub-format eBooks from a number of different websites and retailers. Naturally, Barnes & Noble would prefer that you purchase your eBooks from their own online store.

1. From the Windows Start screen, click or tap the NOOK tile to open the NOOK app.

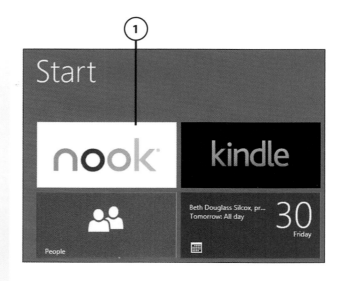

First Time

The first time you open the NOOK app, you're prompted to sign in with either your Microsoft Account or a NOOK account. Your account information is remembered on subsequent logins.

(2) Scroll to the Shop by Department list and click Books.

(3) You now see the NOOK store, with New Releases featured. To browse books by category, click the Browse Categories list and select a category.

(4) To search for a specific book, click the Search (magnifying glass) icon to display the Search pane.

(5) Enter the title or author of the book you want into the Search box and then press Enter.

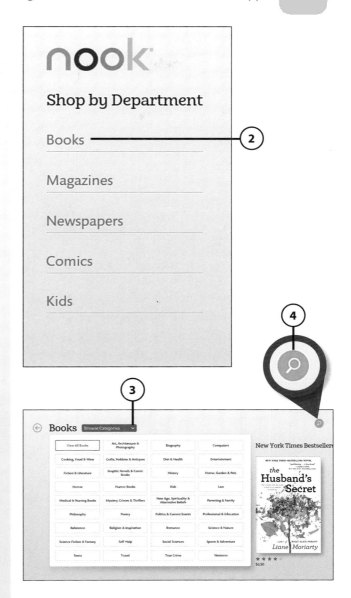

6 When the search results page displays, click the book you want to purchase.

7 When the book page appears, click the Buy button to purchase and download the book.

Free Samples

Barnes & Noble offers free samples for many of the eBooks it sells. Click the Free Sample button to download the sample chapter or section to your PC.

6

Click to read free sample

7

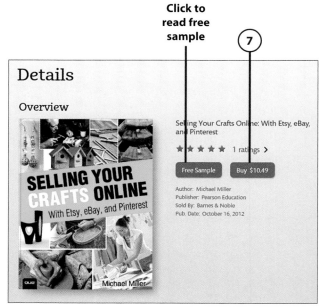

Read an eBook

All the eBooks you purchase from Barnes and Noble are stored online until you're ready to read them. You can use the NOOK app to open and read any book you've purchased from Barnes & Noble, as well as ePub-format eBooks you've purchased elsewhere.

(1) From the Windows Start screen, click or tap the NOOK tile to open the NOOK app.

(2) Scroll to the My Library section and click View All to display all your books.

(3) Click the cover of the book you want to read.

4 To turn the page, press the right arrow key on your keyboard or click the right side of the screen with your mouse.

5 To return to the previous page, press the left arrow key on your keyboard or click the left side of the screen with your mouse.

6 To view additional functions, right-click anywhere on screen to display the top and bottom Options bars.

7 To return to your eBook library, click Library in the top Options bar.

8 To bookmark the current page for future reference, click Add Bookmark in the bottom Options bar.

9 To jump to another location in the book, click and drag the slider in the bottom Options bar.

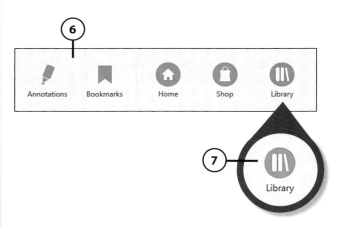

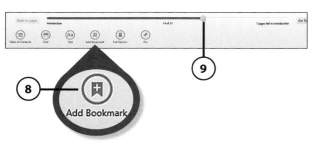

Change How a Book Is Displayed Onscreen

The NOOK app, like the Kindle app, enables you easily change how the text is displayed onscreen. You can make the text larger or smaller, change the page margins, and even change the color of the text and the page background.

(1) From within the book, right-click to display the Options bars.

(2) Click Text in the bottom Options bar to display the Text pane.

(3) To make the text larger or smaller for easier reading, go to the Size section and click one of the seven available font sizes.

(4) To change the spacing between lines, go to the Line Spacing section and click one of the three options.

(5) To change the white space on the sides of the screen, go to the Margins section and click one of the three options.

(6) To change the font used on the page, go to the Font section and make a new selection.

(7) To change the way the text appears onscreen, go to the Theme section and make a selection from Normal, Night, Gray, Butter, Mocha, or Sepia.

(8) To force a book to display as the publisher intended, click "on" the Publisher Defaults control.

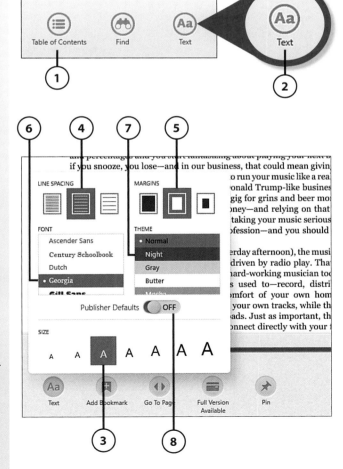

>>>Go Further

MY BOOKS

All of my books published within the past few years are available in all major eBook formats. You can find my books in Kindle format in Amazon's Kindle store, or in ePub format in Barnes & Noble's NOOK store. You can also find ePub and PDF formats of my books on the publisher's website. For example, if you want to buy an electronic version of this particular book, go to the Que Publishing website (www.quepublishing.com), search for **my windows 8.1 computer for seniors**, and purchase and download the version that best suits your needs.

Online movie from Netflix

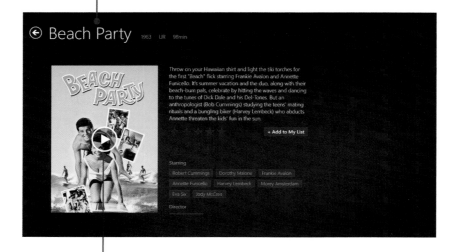

Click to play movie

In this chapter you discover how to watch your favorite TV shows, movies, and other videos on your Windows PC.

→ Watching Movies on Netflix
→ Watching TV Shows on Hulu Plus
→ Sharing Videos on YouTube
→ Purchasing Videos with the Xbox Video App

16

Watching Movies and TV Shows on Your PC

Want to rewatch last night's episode of *Dancing with the Stars*? Or the entire season of *NCIS*? How about a classic episode of *Perry Mason* or *Cheers*? Or that latest "viral video" you've been hearing about?

Here's the latest hot thing on the Web: watching your favorite television programs, films, and videos online, via your web browser. Assuming you have a broadband Internet connection, you can find tens of thousands of free and paid videos to watch at dozens of different websites, including YouTube, Hulu, and Netflix. You can even use the Xbox Video app to purchase and download videos to your PC—and watch them anytime, at your convenience.

Watching Movies on Netflix

When it comes to watching movies and TV shows online, you can't beat Netflix. For a low $7.99/month subscription, you can watch all the movies you want. Netflix offers a mix of both classic and newer movies, as well as a surprising amount of classic and newer television programming, so there should be something there to please just about everyone.

DVD Rental

Netflix also offers a separate DVD-by-mail rental service, with separate subscription fee. That's not what we're talking about here, however.

Sign Up or Sign In

Netflix offers a full-screen Modern Windows app that is the best way to view its programming on your Windows 8.1 PC. (You can also watch Netflix in your web browser, if you like, but the full-screen experience is best.)

Download the Netflix App

To download and install the Netflix app, go to the Start screen and click the Store tile to open the Windows Store. Search for netflix and then click the Netflix tile in the search results. When you see the app screen, click Install. The app is free.

The first time you open the Netflix app, you're prompted to either create a new Netflix account or log into an existing one. Each subsequent time you open the app, it automatically logs in to this account and displays the appropriate content tailored exclusively to your viewing habits.

① From the Windows Start or App screen, click or tap the Netflix tile to open the Netflix app.

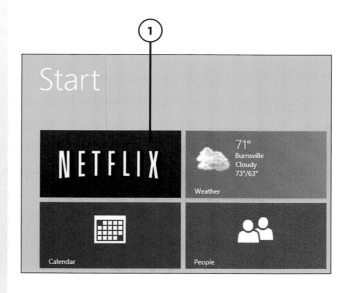

(2) If you don't yet have a Netflix account, you need to create one. Enter your email address and desired password and then click Continue and follow the onscreen instructions.

(3) If you already have a Netflix account that you use on another computer or device, click Member Sign In.

(4) When the next screen appears, enter your email address into the Email box.

(5) Enter your Netflix password into the Password box.

(6) Click Sign In.

Watch a Movie or TV Show

After you've logged into Netflix, you can browse or search for movies and TV shows to watch, and then you can start playback directly on your PC.

(1) From the Windows Start or App screen, click or tap the Netflix tile to open the Netflix app.

(2) By default, Netflix displays its Home screen, which is personalized based on your viewing habits. Scroll right to view Netflix's Instant Queue, your personal Top 10, Popular movies, and more.

(3) Click Top 10 for You to view your top ten items.

(4) Click New Releases to view the latest movies and shows on Netflix.

(5) Click Genres to view a list of popular genres; click a genre to view all items within that category.

(6) To search for a specific movie or show, click the Search (magnifying glass) icon to display the Search panel.

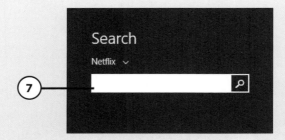

(7) Enter the name of the movie or show into the Search box and then press Enter.

8 Click the movie or show you want to watch. The detail page for that movie or show displays.

9 Click the Play button on the movie image to watch the movie.

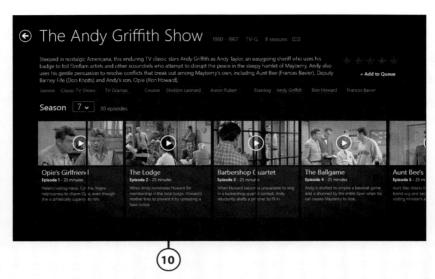

(10) If you choose to watch a TV show, you typically can choose from different episodes in different seasons. Select a season to see all episodes from that season and then click the episode you want to watch.

(11) Netflix begins playing the movie or show you selected. Right-click anywhere on the screen to display the Options bar.

(12) Click the Pause button to pause playback; the Pause button changes to a Play button. Click the Play button to resume playback.

(13) Click and drag the slider control to move directly to another part of the movie.

>>>Go Further

STREAMING VIDEO

Most movies and TV shows you watch online are not downloaded to your computer. Rather, they flow in real time from the host website to your PC, over the Internet, using a technology called *streaming video*. With streaming video, programs can start playing back almost immediately, with no time-consuming downloading necessary.

Watching TV Shows on Hulu Plus

If Netflix is the best website for movies and classic TV shows, Hulu is the best site for newer television programming. Hulu offers episodes from a number of major-network TV shows, as well as some new and classic feature films. (There are also a fair number of programs from Canada, England, and other countries.) The standard free membership offers access to a limited number of videos; Hulu Plus ($7.99/month) offers a larger selection of newer shows. A Hulu Plus subscription is necessary to use the Hulu Plus app.

Sign Up or Sign In

You watch Hulu programming via the full-screen Hulu Plus app. The app is freely available from the Windows Store.

Download the Hulu Plus App

To download and install the Hulu Plus app, go to the Start screen and click the Store tile to open the Windows Store. Search for hulu and then click the Hulu Plus tile in the search results. When you see the app screen, click Install. The app is free.

After you've installed the Hulu Plus app, you can create a new Hulu Plus account or log into an existing one.

(1) From the Windows Start or App screen, click or tap the Hulu Plus tile to open the Hulu Plus app.

(2) If you don't yet have a Hulu account, you need to create one. Click the Try Hulu Plus for Free button and follow the onscreen instructions to register.

(3) If you already have a Hulu account that you use on another computer or device, click the Log In button to display the Log In to Hulu Plus panel.

(4) Enter your username into the Username box.

(5) Enter your Hulu password into the Password box.

(6) Click Log In.

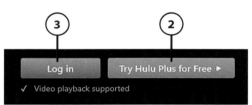

Watch TV Programming

After you've logged into Hulu, you can browse or search for TV shows to watch and then start playback directly on your PC.

(1) From the Windows Start or App screen, click or tap the Hulu Plus tile to open the Hulu Plus app.

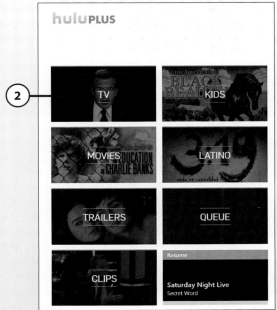

(2) Hulu displays a series of featured programs on its main screen. Scroll right to view recommended programming by type and then click TV to view available TV shows.

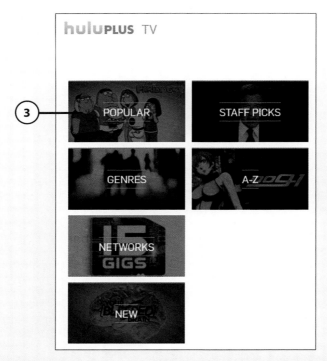

3 Scroll right to browse through TV programs by genre, network, or name.

4 To search for specific shows, click the Search (magnifying glass icon) to display the Search pane.

5 Enter the name of the program into the Search box and press Enter.

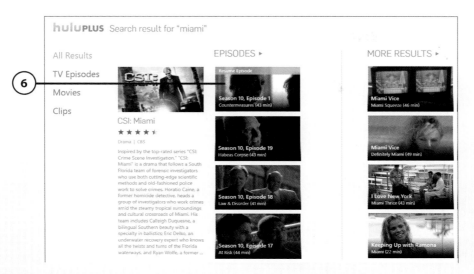

6 Click the show you want to watch.

7 When the detailed program page appears, scroll right to view episodes by season and then click the episode you want to watch.

8 Hulu begins playing the program you selected. Move your mouse over the screen (or tap the screen on a touchscreen) to display the playback controls.

9 Click the Pause button to pause playback; the Pause button changes to a Play button. Click the Play button to resume playback.

10 Click and drag the slider control to move directly to another part of the program.

>>>Go Further

WATCHING NETFLIX AND HULU ON YOUR LIVING ROOM TV

Watching movies and TV shows on your PC is fine if you're on the go, but it's not the same as watching programming on the flat screen TV you have in your living room. Some newer TVs (sometimes called "smart" TVs) have built-in Internet, so you can watch Netflix and Hulu directly from the TV itself. Older TVs, however, don't have Internet connections, which means you're limited to over-the-air and cable/satellite programming.

You can, however, connect many PCs to your TV to watch Internet-based programming. All you need is the right connections on your PC, and the right connecting cable.

If your computer has an HDMI connector, it's an easy task. HDMI is the cable technology used to connect high-definition Blu-ray players, cable boxes, and other equipment to flatscreen TVs; the HDMI cable carries both audio and video signals. Just connect an HDMI cable from your PC to a similar HDMI input on your TV, and you're ready to go. Start Netflix or Hulu on your PC, as you would normally, and then switch your TV to the corresponding HDMI input. The programming you're playing on your PC is displayed on your TV. Sit back and start watching.

Sharing Videos on YouTube

Netflix and Hulu are both popular, but the most popular video site on the Web is YouTube. YouTube doesn't have near as many movies or TV shows as the other video sites, but it does have more videos in total—most them uploaded by members of the site.

YouTube is where you find all those homemade videos of cute cats and laughing babies that everybody's watching. When you find a video you like, you can share it with your friends and family—which is what helps a video go "viral."

View a Video

You access YouTube from Internet Explorer or any web browser. Unlike the commercial video services we've discussed, YouTube is totally free.

1. From within Internet Explorer, go to the YouTube site at www.youtube.com.

2. To search for a particular video, enter what you're looking for into the Search box and then press Enter or click the Search (magnifying glass) button.

3. To browse for videos by category, click one of the categories in the box on the left side of the page.

4. Click the video you want to watch.

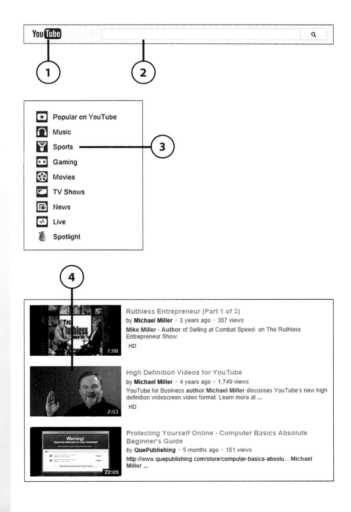

(5) The video begins playing auto-matically when the video page displays.

(6) Click the Pause button to pause playback; click the button again to resume playback.

(7) Click the full-screen button to view the video on your entire computer screen.

(8) Click the thumbs-up button to "like" the video.

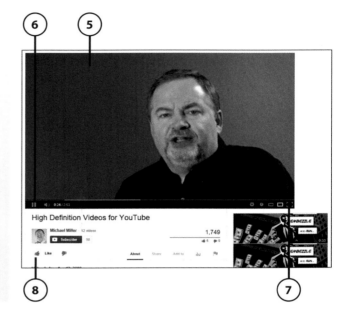

SHARING VIDEOS

Find a video you think a friend would like? YouTube makes it easy to share any video with others.

Click the Share button under the video player to display the Share panel. You can then opt to email a link to the video, "like" the video on Facebook, or tweet a link to the video on Twitter.

>>>Go Further

Upload Your Own Video

If you take movies with your camcorder or smartphone, you can transfer those movies to your computer and then upload them to YouTube. This is a great way to share your home videos with friends and family online.

Uploading from a Smartphone

If you shoot video with your smartphone or tablet, you may be able to upload to YouTube directly from your device or the YouTube mobile app. Check your device or app to see what's available.

Video Formats

YouTube accepts uploads in all major video file formats. You can upload videos up to 15 minutes in length.

1. Click the Upload button at the top of any YouTube page.

2. Click Select Files to Upload. The Files screen displays.

3. Navigate to and select the video file you want to upload.

4. Click the Open button.

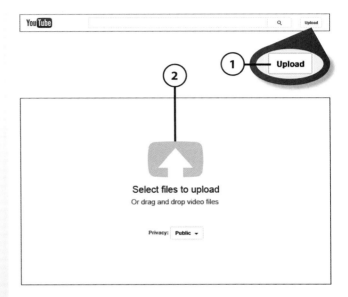

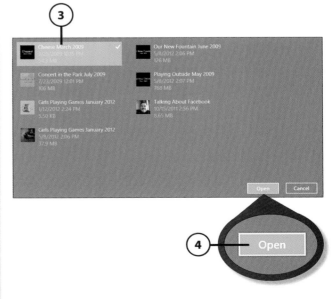

5 As the video is uploaded, YouTube displays the video information page. Enter a title for the video into the Title box.

6 Enter a description for the video into the Description box.

7 Enter one or more keywords to describe the video into the Tags box.

8 Pull down the Category list and select a category for the video.

Thumbnail

After the video is done uploading, you may be prompted to select a thumb-nail image for the video. This thumb-nail is displayed on all search results pages where your video appears.

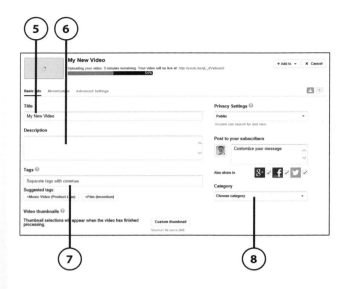

Purchasing Videos with the Xbox Video App

Netflix and Hulu are streaming video services, which means you watch programming stored on their sites and streamed over the Internet to your PC. You can also rent and purchase programming from online stores to download to your PC, for watching at a later time.

Microsoft offers movies and TV shows for sale through its Xbox Video store. You can view the programs you download via the Xbox Video app included with Windows 8.1.

XBOX VIDEO

If you have grandkids who like to play videogames, you're probably familiar with Microsoft's Xbox videogame system. Microsoft has carried over the Xbox brand to the video, music, and games apps built into Windows, dubbing them Xbox Video, Xbox Music, and Xbox Games. Versions of these apps are also available on the Xbox game console.

Purchase a Video

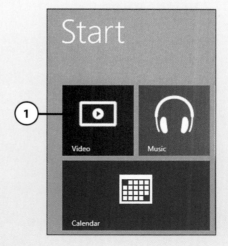

(1) From the Windows Start screen, click or tap the Video tile to open the Xbox Video app.

2) The main screen displays the Home section, with recommendations just for you; scroll right to purchase movies (click New Movies or Featured Movies) and TV shows (click New TV Shows or Featured TV Shows).

3) When you find an item you want to purchase, click or tap the tile for that item.

4. Click or tap the Buy button to purchase and download the selected item.

5. Click or tap the Rent button to rent the item for a specific number of days.

Renting Movies

Many movies can be "rented" for a limited time (14 days), in addition to being available for permanent purchase. If you rent a movie, you have 24 hours to finish watching it once you've started.

View a Video

All the items you've purchased or rented are displayed within the Xbox Video app, and you can view them within the app. You can also use the Xbox Video app to view home movies you've recorded yourself, as well as any other videos you've downloaded to your computer.

(1) From the Windows Start screen, click or tap the Video tile to open the Xbox Video app.

(2) To view all the videos in your collection scroll *left* and click either Personal Videos (your own videos stored on your PC), My TV (televisions shows you've purchased), or My Movies (movies you've purchased).

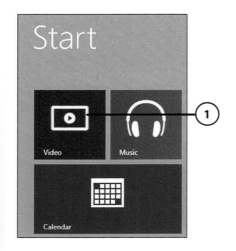

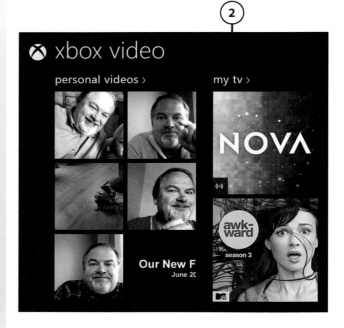

3 You see all the videos of that type stored on your PC. Click or tap the video, program, or movie you want to view.

4 If you selected a television program, click the episode you want to watch.

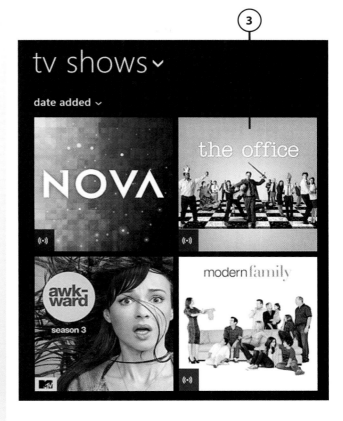

(5) When the video begins to play, move your mouse to display program information and playback controls.

(6) Click the Pause control to pause playback; click the Play control to resume playback.

(7) Click and drag the slider bar to move to any specific part of the program.

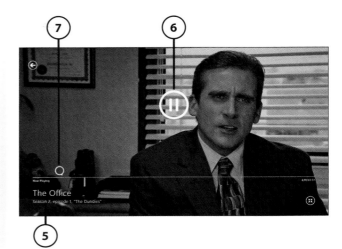

>>>Go Further

OTHER ONLINE VIDEO STORES

The Xbox Video Store is just one place to purchase or rent movies and TV shows online. There are several other sites that offer video programming for purchase or rental, including Amazon Instant Video (www.amazon.com), Apple's iTunes Store (www.apple.com/itunes/), CinemaNow (www.cinemanow.com), and Vudu (www.vudu.com).

Listen to
streaming   Search   Browse music
radio   music   on your PC

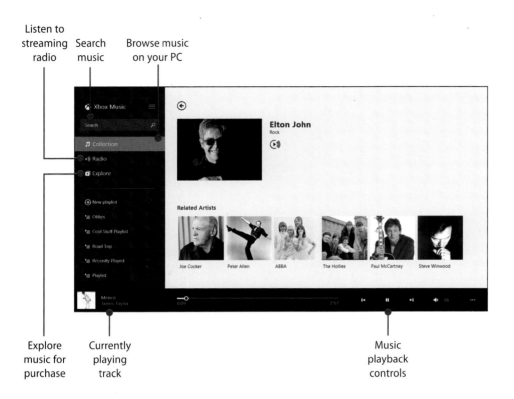

Explore   Currently   Music
music for   playing   playback
purchase   track   controls

In this chapter you find out how to listen to music on your PC, using the Xbox Music app and Apple's iTunes software.

→ Using the Xbox Music App
→ Using iTunes

17

Listening to Music on Your PC

Many folks like to listen to music on their computers. You can use the CD/DVD drive in your PC to play CDs, or "rip" those CDs to electronic format and store them on your PC's hard drive. You can purchase and download tunes from online music stores to your computer's hard drive. You can even stream music over the Internet to your computer, and thus have access to millions of tunes anytime you want.

There are a number of ways to manage digital music on your Windows PC. First and foremost is the Xbox Music app, completely revamped for Windows 8.1. This app lets you play music stored on your computer, purchase and download new music online, and even stream music via your own user-created "radio" stations.

Then there's Apple's iTunes, the program you use to manage the music you store on your iPhone or iPod. It turns out that the iTunes software is a versatile, easy-to-use music player application you can use to download, rip, and burn music in a variety of digital formats.

Using the Xbox Music App

The Xbox Music app in Windows 8.1 is a full-screen, Modern approach to finding and playing digital music. The app enables you to listen to any tunes you've previously downloaded or ripped from CD, purchase and download new tracks from the Xbox Music Store, and even stream tunes in real time over the Internet. Like many seniors, you might find it's the only music player you'll need on your Windows PC.

Play Your Own Music

With the Xbox Music app, you can play any songs you've downloaded from the Internet or ripped from your own CDs. Your music is available from the Collection page of the app.

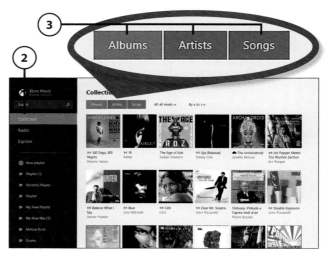

1. From the Start or Apps screen, click or tap the Music tile to launch the Xbox Music app.

2. Click or tap the Collection tab to view the tracks stored on your computer.

3. Click or tap Albums to view your collection by album. Click or tap Artists to view your collection by performing artist. Click or tap Songs to view your collection on a track-by-track basis.

4. Right-click an album to display the Options bar.

5. Click Explore Artist to display information about the current artist.

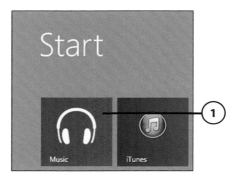

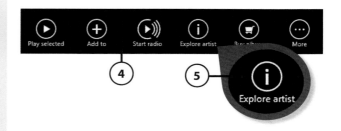

(**6**) Click or tap an album cover to view all the tracks in that album.

(**7**) Click or tap the Play button to play all the tracks in this album.

(**8**) Click or tap any individual track and then click that track's Play button to play that song. Playback controls appear at the bottom of the screen.

(**9**) Click the Pause button to pause playback. Click the Play button to resume playback.

(**10**) Click the Next button to play the next track in an album or play-list. Click the Previous button to play the previous track.

Windows Media Player
If you need more fully featured music playback and management, check out the Windows Media Player app that runs on the traditional Windows desktop. To launch this app, go to the Apps screen, and then scroll to and click the Windows Media Player icon.

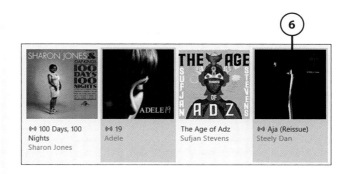

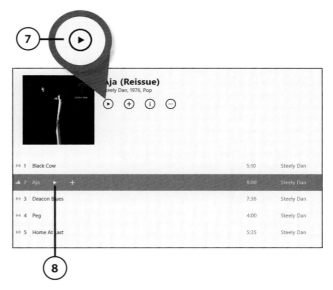

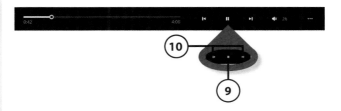

Create and Play a Playlist

A playlist is a collection of tracks, either from the same artist or different artists, that you assemble yourself for future playback. Playlists are great for creating music mixes based on mood or individual taste.

(1) From within the Xbox Music app, tap or click the Collection tab to view the music in your collection.

(2) To play an existing playlist, click or tap the playlist's name in the navigation pane.

(3) Click or tap the Play button to begin playback.

(4) Click or tap New Playlist in the navigation pane to create a new playlist.

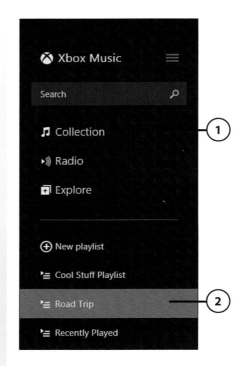

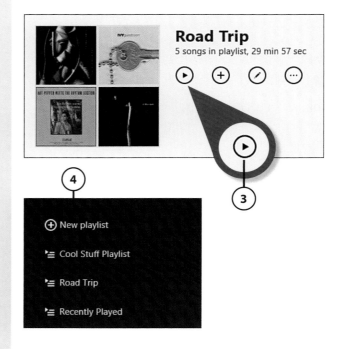

5 Enter a name for this playlist and then click or tap Save.

6 To add a track to a playlist, navigate to and right-click that track to display the Options bar.

7 Click or tap Add To to display the menu of options.

8 Select the name of the playlist to which you want to add this track.

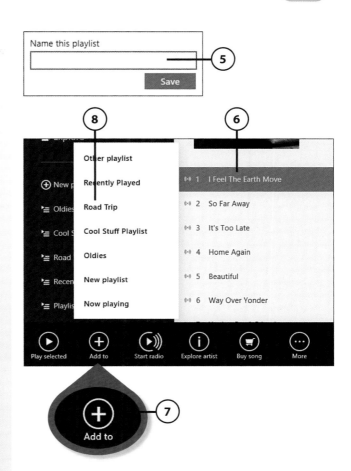

Name this playlist

5

Save

8   **6**

Other playlist

⊕ New   Recently Played   1   I Feel The Earth Move

Oldies   Road Trip   2   So Far Away

Cool S   Cool Stuff Playlist   3   It's Too Late

Road   Oldies   4   Home Again

Recen   New playlist   5   Beautiful

Playlis   Now playing   6   Way Over Yonder

▶ Play selected   ＋ Add to   ▶》 Start radio   ⓘ Explore artist   🛒 Buy song   ⋯ More

＋ Add to   **7**

Purchase and Download New Music

Looking for some new music to listen to? Want an entire album or just a single track? Chances are you can find the music you want in the Xbox Music Store, so fire up the Xbox Music app, pull out your credit card, and get ready to shop!

1 From within the Xbox Music app, click the Explore tab to display the Xbox Music Store. You see a selection of albums for purchase.

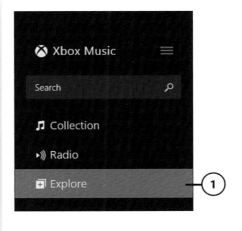

⊗ Xbox Music   ≡

Search   ⌕

♫ Collection

》 Radio

⊞ Explore   **1**

(2) Scroll to the Top Albums section and click View All.

Search for Music

To search for a specific song, album, or artist, enter the name or title into the Search box at the top of the Xbox Music navigation pane and press Enter.

(3) Click the down arrow next to All Genres to view a selection of musical genres.

(4) Click a genre to view all music in that genre.

(5) Click the All Subgenres down arrow to view and select additional subgenres within the main genre.

(6) To purchase an album or tracks from that album, click the album to display the album's page.

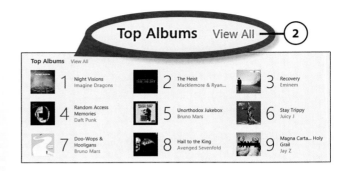

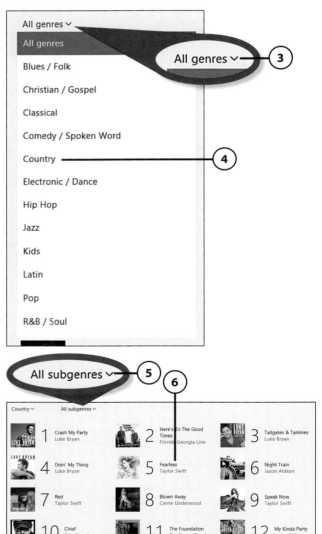

7 To search for a particular song, album, or artist, enter the name or title into the Search box in the navigation pane.

8 When the search results page appears, click to view only Artists, Albums, or Songs.

9 Click an album cover to view the Album page.

10 Click Buy Album to purchase the entire album.

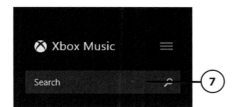

11 Right-click the track to display the options bar and then click Buy Song to purchase and individual song.

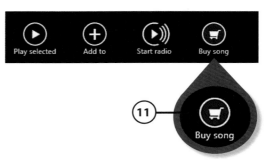

12 Sign in to your Microsoft account and confirm your purchase via credit card. Click Confirm to purchase with your currently registered card; click Change Payment Options to pay with a different card.

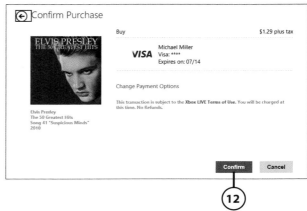

Stream Music Online

People our age have been conditioned to purchase the music we like, whether on vinyl, cassette tape, compact disc, or via digital download. But there's an entire world of music on the Internet that you don't have to purchase and download. It's called streaming music, and it gives you pretty much all you can listen to for a low monthly subscription price—or even for free. There's nothing to download; the music is streamed to your computer in real time, over the Internet.

Microsoft's streaming music service is called Xbox Music Pass, and it offers millions of songs for your listening pleasure. You can listen to individual tracks on demand or create your own personalized online radio stations.

Xbox Music Pass comes in both free and premium versions. The free version makes you listen to occasional ads and limits you to just 10 hours of music a month. Xbox Music Pass Premium costs $9.99/month but gets rid of the ads and gives you unlimited music streaming. A yearly subscription and 30-day free trial are also available.

1. From the Xbox Music Store, navigate to and click a track or album you want to play.

2. Click the Play button to begin streaming this track or album in real time.

3. To create a new online radio station, go to the main screen of the Xbox Music app and click Radio.

4. Click Start a Station.

5. Enter the name of an artist. As you type, Xbox Music lists matching artists.

6. Click the name of the artist you want. Xbox Music creates a radio station based on this artist and begins playback.

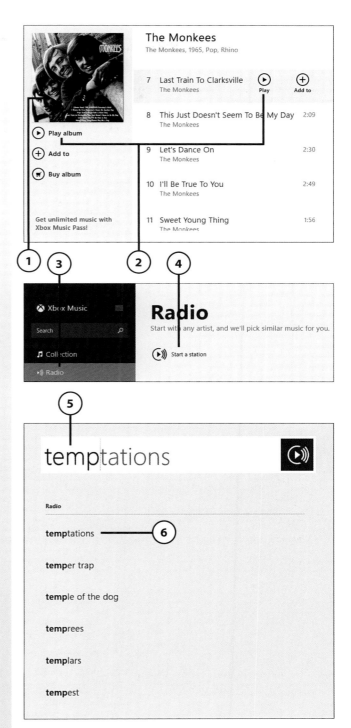

(7) To listen to a radio station you've previously created, click Radio on the main Xbox Music screen and then click the image for that station.

(8) The currently playing track is displayed in the playback bar at the bottom of the screen. Press Pause to pause playback; press Play to resume playback.

Radio

Start with any artist, and we'll pick similar music for you.

(▶)) Start a station

Aretha Franklin
Includes artists like Deniece Williams, Donny Hathaway

Neil Diamond
Includes artists like Barbra Streisand, John Denver

James Taylor
Includes artists like Neil Diamond, Carly Simon

Burt Bacharach
Includes artists like The Drifters, Carpenters

OTHER STREAMING MUSIC SERVICES

Xbox Music Pass isn't the only (or even the most popular) streaming music service on the Internet. You can check out and listen to any of these popular streaming music services using your web browser:

- iTunes Radio (www.apple.com/itunes/itunes-radio/)

- Last.fm (www.last.fm)

- Pandora (www.pandora.com)

- Rdio (www.rdio.com)

- Rhapsody (www.rhapsody.com)

- Spotify (www.spotify.com)

Using iTunes

If you have an iPhone, iPad, or iPod, you're familiar with Apple's iTunes. As you no doubt know, you use iTunes to manage the content of your iDevice. What you might not know is that you can use iTunes as a standalone music player for use on the Windows desktop.

Download and Install iTunes

To download and install the iTunes software on your PC, go to www.apple.com/ itunes/. It's free.

Play Digital Music

After you've installed the iTunes software, you can use it to play any music you've downloaded to your PC or that you've ripped from your own personal CDs.

1. Go to the Windows Start or Apps screen and click or tap the iTunes tile to launch the iTunes program on the Windows desktop.

2. Click Songs to view all the songs in your music library.

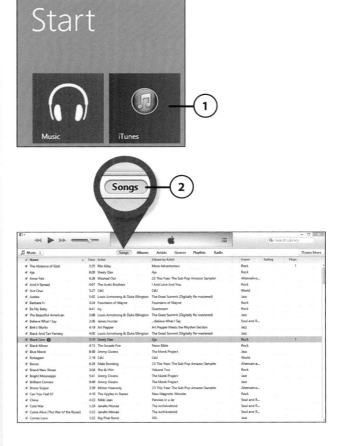

3   Click Albums to view your music by album.

4   Click Artists to view your music by recording artist. Click an artist name in the left-hand column to view all the music by that artist.

5   Click Genres to view music by genre. Click a genre in the left-hand column to view all the music in that category.

6   To play an individual track or album, double-click that item. A mini-player displays at the top of the iTunes window, along with a set of playback controls.

(7) Click the Pause button to pause playback; click the Play button to resume playback.

7

Copying Music to Your Portable Device

If you have an iPhone, iPod, or iPad, you use the iTunes software to synchronize ("sync") music from your computer to your portable device. If you've downloaded or ripped new music to your PC, it will be automatically copied to your portable device the next time you connect your device to your computer.

Create and Play Playlists

The iTunes program lets you combine multiple songs into a single playlist. It's a great way to create personalized music mixes.

(1) From within iTunes, click the Playlists button to display the Playlists pane.

(2) Click the playlist you want to play and the contents of that playlist are displayed in the content pane.

(3) Click the Play button at the top of the content pane.

Shuffle

To play the tracks in the playlist in random order, click the Shuffle icon in the mini-player. (When activated, the Shuffle icon turns blue.)

(4) To create a new playlist, click the + button at the bottom of the Playlists pane and then click New Playlist.

(5) When the new playlist pane appears on the right side of the window, enter a title for this playlist into the first text box.

(6) To add a song to this playlist, drag it from the content pane into the playlist pane. Repeat this step to add multiple songs to the playlist.

(7) When you're finished adding tracks to the playlist, click the Done button.

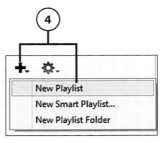

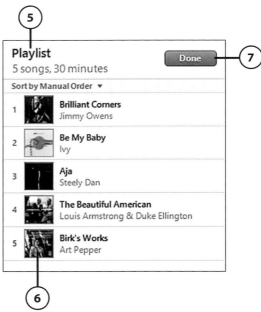

Play a CD

If your PC has a CD/DVD drive, it's easy enough to use iTunes to play the music on that CD.

(1) From the Windows Start screen, click the iTunes tile to launch iTunes.

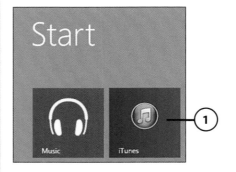

2 Insert the music CD into your PC's CD/DVD drive.

3 The CD should automatically appear in the iTunes window, with all the tracks listed. Click the Play button to begin play-back; click Pause to pause play-back.

4 Click the Forward arrow to skip to the next track on the CD.

5 Click the Back arrow to skip to the previous track.

6 Double-click a specific track to jump to that track.

Think About The Days
The Beach Boys — That's Why God Made The Radio

That's Why God Made... ↕

That's Why God Made The Radio ▶ ⤬ ⏏
12 songs, 39 minutes

		Name	Time	Artist	Album	Genre
1	✔	Think About The Days	1:28	The Beach Boys	That's Why God Made The Radio	Rock
2	✔	That's Why God Made The Radio	3:19	The Beach Boys	That's Why God Made The Radio	Rock
3	✔	Isn't It Time	3:45	The Beach Boys	That's Why God Made The Radio	Rock
4	✔	Spring Vacation	3:07	The Beach Boys	That's Why God Made The Radio	Rock
5	✔	The Private Life Of Bill And Sue	4:17	The Beach Boys	That's Why God Made The Radio	Rock
6	✔	Shelter	3:02	The Beach Boys	That's Why God Made The Radio	Rock
7	✔	Daybreak Over The Ocean	4:20	The Beach Boys	That's Why God Made The Radio	Rock
8	✔	Beaches In Mind	2:38	The Beach Boys	That's Why God Made The Radio	Rock
9	✔	Strange World	3:03	The Beach Boys	That's Why God Made The Radio	Rock
10	✔	From There To Back Again	3:24	The Beach Boys	That's Why God Made The Radio	Rock
11	✔	Pacific Coast Highway	1:47	The Beach Boys	That's Why God Made The Radio	Rock
12	✔	Summer's Gone	4:42	The Beach Boys	That's Why God Made The Radio	Rock

Rip a CD to Your PC

You can use iTunes to copy songs from any CD to your PC's hard drive. This lets you take all your music with you, without having to carry dozens (or hundred) of CDs along for the ride. In addition, when you rip a CD to your PC using iTunes, you can then transfer it to your iPhone or iPod for listening on the go.

(1) From the Windows Start screen, click the iTunes tile to launch iTunes.

(2) Insert the music CD into your PC's CD/DVD drive.

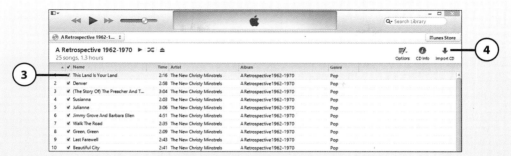

(**3**) The CD should automatically appear in the iTunes window, with all the tracks listed. Leave checked those tracks you want to copy to your computer, and uncheck those you don't want to copy.

(**4**) Click the Import CD button. (If the Import Settings dialog box appears at this point, click OK to proceed.) The selected tracks are now copied to your PC's hard disk and automatically added to the iTunes library.

Connect to the Internet

Make sure you're connected to the Internet before you start ripping so that iTunes can download album and track details. If you don't connect, you won't see the proper track names or CD cover art for the CD you're ripping.

Burn Your Own CDs

You might prefer to take CDs with you to play in your car or on the go. Did you know that you can use iTunes to create your own "mix" CDs, with tracks from multiple artists and albums? It's called burning a CD, and it's relatively easy to do.

(**1**) In iTunes, create a new playlist containing all the songs you want to burn to CD. (Read the "Create and Play a Playlist" task earlier in this chapter for more information.) Make sure that your playlist is less than 80 minutes long.

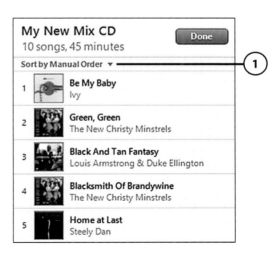

2 Insert a blank CD into your PC's CD drive.

3 Select the playlist that contains the songs you want to burn, and make sure that all the songs in the playlist are checked.

4 Click the Gear button and select Burn Playlist to Disc. iTunes copies the selected tracks to the blank CD and ejects the disc when it's done.

Ripping and Burning

The process of copying music from a CD to a computer's hard drive, in digital format, is called ripping. The reverse process, copying music from your PC to a blank CD, is called burning.

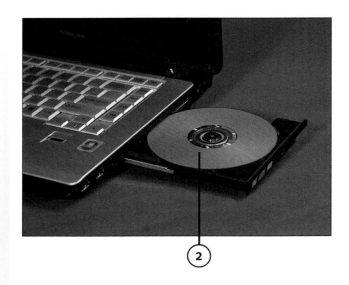

2

3

4

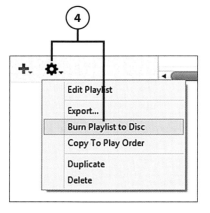

Download Music from the iTunes Store

When you want to add new music to your library, you can either rip music from a CD, as just discussed, or purchase new digital music online—which you can do from Apple's iTunes Store. The iTunes Store is the largest online music store today, with more than 20 million tracks available for downloading at prices ranging from 69 cents to $1.29 each. (It also offers complete albums for download, too.) It's a much bigger store than any local music store you've ever seen in your life.

MORE THAN MUSIC

The iTunes Store offers more than just music for download. iTunes also sells (or rents) movies, TV shows, music videos, podcasts, audiobooks, and eBooks (in the ePub format). You even get access to iTunes U, which offers all manner of textbooks, courses, and educational materials, and Apple's App Store for the iPhone and iPad.

>>>Go Further

Apple Account

Before you can purchase items from the iTunes Store, you have to create an Apple account. You might be prompted to do this the first time you click to purchase, or you can create your account manually, at any time, by clicking the Sign In button and, when prompted, clicking the Create New Account button.

(1) In iTunes, click the iTunes Store button in the top-right corner. This connects you to the Internet and displays the Store's home page.

(2) To view only music items, click Music in the iTunes toolbar.

(3) To browse music by category, click the All Categories list and select a category.

(4) To search for something specific, enter the song title, album title, or artist name into the search box at the top of the window and then press Enter.

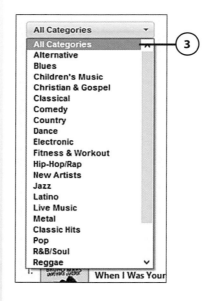

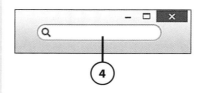

5 To view all the tracks in an album, click the album cover.

6 To purchase an individual track, click the Buy (price) button for that track.

7 To purchase an entire album, click the Buy button for that album.

8 If prompted to confirm your purchase, click the Buy button.

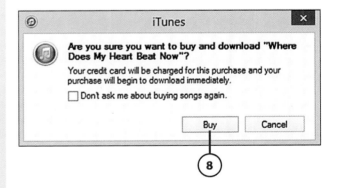

Ribbon   File Explorer   Folders

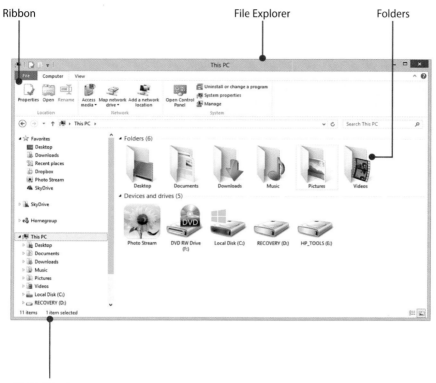

Navigation pane

In this chapter you see how to use File Explorer to manage the files and folders on your PC's hard drive.

→ Using File Explorer

→ Working with Folders

→ Managing Files

→ Working with Microsoft SkyDrive

18

Using Files and Folders

All the data for documents and programs on your computer is stored in electronic files. A file can be a word processing document, a music track, a digital photograph—just about anything, really.

The files on your computer are organized into a series of folders and subfolders. It's just like the way you organize paper files in a series of file folders in a filing cabinet—only it's all done electronically.

Using File Explorer

You might, from time to time, need to work with the files on your computer. You might want to copy files from an external USB memory drive, for example, or move a file from one folder to another. You might even want to delete unused files to free up space on your hard drive.

When you need to manage the files on your Windows 8.1 computer, you use an app called File Explorer. This app runs on the traditional Windows Desktop, and with it you can view and manage all the files and folders on your PC.

Windows Explorer

Prior to Windows 8, File Explorer was called Windows Explorer—or just My Computer.

Open File Explorer

You open and run File Explorer from the Windows Desktop. That's also where you do all your file management.

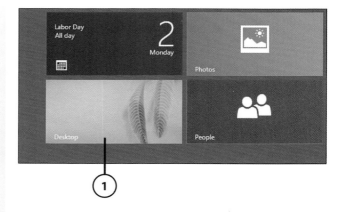

1. From the Windows Start screen, click the Desktop tile to open the Desktop.

2. Click the File Explorer icon in the Taskbar.

Navigate Folders and Libraries

All the files on your computer are organized into folders. Some folders have subfolders—that is, folders within folders. There are even sub-sub-folders, and sub-sub-subfolders. It's a matter of nesting folders within folders, in a kind of hierarchy. Naturally, you use File Explorer to navigate the various folders and subfolders on your PC's hard disk.

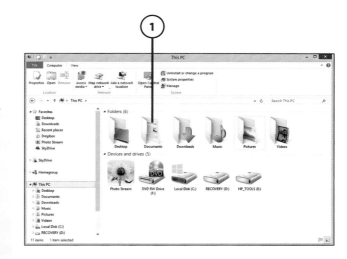

(1) In File Explorer's default view, This PC is selected and your documents are organized into the following folders: Desktop, Documents, Downloads, Music, Pictures, and Videos. Double-click any folder to view the contents.

(2) A given folder may contain multiple folders and subfolders. Double-click any item to view its contents

(3) To move back to the disk or folder previously selected, click the Back button on the toolbar.

(4) To move up the hierarchy of folders and subfolders to the next highest item, click the up-arrow button on the toolbar.

>>>Go Further

BREADCRUMBS

File Explorer includes an Address box at the top of the window, which displays your current location, in terms of folders and subfolders. This list of folders and subfolders presents a "breadcrumb" approach to navigation; it's like leaving a series of breadcrumbs behind as you delve deeper into the hierarchy of subfolders.

You can view additional folders within the hierarchy by clicking the separator arrow next to the folder icon in the Address box. This displays a pull-down menu of the recently visited and most popular items.

Use the Navigation Pane

Another way to navigate your files and folders is to use the navigation pane on the left side of the File Explorer window. This pane displays both favorite links and hierarchical folder trees for your computer, libraries, and networks.

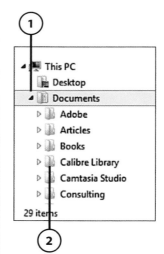

(1) Click the arrow icon next to any folder to display all the subfolders it contains.

(2) Click an icon in the navigation pane to open the contents of the selected item.

Change the Folder View

You can choose to view the contents of a folder in a variety of ways. File Explorer lets you display files as Small Icons, Medium Icons, Large Icons, or Extra Large Icons. You also have the option of displaying files as Tiles, Details, or a List. There's even a Content view that displays information about the file beside it.

① From within File Explorer, click the View tab on the ribbon bar.

② Click Content to display files with content descriptions.

③ Click Details to display columns of details about each file.

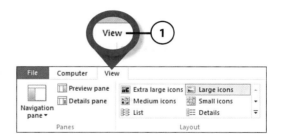

(4) Click List to display files in a simple list.

(5) Click Tiles to display files as small tiles.

(6) Click Small Icons, Medium Icons, Large Icons, or Extra Large Icons to display files as icons of various sizes.

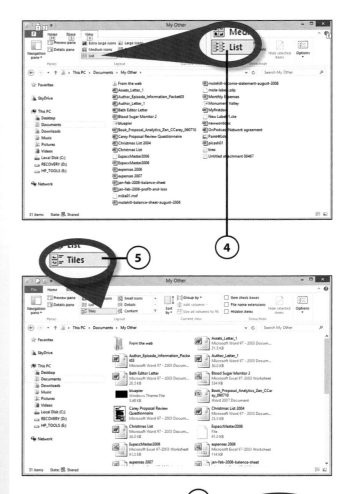

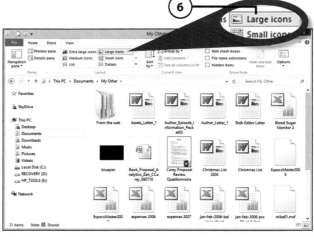

Sort Files and Folders

When viewing files in File Explorer, you can sort your files and folders in a number of ways. To view your files in alphabetic order, choose to sort by Name. To see all similar files grouped together, choose to sort by Type. To sort your files by the date and time they were last edited, select Date Modified.

(1) From within File Explorer, click the View tab on the ribbon bar.

(2) Click the Sort By button.

(3) Choose to sort by Name, Date Modified, Type, Size, Date Created, Folder Path, Authors, Categories, Tags, or Title.

(4) By default, Windows sorts items in ascending order. To change the sort order, click Descending.

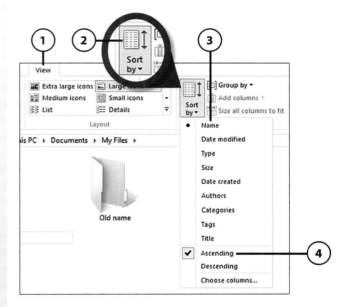

Different Sorting Options

Different types of files have different sorting options. For example, if you're viewing music files, you can sort by Album, Artists, Bit Rate, Composers, Genre, and the like.

Working with Folders

Windows organizes like files into folders. You can create new folders to hold new files, or rename existing folders if you like.

Create a New Folder

The more files you create, the harder it is to organize and find things on your hard disk. When the number of files you have becomes unmanageable, you need to create more folders—and subfolders—to better categorize your files.

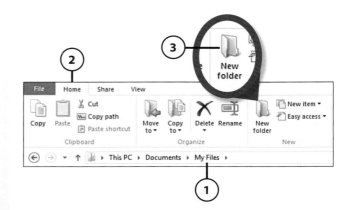

(1) From within File Explorer, navigate to the drive or folder where you want to place the new folder.

(2) Click the Home tab on the ribbon bar.

(3) Click the New Folder button.

(4) A new, empty folder now appears with the filename New Folder highlighted. Type a name for your folder and press Enter.

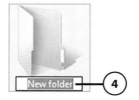

It's Not All Good

Don't Click

When creating a new folder, do *not* click the folder until you've entered a new name for it. Clicking the folder locks in the current name as New Folder. You would then have to rename the folder (as described next) to change that name.

Rename a Folder

When you create a new folder, it helps to give it a name that describes its contents. Sometimes, however, you might need to change a folder's name. Fortunately, Windows makes renaming an item relatively easy.

Renaming Files
The steps in this lesson also apply to renaming files, not just folders.

---

① Click the file or folder you want to rename.

② Click the Home tab on the ribbon bar.

③ Click the Rename button; this highlights the filename.

④ Type a new name for your folder (which overwrites the current name) and press Enter.

Keyboard Shortcut
You can also rename a folder or file by selecting the item and pressing F2 on your computer keyboard. This highlights the name and readies it for editing.

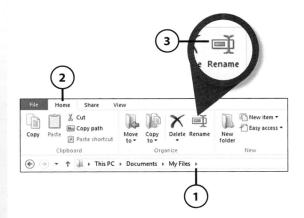

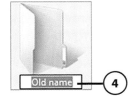

WHY ORGANIZE YOUR FOLDERS?

You might never have occasion to open File Explorer and work with your files and folders. But there's some value in doing so, especially when it comes to organizing your own personal files.

Perhaps the best example of this is when you have a large number of digital photos—which, if you're a grandparent, you surely do. Instead of lumping hundreds or thousands of photos into a single Photos folder, you can instead create different subfolders for different types of photos. For example, you might want to create folders named Vacation Photos, Family Photos, Holiday Photos, and the like.

Personally, I like organizing my photos by year and month. Within my main Photos folder I have subfolders for 2010, 2011, 2012, 2013, and the like. Then, within each year folder, I have subfolders for each month—January, February, March, and such. This way I can quickly click through the folders to find photos taken in a particular month.

You can organize your photos and other files similarly, or use whatever type of organization suits you best. The point is to make all of your files easier to find, however you choose to do so.

Managing Files

There are tens of thousands of files stored on a typical personal computer. From time to time you might need to manage them in various ways. You can copy a file to create a duplicate in another location, or move a file from one location to another. You can even delete files from your hard drive, if you like. And you do all this with File Explorer.

Copy a File

Copying a file places a duplicate of the original file into a new location. There are many ways to copy a file in Windows 8.1, the easiest of which is to use the Copy To button on File Explorer's Home ribbon.

1. From within File Explorer, navigate to and click the item you want to copy.
2. Click the Home tab on the ribbon bar.
3. Click the Copy To button.
4. Select Choose Location from the pull-down menu. The Copy Items dialog box displays.
5. Navigate to the new location for the item.
6. Click the Copy button.

Primary Folders

To copy an item directly to one of Windows' primary folders, click either Documents, Music, Pictures, or Videos from the Copy To menu.

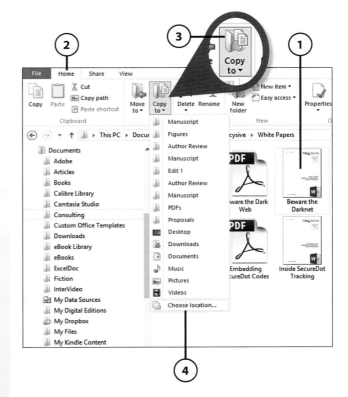

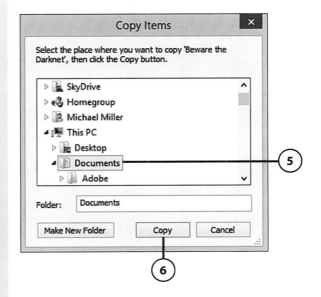

Move a File

Moving a file or folder is different from copying it. Moving cuts the item from its previous location and pastes it into a new location. Copying leaves the original item where it was and creates a copy of the item elsewhere.

1. From within File Explorer, navigate to and click the item you want to move.

2. Click the Home tab on the ribbon bar.

3. Click the Move To button.

4. Select Choose Location from the pull-down menu. The Move Items dialog box displays.

5. Navigate to the new location for the item.

6. Click the Move button.

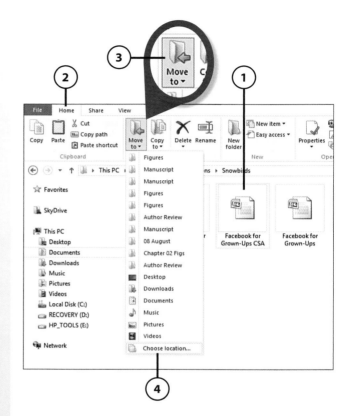

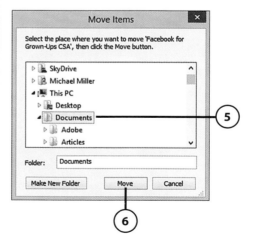

Delete a File

Keeping too many files eats up a lot of hard disk space on your computer—which can be a bad thing. Because you don't want to waste disk space, you should periodically delete those files (and folders) you no longer need. When you delete a file, you send it to the Windows Recycle Bin, which is kind of a trash can for deleted files.

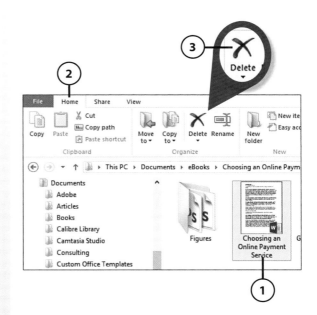

1. From within File Explorer, navigate to and click the item you want to delete.

2. Click the Home tab on the ribbon bar.

3. Click the Delete button.

Other Ways to Delete
You can also delete a file by dragging it from the File Explorer window onto the Recycle Bin icon on the desktop, or by highlighting it and pressing the Delete key on your computer keyboard.

Restore a Deleted File

Have you ever accidentally deleted the wrong file? If so, you're in luck. Windows stores the files you delete in the Recycle Bin, which is actually a special folder on your hard disk. For a short period of time, you can "undelete" files from the Recycle Bin back to their original locations—and save yourself from making a bad mistake.

(1) From the Windows Start screen, click the Desktop tile to open the Desktop.

(2) Double-click the Recycle Bin icon to open the Recycle Bin folder.

(3) Click the file you want to restore.

(4) Click the Manage tab on the ribbon bar.

(5) Click the Restore the Selected Items button.

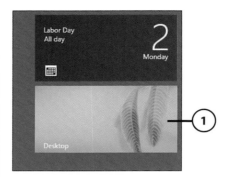

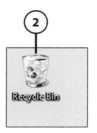

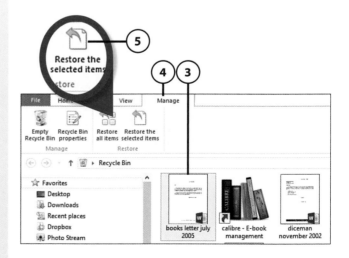

Empty the Recycle Bin

By default, the deleted files in the Recycle Bin can occupy 4GB plus 5 percent of your hard disk space. When you've deleted enough files to exceed this limit, the oldest files in the Recycle Bin are automatically and permanently deleted from your hard disk. You can also manually empty the Recycle Bin and thus free up some hard disk space.

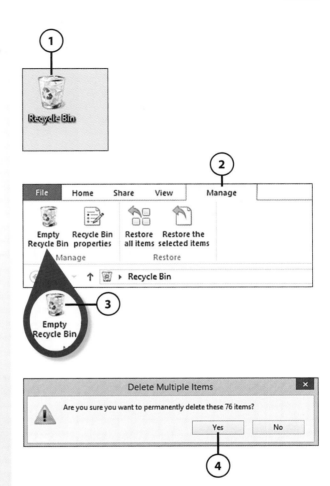

(1) From the Windows desktop, double-click the Recycle Bin icon to open the Recycle Bin folder.

(2) Click the Manage tab on the ribbon bar.

(3) Click the Empty Recycle Bin button.

(4) Click Yes in the Delete Multiple Items dialog box to completely erase the files.

Working with Microsoft SkyDrive

Microsoft offers online storage for all your documents and data, via its SkyDrive service. When you store your files on SkyDrive, you can access them via any computer or mobile device connected to the Internet.

Cloud Storage

Online file storage, such as that offered by SkyDrive, Apple's iCloud, and Google Drive, is called cloud storage. The advantages of cloud storage is that you can access files from any computer (work, home, or other) at any location. You're not limited to using a given file on one particular computer.

Manage Files with the SkyDrive App

You use the Windows SkyDrive app, included with Windows 8.1, to manage all your online files. You can also use the SkyDrive app to manage your local files—although File Explorer is easier for that.

(**1**) From the Windows Start screen, click or tap the SkyDrive tile to launch the SkyDrive app.

(**2**) By default, SkyDrive shows your online files. To view and manage your local files, click the SkyDrive down arrow and select This PC.

(**3**) Your SkyDrive files are stored in folders—Documents, Favorites, Photos, and so forth. Click a folder to view its contents.

(**4**) Click a file to view it or, in the case of an Office document, open it in its host application.

(**5**) To copy, cut, or rename a file, right-click the file to display the options bar, and then select the action you want to perform.

(**6**) To download a file from SkyDrive to your local hard disk, click Make Offline in the Options bar.

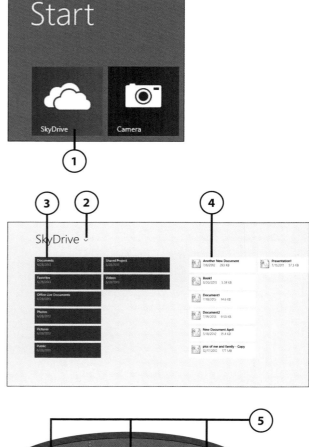

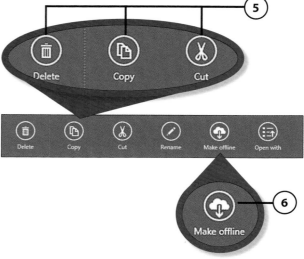

Storage Plans

Microsoft gives you 7GB of storage in your free SkyDrive account, which is more than enough to store most users' documents, digital photos, and the like. If you need more storage, you can purchase an additional 20GB for $10/year.

Windows Start screen in
high-contrast colors

In this chapter you discover how to use Windows' built-in accessibility functions and other ways to make Windows easier to use if you have vision or mobility issues.

→ Employing Ease of Access Functions
→ Using Alternative Input Devices
→ Connecting a Larger Screen

Making Windows Easier to Use by Seniors

As we get older, certain things become more difficult to do. It's a simple fact of aging—our hearing starts to go, our eyesight gets a little worse, and it's more challenging to grasp small objects in our hands.

Now, if you still have 20/20 vision, perfect hearing, and the Samson-like grip of a circus strongman, good for you. For the rest of us, however, the effects of aging can affect our ability to use our PCs—particularly notebook models with smaller screens and cramped keyboards.

Fortunately, Microsoft offers some Ease of Access features that can make Windows 8.1—and your new PC—a little easier to use. Let's take a look.

Employing Ease of Access Functions

Windows 8.1's Ease of Access features are designed to improve accessibility—that is, to make your computer easier and more comfortable to use, especially for seniors and those with specific disabilities. Windows 8.1 includes several useful Ease of Access functions, including the capability to enlarge text on the screen, change the contrast to make text more readable, and read the screen to aid those with vision problems. It can even enable you to operate your computer with voice commands.

Access Ease of Access Features

Windows 8.1 still offers the desktop-based Ease of Access Center utility, but it's actually easier to access these features from the Modern PC Settings screen.

1 Press Windows+C to display the Charms bar and click Settings to display the Settings panel.

2 Click Change PC Settings to display the PC Settings page.

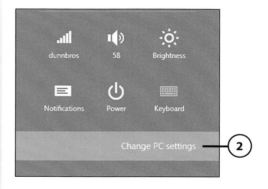

3 Click Ease of Access to display the Ease of Access screen.

Ease of Access Center

To open the desktop-based Ease of Access Center utility, press Windows+U or, from the Windows sign-in screen, click the Ease of Access button in the lower-left corner.

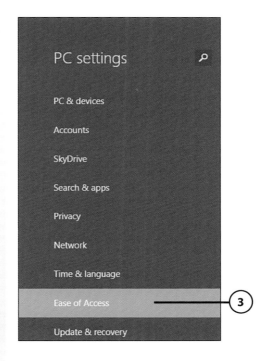

Enlarge the Screen

If you're having trouble reading what's onscreen because the text is too small, you turn on the Magnifier tool. The Magnifier does just what the name implies—magnifies an area of the screen to make it larger, for easier reading.

1 From the Ease of Access screen, click Magnifier.

2 Click "on" the Magnifier control. (If you want to use Magnifier full-time, click "on" the Start Magnifier Automatically control, instead.)

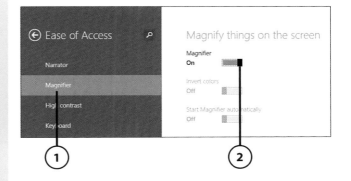

(3) The screen enlarges to 200% of its original size. Navigate around the screen by moving your mouse to the edge of the screen. (For example, to move the screen to the right, move your mouse to the right edge of the screen.)

(4) To adjust Magnifier settings, click the onscreen magnifying glass icon to display the Magnifier dialog box.

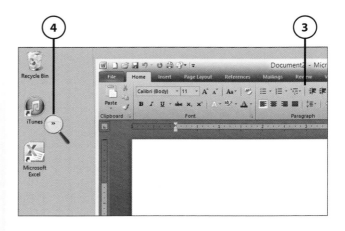

(5) Click the + button to enlarge the screen further.

(6) Click the – (minus) button to reduce the size of the screen.

(7) Click the X to turn off the Magnifier.

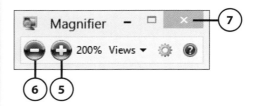

Improve Onscreen Contrast

Some people find it easier to view onscreen text if there's more of a contrast between the text and the background. To that end, Windows 8.1 offers a High Contrast option that displays lighter text on a dark background, instead of the normal black-on-white theme.

(1) From the Ease of Access screen, click High Contrast.

(2) Pull down the Choose a Theme list and select one of the four High Contrast color schemes.

(3) Click the Apply button.

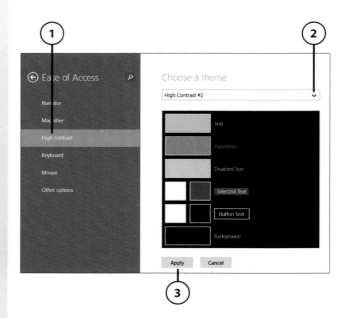

Make the Cursor Easier to See

Another issue that many seniors have is seeing the cursor onscreen. The default cursor in Windows can be a little small and difficult to locate on a busy desktop; you can change the size and color of the cursor to make it easier to see. You can choose from Regular, Large, and Extra Large sizes, and from White, Black, or Inverting colors.

1. From the Ease of Access screen, click Mouse.

2. In the Pointer Size section, select a larger pointer size.

3. In the Pointer Color section, select a different pointer color—ideally one that's easier to see onscreen.

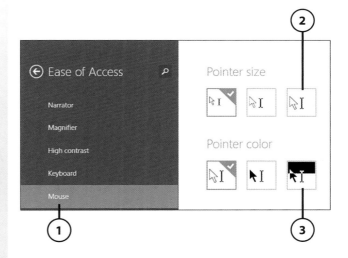

Read Text Aloud with Narrator

If your eyesight is really bad, even making the onscreen text and cursor super large won't help. To that end, Windows offers the Narrator utility, which speaks to you through your PC's speakers. When you press a key, Narrator tells you the name of that key. When you mouse over an item onscreen, Narrator tells you what it is. Narrator helps you operate your PC without having to see what's onscreen.

(1) From the Ease of Access screen, click Narrator.

(2) Click "on" the Start Narrator control. (If you want to use Narrator full-time, click "on" the Start Narrator Automatically control, instead.)

Keyboard Shortcut

You can also enable Narrator by pressing Windows+Enter on your keyboard.

(3) Pull down the Choose a Voice list and select from one of the three available voices (David, Hazel, or Zira).

(4) Use the Speed and Pitch controls to adjust how the voice sounds to you.

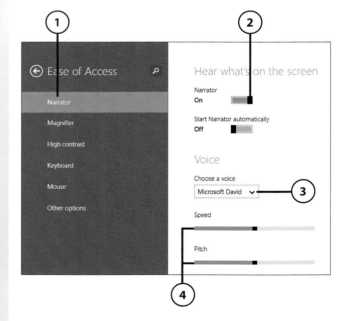

(5) Go to the Sounds You Hear section and click "on" those items you want narrated.

(6) Go to the Cursor and Keys section and click "on" those settings you prefer.

(5)

Sounds you hear

Read hints for controls and buttons
On

Characters you type
On

Words you type
On

Lower the volume of other apps when Narrator is running
On

Play audio cues
On

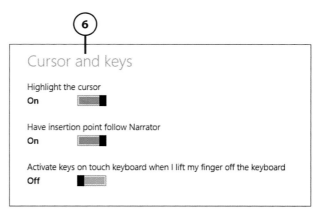

(6)

Cursor and keys

Highlight the cursor
On

Have insertion point follow Narrator
On

Activate keys on touch keyboard when I lift my finger off the keyboard
Off

Operate Your PC via Voice Command

If you're having difficulty using your computer with the normal keyboard and mouse, you can instead opt to control your PC by voice. Windows 8.1 includes a rudimentary speech recognition feature that lets you speak various commands and have them executed by Windows. You can also use Speech Recognition, as it's called, to speak the text you would normally type into a form or document.

Microphone Needed

To use the Speech Recognition feature in Windows, you need to have a microphone of some sort connected to your PC. This can be a standard USB desktop microphone, or a USB headset with microphone.

(1) Press Windows+U to open the Ease of Access Center on the Windows desktop.

(2) Scroll to the Explore All Settings section and click Use the Computer Without a Mouse or Keyboard.

(3) When the next page appears, go to the Avoid Using the Mouse or Keyboard section and click Use Speech Recognition.

(4) Click Start Speech Recognition to enable the feature.

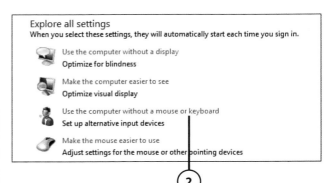

Explore all settings
When you select these settings, they will automatically start each time you sign in.

Use the computer without a display
Optimize for blindness

Make the computer easier to see
Optimize visual display

Use the computer without a mouse or keyboard
Set up alternative input devices

Make the mouse easier to use
Adjust settings for the mouse or other pointing devices

(2)

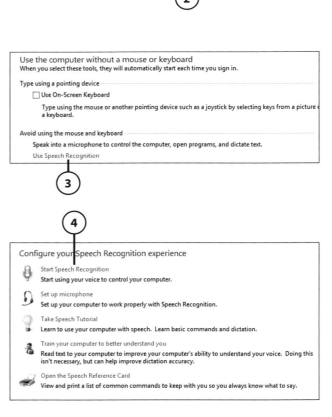

Use the computer without a mouse or keyboard
When you select these tools, they will automatically start each time you sign in.

Type using a pointing device
☐ Use On-Screen Keyboard
Type using the mouse or another pointing device such as a joystick by selecting keys from a picture of a keyboard.

Avoid using the mouse and keyboard
Speak into a microphone to control the computer, open programs, and dictate text.
Use Speech Recognition

(3)

(4)

Configure your Speech Recognition experience

Start Speech Recognition
Start using your voice to control your computer.

Set up microphone
Set up your computer to work properly with Speech Recognition.

Take Speech Tutorial
Learn to use your computer with speech. Learn basic commands and dictation.

Train your computer to better understand you
Read text to your computer to improve your computer's ability to understand your voice. Doing this isn't necessary, but can help improve dictation accuracy.

Open the Speech Reference Card
View and print a list of common commands to keep with you so you always know what to say.

First Time Use

The first time you use Speech Recognition, you might be prompted to select which type of microphone you're using (Headset Microphone, Desktop Microphone, or Other) and to set up your system. Follow the onscreen prompts to continue.

(5) You see the small control panel that displays the commands it "hears." Start speaking.

(6) To disable Speech Recognition, click the X.

Use the On-Screen Keyboard

If you find that pressing the keys on your computer keyboard with your fingers is becoming too difficult, especially on a notebook PC with smaller keys, you might want to use Windows 8.1's On-Screen Keyboard. This is a virtual keyboard, displayed on your computer screen, that you can operate with your mouse instead of your fingers. (Or with your fingers, if you have a tablet PC without a traditional keyboard.)

(1) From the Ease of Access screen, click Keyboard.

(2) Click "on" the On-Screen Keyboard control. The On-Screen Keyboard displays.

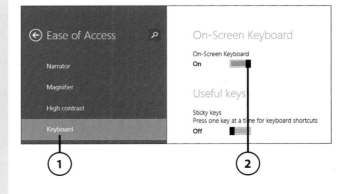

(3) To "press" a key, click it with your mouse—or, on a touchscreen display, tap it with your finger.

(4) To close the On-Screen Keyboard, click the X in the top-right corner.

MORE ACCESSIBILITY OPTIONS

>>>Go Further

I've covered the major Ease of Access functions here, but there are more where these came from. If you're having difficulty seeing items onscreen or operating Windows, you should explore all the options present on the Ease of Access screen and in the Ease of Access Center. You can, for example, enable visual notifications for Windows sounds, opt to use the numeric keypad to move the mouse around the screen, and choose to activate a window by hovering over it with your mouse. You can also let Windows figure out which Ease of Access functions are best for you. Open the Ease of Access Center and click Get Recommendations to Make Your Computer Easier to Use. You'll be asked five simple questions; your answers help Windows determine which Ease of Access features to activate.

Using Alternative Input Devices

As you get older, you might begin to lose fine mobility in your hands and fingers, whether due to arthritis or some other condition. This might make it difficult for you to use the small touchpad found on most notebook PCs or to type on normal-sized keyboard keys.

The solution for this problem is to attach different input devices. You can easily connect an external mouse to a notebook PC that then replaces the built-in touchpad, or attach a keyboard with larger keys for easier use.

Replace the Touchpad

Touchpads are convenient pointing devices for notebook PC users, but they can be difficult to use, especially if you have difficulty moving or holding steady your hand and fingers. The solution is to attach an external pointing device to a USB port on your notebook PC; when you do this, you use the (hopefully easier to use) external device instead of the built-in touchpad. There are two primary types of devices to choose from.

(1) An external mouse, such as the model from Microsoft (www. microsoft.com) that's shown in the figure, might prove easier to control than the internal touch-pad. It fits comfortably in your hand, and makes it easier to perform fine movements of the cursor onscreen.

(2) Many seniors prefer an even larger trackball controller, such as the model from Logitech (www.logitech.com) that's shown in the figure. This type of controller is preferred by young-sters who play computer games, but is also easy to use for those with mobility issues. Use the large roller ball on top to move the cursor around the screen.

Attach a Different Keyboard

Some notebook PC keyboards are a little smaller than the keyboard on a typical desktop PC. Even the keys on a standard-sized keyboard might not be big enough if you have mobility issues. The solution is to attach an external keyboard to your PC's USB port—one with big enough keys for you to use comfortably.

(1) Many external keyboards, such as the model from Logitech (www.logitech) that's shown in the figure, are easier to use and more ergonomic than the smaller keyboards found on most notebook PCs.

(2) Several companies make keyboards specifically for seniors, with enlarged keys that are both easier to see and easier to use. The most popular of these include the Chester Creek VisionBoard2 (www.chester-creek.com, shown here) and the BigKeys LX (www.bigkeys.com).

Connecting a Larger Screen

The easiest solution if you're having trouble seeing what's onscreen is to make the screen bigger—literally. This means connecting a larger computer monitor to your computer. Many seniors find that monitors sized 22" and larger are a lot easier to see than the standard 15" screens that are common today.

TOUCHSCREEN MONITORS

If you're in the market for a larger computer monitor, consider going with a touchscreen model. Not only is Windows 8.1 optimized for touchscreen use, as you know, but many seniors find using a touchscreen easier than using a mouse or keyboard for many tasks.

Connect a New Monitor

With most new computer monitors, you have the option of connecting via the traditional Video Graphics Array (VGA) connector or the newer Digital Visual Interface (DVI) connector. A DVI cable costs more than a VGA cable, but it provides a sharper digital picture.

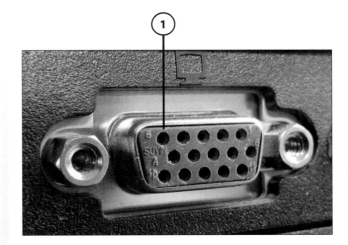

(1) If your monitor has only a VGA output, connect a VGA cable from the monitor to the VGA connector on your computer.

(2) If your monitor has a DVI output, connect a DVI cable from the monitor to the DVI connector on your computer.

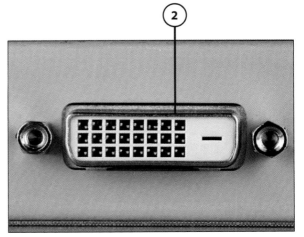

The Windows Task Manager

Name	Status	90% CPU	74% Memory	0% Disk	0% Network
Apps (14)					
▷ FullShot 9.5 (32 bit)		0%	9.3 MB	0 MB/s	0 Mbps
▷ Google Chrome (32 bit) (2)		0.1%	133.1 MB	0 MB/s	0 Mbps
Hulu Plus		0%	1.7 MB	0 MB/s	0 Mbps
Internet Explorer		0%	4.3 MB	0 MB/s	0 Mbps
▷ Microsoft Outlook (32 bit)		0%	71.9 MB	0 MB/s	0 Mbps
▷ Microsoft Word (32 bit)		0%	78.0 MB	0 MB/s	0 Mbps
Music		0%	1.6 MB	0 MB/s	0 Mbps
NOOK – Books, Magazines, Ne...		0%	1.7 MB	0 MB/s	0 Mbps
PC settings		0%	0.8 MB	0 MB/s	0 Mbps
SkyDrive		0%	0.9 MB	0 MB/s	0 Mbps
Store		0%	1.5 MB	0 MB/s	0 Mbps
▷ Task Manager		0.4%	12.4 MB	0 MB/s	0 Mbps
▷ Windows Explorer (3)		0.1%	75.5 MB	0 MB/s	0 Mbps

Task Manager

File   Options   View

Processes | Performance | App history | Startup | Users | Details | Services

⌃ Fewer details   End task

Dealing with Common Problems

Have you ever had your computer freeze on you? Or refuse to start? Or just start acting weird? Maybe you've had problems trying to print a document, or open a given program, or find a particular file. Or maybe you just can't figure out how to do a specific something.

Computer problems happen. When issues do occur, you want to get things fixed and running again as fast and as painlessly as possible. That's what this chapter is all about—dealing with those relatively common computer problems you might encounter.

Performing Necessary Maintenance

Before we deal with fixing computer problems, let's deal with how to prevent those problems. That's right—a little preventive maintenance can stave off a lot of future problems. Take care of your PC on a regular basis, and it will take care of you.

To ease the task of protecting and maintaining your system, Windows 8.1 includes several utilities to help you keep your computer running smoothly. You should use these tools as part of your regular maintenance routine—or if you experience specific problems with your computer system.

How Often to Run?

It's a good idea to run all these system utilities at least once a month, just to ensure that your system stays in tip-top condition.

Delete Unnecessary Files

Even with today's very large hard disks, you can still end up with too many useless files taking up too much hard disk space—especially if you're a grandparent obsessed with taking pictures of your very cute grandkids. Fortunately, Windows includes a utility that identifies and deletes unused files. The Disk Cleanup tool is what you should use when you need to free up extra hard disk space for more frequently used files.

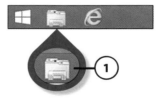

1. From the Windows desktop, open File Explorer.

2. Navigate to the This PC section, right-click the drive you want to clean up (usually the C: drive), and click Properties to open the Properties dialog box.

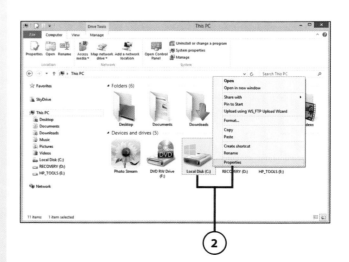

3 Select the General tab (displayed by default) and click the Disk Cleanup button.

4 Disk Cleanup automatically analyzes the contents of your hard disk drive. When it's finished analyzing, it presents its results in the Disk Cleanup dialog box. Select which types of files you want to delete.

5 Click OK to begin deleting.

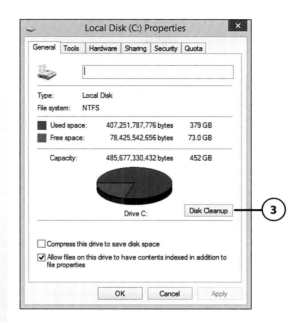

It's Not All Good

Which Files to Delete?

You can safely choose to delete all files suggested by Disk Cleanup *except* the setup log files and hibernation files. These files are needed by the Windows operating system, and you should not delete them.

Delete Unused Programs

Another way to free up valuable hard disk space is to delete those programs you never use. This is accomplished using the Uninstall or Change a Program utility.

(1) From the Windows Start screen, right-click in the lower-left corner to display the Quick Access menu and then click Programs and Features.

(2) Click the program you want to delete.

(3) Click Uninstall.

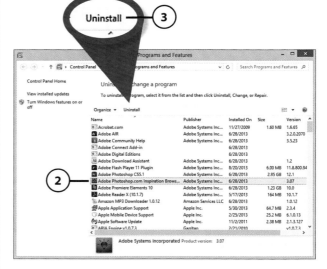

Check Your Hard Drive for Errors

Any time you move or delete a file or accidentally turn off the power while the system is running, you run the risk of introducing errors to your hard disk. Fortunately, you can find and fix most of these errors directly from within Windows using the ScanDisk utility.

(1) From Windows desktop, click the File Explorer icon in the Taskbar to open File Explorer.

(2) Click This PC in the navigation pane.

(3) Right-click the icon for the drive you want to scan and then select Properties from the pop-up menu. The Properties dialog box displays.

(4) Select the Tools tab.

(5) Click the Check button in the Error-Checking section.

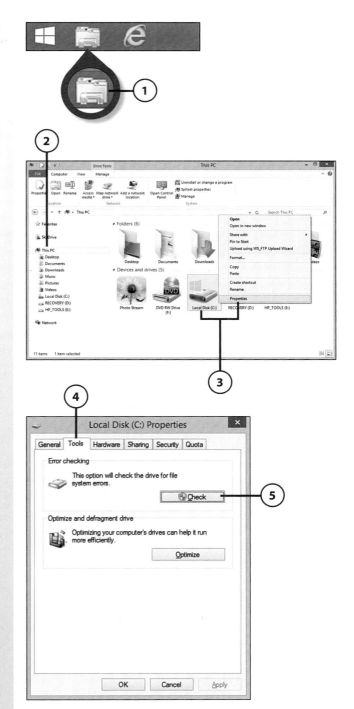

6 Click Scan Drive in the Error
Checking dialog box.

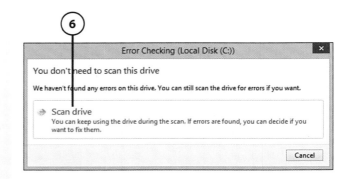

Scanning and Fixing
ScanDisk not only scans your hard disk
for errors but also automatically fixes
any errors it finds. (If it finds errors,
however, you might need to reboot
your system.)

Backing Up Important Files

The data stored on your computer's hard disk is valuable, and perhaps irreplacable.
We're talking about your personal photos, home movies, favorite music, spread-
sheets and word processing documents, and maybe even a tax return or two.

That's why you want to keep a backup copy of all these valuable files. The easiest
way to store backup copies is on an external hard disk drive. These drives provide
lots of storage space for a relatively low cost, and they connect to your PC via
USB. There's no excuse not to do it!

Activate File History

In Windows 8.1, you back up important data files using the new File
History feature. When enabled, File
History automatically creates copies
of all the different versions of your
files and enables you to restore them
in case they get lost or destroyed.
To protect your valuable files, then,
there's little you need to do except
turn on File History.

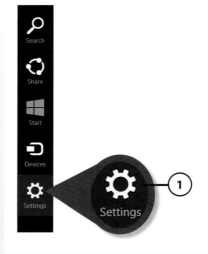

1 Press Windows+C to display the
charms bar and click or tap Settings to display the Settings pane.

(2) Click or tap Change PC Settings to display the PC Settings panel.

(3) Click or tap Update & Recovery.

(4) Click or tap File History to display the File History screen.

(5) Click "on" the File History control.

(6) File History automatically uses the first external drive on your system for its backup. If you want to use a different backup drive, click Select a Different Drive and, when the drive pane appears, select a different drive or network location.

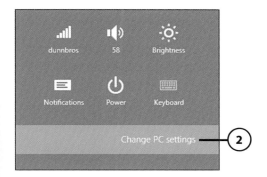

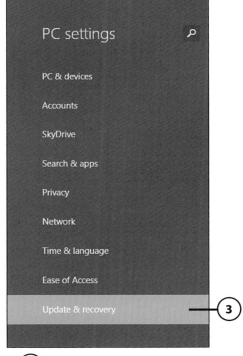

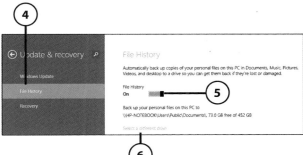

Restore Backup Files

File History makes it easy to restore any or all files you've backed up. It's a matter of selecting which files to restore, and to where.

Restoring Changed Files

You can also use File History to restore a given file to an earlier state. This is useful if you're editing a document, for example, and want to use an earlier version of the document before more recent editing.

(1) Press Windows+Q to display the search panel.

(2) Enter **restore your files** into the search box and press Enter.

(3) From the search results screen, click or tap Restore Your Files with File History to launch the File History desktop app.

(4) Navigate to and select those files or folders you want to restore.

(5) Click the green Restore button to restore these files to their original locations.

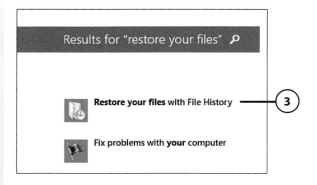

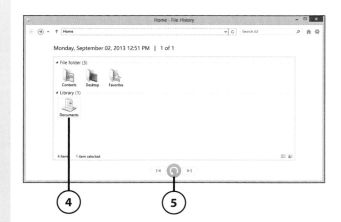

Fixing Simple Problems

Computers aren't perfect—even new ones. It's always possible that at some point in time, something will go wrong with your PC. It might refuse to start; it might freeze up; it might crash and go dead. Then what do you do?

When something goes wrong with your computer, there's no need to panic (even though that's what you'll probably feel like doing). Most PC problems have easy-to-find causes and simple solutions. The key thing is to keep your wits about you and attack the situation calmly and logically.

You Can't Connect to the Internet

This problem is likely caused by a bad connection to your Wi-Fi network or hotspot. Fix the Wi-Fi problem and you can get back online lickity-split.

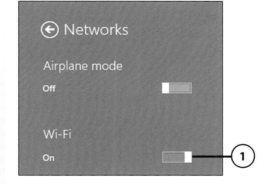

(1) Try turning off and then turn-ing back on your PC's wireless functionality. You might be able to do this from a button or switch on your computer, or you can do it within Windows. Press Windows+C to display the Charms bar, click Settings, click the Wi-Fi connection icon, and then turn "off" the Wi-Fi option. Wait a few moments, then turn back "on" the Wi-Fi option and reconnect to your network.

(2) It's possible that your computer is too far away from the wire-less signal. Move your computer nearer to the closet Wi-Fi router or hotspot.

(3) If you're using a public Wi-Fi hotspot, you might need to log onto the hotspot to access the Internet. Open Internet Explorer and try to access any web page; if you're greeted with a log-in page for the hotspot, enter the appropriate information to get connected.

(4) If nothing else works, it's possible that the hotspot to which you're trying to connect has Internet issues. Report your problem to whomever is in charge at the moment.

(5) If you're on your home network, it's possible that your Internet service provider is having issues. Call your ISP and report the problem.

You Can't Go to a Specific Web Page

If you have a good connection to the Internet and can open some web pages, trouble opening a specific web page is probably isolated to that particular website.

(1) The site might be having temporary connection issues. Refresh the web page to try loading it again.

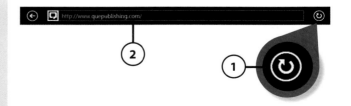

(2) You might have typed the wrong address for this particular site. Try entering the address again.

(**3**) You might have the wrong address for a specific page on the website. Try shortening the address to include only the main URL—that is, go directly to the site's home page, not to an individual page on the site. For example, instead of going to www.quepublishing.com/articles/article.aspx?p=1951178, just go to the main page at www.quepublishing.com.

(**4**) If you continue to have issues with this website, it's probably a problem with the site itself. That is, it's nothing you're doing wrong. Wait a few moments and try again to see if the problem is fixed.

You Can't Print

What do you do when you try to print a document on your printer and nothing happens? This problem could have several causes.

(**1**) Click the Print button or command to open the Printer page or dialog box and then make sure the correct printer is selected.

(**2**) Make sure the printer is turned on. (You'd be surprised…)

(**3**) Check the printer to make sure it has plenty of paper and isn't jammed. (And if it is jammed, follow the manufacturer's instructions to unjam it.)

(4) Check the cable between your computer and the printer. Make sure both ends are firmly connected. Lots of printer problems are the result of loose cables.

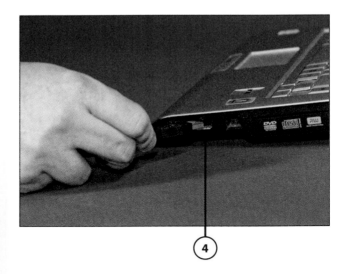

Your Computer Is Slow

Many computers will start to slow down over time. There are many reasons for this, from an overly full hard disk to an unwanted malware infection.

(1) Close any open programs that don't need to be open at the moment.

(2) Run the Disk Cleanup utility to remove unnecessary files and free up hard disk space. (See the "Delete Unnecessary Files" task earlier in this chapter for more information on the Disk Cleanup Utility.)

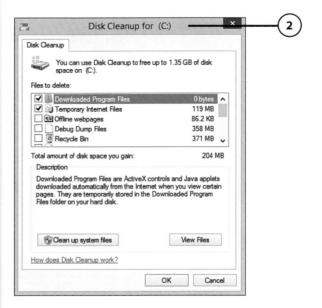

3 Install and run a reputable anti-malware utility to find and remove any computer viruses or malware unknowingly installed on your system. (Learn more about anti-malware utilities in Chapter 9, "Protecting Yourself from Online Scams.")

4 Ask a knowledgeable friend or professional computer technician to check your computer's startup programs; these are programs that load automatically when Windows starts up and run in the background, using valuable computer memory. Have your friend or technician remove those unnecessary start-up programs.

Task Manager

You can view and manage your start-up programs from the Task Manager utility. Open the Task Manager by pressing Ctrl+Alt+Del and then selecting Task Manager.

A Specific Program Freezes

Sometimes Windows works fine but an individual software program stops working. Fortunately, Windows 8.1 presents an exceptionally safe environment; when an individual application crashes or freezes or otherwise quits working, it seldom messes up your entire system. You can then use the Task Manager utility to close any frozen program without affecting other Windows programs.

(**1**) When an application freezes, press Ctrl+Alt+Del.

(**2**) Click the Task Manager option to launch the Task Manager utility.

(**3**) Click the Processes tab.

(**4**) Go to the Apps section and click the program that's frozen.

(**5**) Click the End Task button.

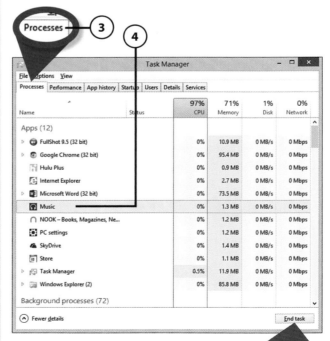

Your Entire Computer Freezes

For many users, the worst thing that can happen is that your computer totally freezes, and you can't do anything—including shut it off. Well, there is a way to shut down a frozen computer and then restart your system.

1. Hold down the Windows key on your keyboard and simultaneously press your PC's power button. If that doesn't work, press and hold the PC's power button for several seconds, until the PC shuts down.

2. Wait a few moments and then turn your computer back on. It should restart normally. If not, you might need to consult a computer technician or repair service.

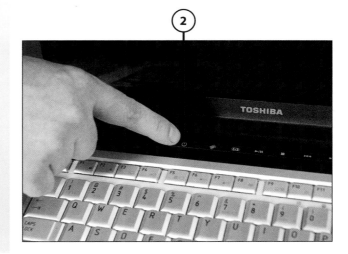

TROUBLESHOOTING PC PROBLEMS

No matter what kind of computer-related problem you're experiencing, there are six basic steps you can take to track down the cause of the problem. Work through these steps calmly and deliberately, and you're likely to find what's causing the current problem—and then be in a good position to fix it yourself:

1. Don't panic! Just because there's something wrong with your PC is no reason to get frustrated or angry or just plain crazy. That's because it's likely that there's nothing seriously wrong. Besides, getting all panicky won't solve anything. Keep your wits about you and proceed logically, and you can probably find what's causing your problem and get it fixed.

2. Check for operator errors. That is, look for something that you did wrong. Maybe you clicked the wrong button, pressed the wrong key, or plugged something into the wrong port. Retrace your steps and try to duplicate your problem. Chances are the problem won't recur if you don't make the same mistake twice.

3. Check that everything is plugged into the proper place and that the system unit itself is getting power. Take special care to ensure that all your cables are securely connected—loose connections can cause all sorts of strange results.

4. Make sure you have the latest versions of all the software and apps installed on your system. That's because old versions of most problems probably haven't been updated with the latest bug fixes and compatibility patches. (These are small updates that typically fix known issues within a program.)

5. Try to isolate the problem by when and how it occurs. Walk through each step of the process to see if you can identify a particular program or process that might be causing the problem.

6. When all else fails, call in professional help. If you have a brand-new PC and you think it's a Windows-related issue, contact Microsoft's technical support department. If you think it's a problem with a particular program or app, contact the tech support department of the program's manufacturer. If you think it's a hardware-related problem, contact the manufacturer of your PC or the dealer you bought it from. The pros are there for a reason—when you need technical support, go and get it.

Above all, don't be afraid of your PC. It's really difficult to break a computer these days; even if you did something wrong, most mistakes can be easily fixed.

Recovering from Serious Problems

If you have a frozen computer that won't unfreeze or a computer that refuses to start properly, and this issue continues over time (that is, restarting your computer doesn't fix it), you might have a serious problem on your hands. At this point, you bring in a professional computer technician or attempt a few simple fixes on your own.

Restore Your Computer to a Previous State

If your computer system crashes or freezes on a regular basis, your best course of action is to reboot your system and then run the System Restore utility. This utility can automatically restore your system to the state it was in before the crash occurred—and save you the trouble of reinstalling any damaged software programs. It's a great safety net for when things go wrong!

Before You Restore

Be sure to close all programs before you use System Restore because Windows will need to be restarted when the utility has done its work. The full process might take a half-hour or more.

(1) From the Windows Start screen, right-click in the lower-left corner to display the Quick Access menu and then click System to display the System window.

(2) Click System Protection in the navigation pane to open the System Properties dialog box.

(3) Make sure the System Protection tab is selected.

(4) Click the System Restore button to display the System Restore window.

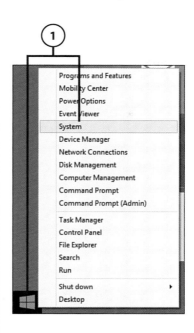

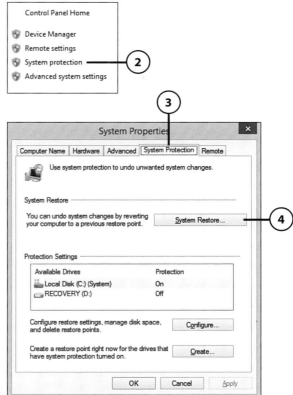

5 Click the Next button.

6 Click the restore point you want to return to.

7 Click the Next button to display the Confirm Your Restore Point screen.

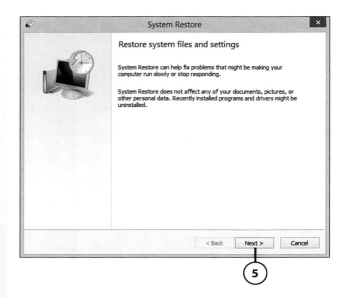

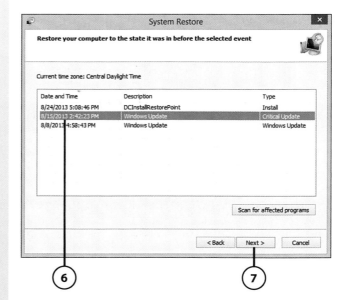

8 Click the Finish button to begin the restore process.

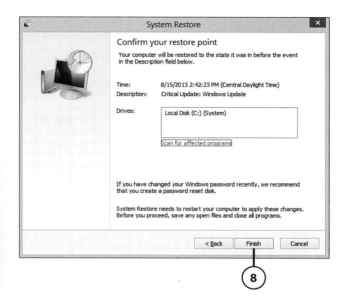

8

It's Not All Good

System Files Only—No Documents

System Restore helps you recover any damaged programs and system files, but it doesn't help you recover any documents or data files. This is why you need to use the File History utility to back up all your data on a regular basis—and restore that backed-up data in the case of an emergency. Read the "Activate File History" task earlier in this chapter for more information about the File History utility.

Refresh System Files

Your computer can get seriously out of whack if key system files somehow become damaged or deleted. Fortunately, Windows 8.1 includes the ability to "refresh" your system with the current versions of important system files. The Refresh PC utility works by checking whether key system files are working properly or not; if it finds any issues, it attempts to repair those files—and only those files.

System Files Only

The Refresh PC utility doesn't remove any of your personal files or documents. It only refreshes Windows system files.

1. Press Windows+C to display the Charms bar.

2. Click Settings to display the Settings panel.

3. Click Change PC Settings to display the PC Settings page.

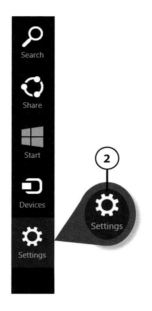

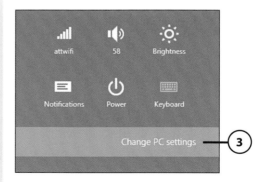

(4) Click Update & Recovery.

(5) Click Recovery.

(6) Go to the Refresh Your PC Without Affecting Your Files section and click Get Started. Follow the onscreen instructions to complete the refresh.

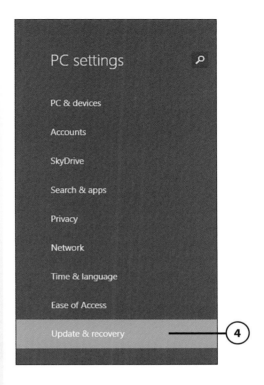

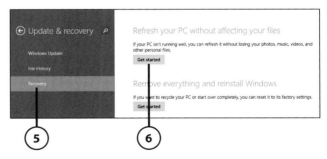

Reset Your System

In the event of a catastrophic system failure, you can reset your computer to its factory-fresh condition by wiping clean the hard disk and reinstalling Windows from scratch.

Resetting your system is more drastic than simply refreshing it. The Reset PC utility wipes your hard disk clean and reinstalls Windows from scratch. That leaves you with a completely reset system—but without any of the apps you've installed or the files you created.

It's Not All Good

Everything Is Deleted

The Reset PC utility completely deletes all the files, documents, and programs you have on your system. You'll want to back up your files before taking this extreme step, and then restore your files from the backup and reinstall all the apps you use.

(1) Press Windows+C to display the Charms bar.

(2) Click Settings to display the Settings panel.

(3) Click Change PC Settings to display the PC Settings page.

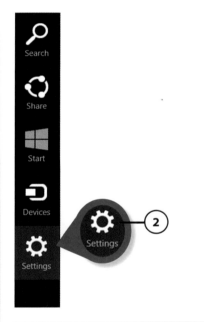

(4) Click Update & Recovery.

(5) Click Recovery.

(6) Go to the Remove Everything
and Reinstall Windows section
and click Get Started. Follow the
onscreen instructions to complete the reset process.

Multiple Drives

If your PC has more than one drive,
the Reset utility asks you whether you
want to remove files from all drives
or only the drive where Windows is
installed. Make your choice.

(7) Windows begins resetting your
system by deleting everything
on your hard drive and reinstalling the Windows operating
system. This might take some
time. When the process is complete, you need to re-enter your
Windows product key and other
personal information—but
you'll have a like-new system
that's ready to start being used
again. (Learn more about product keys and Windows setup
in Chapter 2, "Using Windows
8.1—If You've Never Used a
Computer Before.")

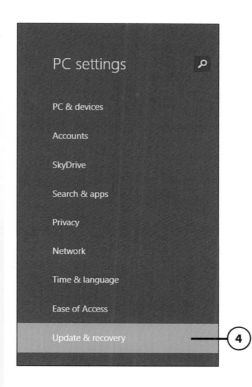

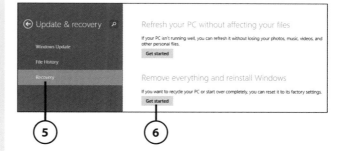

>>>Go Further

GETTING HELP

Many older computer users easily become befuddled when it comes to dealing with even relatively simple computer problems. I understand completely; there's little that's readily apparent or intuitive about figuring out how to fix many PC-related issues.

If you feel over your head or out of your element when it comes to dealing with a particular computer problem, that's okay; you don't have to try to fix everything yourself. There are many options available to you, from Best Buy's ubiquitous Geek Squad to any number of local computer repair shops. Google **computer repair** for your location, check your local Yellow Pages, or just ask around to see who your friends use for computer support. It might prove faster and less aggravating in the long run to pay a professional to get your computer working properly again.

Index

X

Y

Z

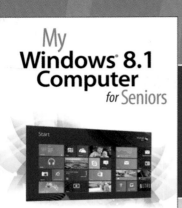

FREE
Online Edition

Your purchase of *My Windows® 8.1 Computer for Seniors* includes access to a free online edition for 45 days through the **Safari Books Online** subscription service. Nearly every Que book is available online through **Safari Books Online**, along with thousands of books and videos from publishers such as Addison-Wesley Professional, Cisco Press, Exam Cram, IBM Press, O'Reilly Media, Prentice Hall, Sams, and VMware Press.

Safari Books Online is a digital library providing searchable, on-demand access to thousands of technology, digital media, and professional development books and videos from leading publishers. With one monthly or yearly subscription price, you get unlimited access to learning tools and information on topics including mobile app and software development, tips and tricks on using your favorite gadgets, networking, project management, graphic design, and much more.

Activate your FREE Online Edition at
informit.com/safarifree

STEP 1: Enter the coupon code: LYTIDDB.

STEP 2: New Safari users, complete the brief registration form.
Safari subscribers, just log in.

If you have difficulty registering on Safari or accessing the online edition,
please e-mail customer-service@safaribooksonline.com